STEADY DRUMMER

TO

K. E. C. AND W. A. C.

The Fire of Salonika from the air

STEADY DRUMMER

BY

STANLEY CASSON

The Naval & Military Press Ltd

Published and © by the
The Naval & Military Press

'As in a dream a man strives to pursue one that flees before him, and yet cannot reach him—the one cannot escape nor the other pursue.'

HOMER, *Iliad*: 22.199

On the idle hill of summer,
  Sleepy with the flow of streams,
Far I hear the steady drummer
  Drumming like a noise in dreams.

Far and near and low and louder
  On the roads of earth go by,
Dear to friends and food for powder,
  Soldiers marching, all to die.

East and west on fields forgotten
  Bleach the bones of comrades slain,
Lovely lads and dead and rotten;
  None that go return again.

A. E. HOUSMAN

CONTENTS

ILLUSTRATIONS

MAPS

PREFACE

The complacency with which large numbers of people to-day contemplate another world-war, or at least a European war, is to me a certain sign that civilisation has not advanced its cause since 1914. It is the complacency that disturbs me, not the situation itself, for complacency is but another name for ineptitude. The Austrian destruction of the Austrian Social-Democratic party in February 1933 and the recent German re-introduction of conscription appear to me to be two events more pregnant with the germs of universal ruin than any single event that has occurred during my lifetime, either during, or after, or before, the War itself. That one nation can deliberately suppress political opponents by means of artillery in the centre of a great city and that another can consciously revel in the prospect of barrack life are indications of the way in which the whole structure of civilisation is crumbling. Political situations can be remedied and international sores healed, but nothing can eradicate tendencies such as these except an increased respect for the development of civilisation itself.

Had the last war been prolonged another two years I fully believe that civilisation itself would have crumbled, not in a material but in a moral and spiritual sense. As things are, the most characteristic features of life to-day are an increased disrespect for human life, a scorn of personal and public liberty and the deliberate propagation of intolerance as a political virtue. From these defects all countries alike are suffering, differing only in degree. Before 1914 men did not think along those lines at all.

I have written this book in order to give to those who are

interested in such things an account of how one ordinary and unimportant person was affected by the crisis of war and its consequences. What I personally thought about the war and its development is not of the slightest value to anybody in itself, but how my life and outlook were affected may, perhaps, serve as a guide to those younger than myself who are likely to be implicated in further disturbances of the same kind; for in 1914 I was indistinguishable from many millions of other men of the same age and from many million men who are of that same age to-day.

The events recorded in these pages may give the reader some idea of the process by which war slowly assimilates those who take part in it to the conditions which it prescribes. They may help to show how the supports of civilisation have come to be cracked and weakened.

A large part of this book deals with the Balkan campaign and with the other campaigns that developed from it. The Balkan campaign was generally considered at the time as a subsidiary affair. The Germans called it their 'largest concentration camp.' British and French alike thought it was a troublesome side-show. But the flanks of a hostile front are not rolled up by subsidiary expeditions. The fact that the Balkan campaign opened the way to the Danube and to Austria and so brought about the final collapse of the whole opposing front suggests that we held a key position in the Balkans. That position was the right flank of the whole Allied front, and the war ended, as most large battles have always ended, by the turning of a flank. The German negotiations with Bulgaria immediately before the Bulgarian collapse and the realisation of the *débâcle* by the German High Command are evidence that the Germans knew well enough that their flank had been turned and that their own resistance was only possible in a very restricted field, and for a very restricted period. Germans lost the war on the field of battle, but they have ever since tried to atone for that loss by shouting their way to victory. The first movements which led to their defeat in battle are those recorded in the last part of this book.

I have to express my gratitude to Messrs A. & C. Black for permission to use two coloured plates which originally appeared in *The Salonika Front* and to the artist Mr W. T. Wood for his concurrence. I must also thank the Editor of the *Atlantic Monthly* for allowing me to reproduce in Chapter XIII certain passages from an article I wrote for that journal. I have also to acknowledge to the War Office permission to reproduce the military documents here published.

S. C.

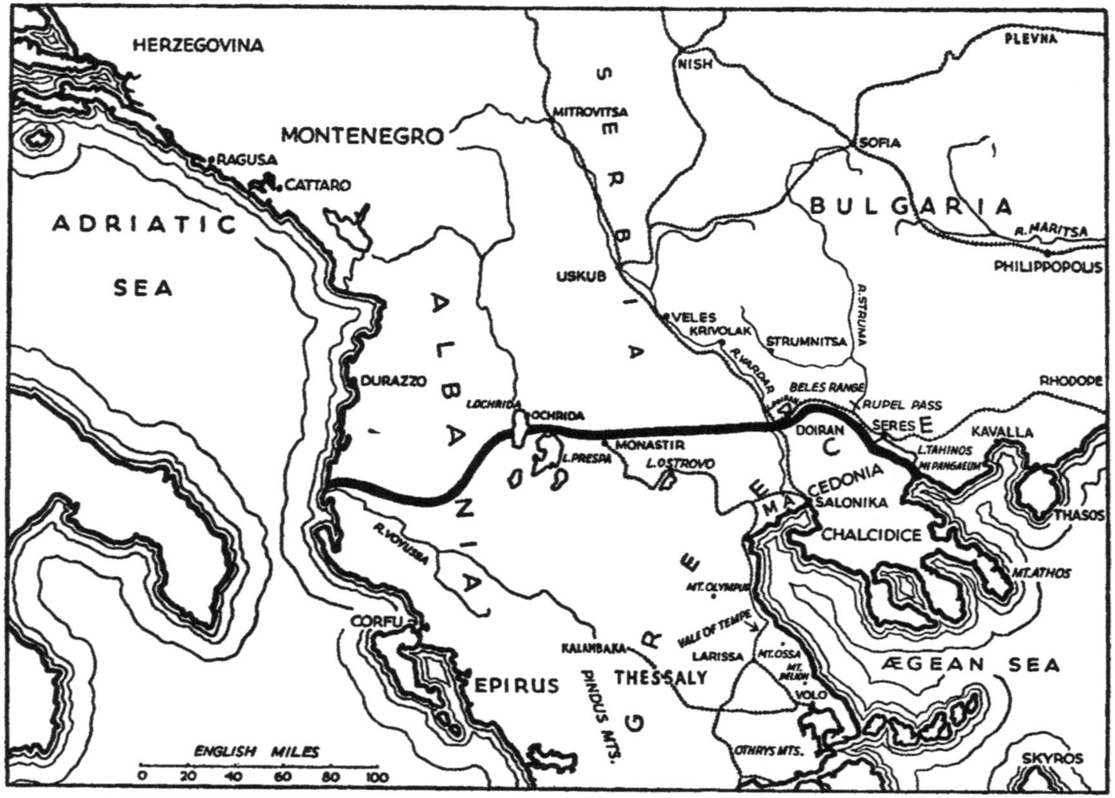

THE SALONIKA FRONT

The Allied Front is shown by the heavy black line

CHAPTER I

HINTS AND PRELIMINARIES

For me the war began at Bonn am Rhein, far away in 1909. I even took part in a Three-Power Conference. The parties to the conference were myself, raw, nineteen and eager; a Frenchman, Marcel Malbrancq, rapidly domesticated as Malbranckelschen; and Max, the dissolute son of the family with whom the Frenchman and myself lived as paying guests. Max was the head of the family, which he interpreted as meaning that he could take as much of the earnings of the fourteen other members of the family as he would (including our modest contributions as paying guests) and spend them on riotous living of the traditional kind, periodically emerging to be ploughed in another medical examination. Max was burly and forty, and had been a student for the phenomenal period of ten years! His brothers and sisters, the youngest of whom was nineteen, never raised against him any protest but that of unavailing tears. The great Max continued as a scandal without deterrent.

The Frenchman was small, square, sallow and simple. Like me, he was there to learn the language. Like me, he was eager and young, and willing to believe most of what he was told.

Our Conference met at irregular intervals either at Godesberg, among the flowers and beer gardens, or else in some small tavern below the woods on the hills behind Bonn.

At every meeting we slowly worked round to one topic, and that was war. We talked of war not in a general way, but rather as of a thing that would one day most certainly involve us all. It did not alarm us, nor did we look upon its coming with the slightest disapproval. It was just, as it were, one of the inevitable seasons, like winter, and we discussed the prospects of its being severe or long or slight or unpleasant. The one thing that never occurred to one of us was to discuss the likelihood of its never happening at all. Such a thing never entered our heads. 'I have not yet done my service,' said Malbrancq, 'but I doubt if it will be necessary, because I shall probably be drafted at once into active service.' 'I shall be the first to go,' said Max, with a chuckle, 'for the medicals are all wanted at the very start.' My own contribution to the conference was more tentative. I had done one season at Aldershot in the Officers Training Corps from Oxford, and knew with perfect certainty that my capacity as a soldier was almost nil. But I was prepared to admit to the Frenchman and the German that I should probably be in it somehow. Max with a friendly guffaw reminded me that we had no army, and wondered exactly how I should become a soldier. I did my best to tell him what I had only vaguely heard of the Expeditionary Force, which was at that time being tentatively discussed. I knew, however, quite certainly that I should be in it somehow. For several years my father, with just the same certainty as Max and Marcel, had considered the war as a normal event due to occur in the course of time. Himself a man of the most advanced and pacific views, he was yet sure of one thing, that England would fight Germany, and he was sure of that because, as he always said, the Franco-German war had left Germany with a taste for more of the same sort of thing. Why we should be involved he never troubled to explain, because he considered it axiomatic.

Oddly enough, Max and Marcel and I, together with various contingents of the family of fourteen, never roused the smallest animosity or opposition among ourselves during these discussions. There was not the faintest suggestion of rancour or rivalry or racial strife; we were all singularly good friends. We talked it all over as one would discuss a game of cards. The atmosphere of peace was almost oppressive; we never even approached a quarrel. In all the polyglot meetings that I have experienced during and after the war there has always been a large element of racial envy, racial rivalry, and racial assertion. With us in those summer days on the Rhine, with our beer or our Pfissirch-bowle before us, we never roused the faintest instinct of dispute. Once on a superb August day a Zeppelin—one of the very first—came sailing majestically over Bonn, from the direction of Cologne. 'What is it for?' I asked amiably, and innocently. 'Why, my dear sir,' replied Max jovially, 'its purpose is to drop bombs on your British Navy.' The answer satisfied me perfectly and there seemed nothing that was in the smallest degree odd or hostile or even impolite in it. A few hours later the Zeppelin in landing hit the ground with a thud and was completely destroyed. The *Kölnische Zeitung* at once opened a subscription list in order to provide a new one. My kindly hosts asked if I would like to contribute. 'Of course not,' I replied, 'I am very glad it is destroyed.' 'But how could you be so cruel?' cried the family, outraged. 'You said it was to be used to destroy our fleet, so of course I am glad we are now safe,' I retorted, with elementary logic but complete sincerity. 'Yes, of course he is right,' piped the youngest sister, Agnes of the corkscrew plaits. And they all agreed at once, seeing that I was at least reasonable.

That was the nearest we ever got to a dispute and it bore about as much relation to the form a similar discussion would take now as would the conversation of two racing enthusiasts bear to an all-in wrestling bout. Yet I was vaguely disturbed. A statue in the gardens by the river of the poet Arndt, bearing on its pedestal the inscription '*Der Rhein: Deutschlands Fluss, nicht Deutschlands Grenze*,' made me pause and wonder why exactly it was put up. I was to find out later on.

* * * * * * *

Visits to the villages of Westphalia, varied with excursions down the Rhine by moonlight, with the inevitable Lorelei sung mournfully by the entire party, Marcel and myself included, made the summer pass lightly and charmingly. Now and again Max and I would try our luck at one of the many hundred shooting-galleries among the beer-gardens either at Godesberg or at Königswinter. Each gallery was plastered with patriotic inscriptions 'Learn to shoot for your Country' and the rest, and Max, with a chuckle, always said it was good to keep one's eye in training. He and I would shoot together, each thinking perfectly seriously that we were in fact shooting at what was, in not a very long time, to be each other. 'That's where I shall hit you, Max,' I would say as I got my bottle in the middle. And Max would ripost with an appropriate remark. Our friendship was sealed and settled.

From that day to this I have never heard any word of that large and homely family except once in 1917. Then I was questioning a young German airman who had been brought down in Salonika. 'Where do you come from?' I asked him as a formality. 'From Bonn,' he replied. 'Do you by any chance know the Familie Joerrens?' I hazarded. 'Certainly,' he answered. And then he explained how the two men, Max and Alfred, had both joined up at the very start. But he knew no more and I have often wondered what have been the sufferings of those twelve sisters on whose *hausfrauliche* energies depended in those days at Bonn all the worldly comforts of poor Max and Alfred.

* * * * * * *

A summer term at Oxford had barely begun when suddenly the death of Edward VII involved our amiable and amateur Officers Training Corps in a terrifying ceremonial. We were ordered to Windsor to line the last stretch of roadway up to the chapel, the roadway along which all the crowned heads of Europe were to walk on foot. Our officers, alarmed, spent exhausting mornings before breakfast instructing us in the incredibly complicated drill concerned with funerals and Royal Passings. 'Rest on your arms reversed!' was an order which for many days resulted only in a clatter of falling rifles and a confusion of whirlings and crashings which, we all felt, would freeze the marrow even of a Balkan king. But practice made perfect and a week later we all entrained for Windsor, feeling almost like soldiers. But on arrival there we once more felt less soldierly than ever, for on one flank were the Coldstream Guards and on the other the Scots Guards. We felt like Boy Scouts. Still we hoped that in the general atmosphere of khaki we should be overlooked by the more critical of the potentates.

Funerals of the great are always massive and profound. The playing of the 'Dead March' away below in the background, the complete silence of the crowd, and the odd bunch of shining figures approaching us behind the hearse stiffened us into a tolerable semblance of soldiers. The dread command 'Rest on your arms reversed' was responded to with a minimum of clatter and some little decorum. We all felt we had escaped general notice. As the Kings of Europe approached they looked for all the world like a segment of the Lord Mayor's Show. Screwing up my eyes below my bowed head I was able to detect Ferdinand of Bulgaria, by far the most kingly of them all, Manuel of Portugal the least kingly, and suddenly close by my side came Wilhelm of Germany, stiff and rigid, white and silver, with his superb helmet and his withered arm. Near him, in ludicrous contrast, some strange Oriental. All the kings and princes deliberately walking out of step in order that they might emphasise their individuality.

The strange party passed, the music faded down and we rested at ease until the vast ceremonial had dispersed. Then off we marched with Guards behind and before us, feeling every inch soldiers now that we no longer had to fear that awful command 'Rest on your arms reversed.'

Back to Oxford and our studies and our imitation soldiering. Proclamations and trumpetings in the ensuing days and a new era had dawned with a new king.

A year later, in that hot summer of 1911, our war nearly came. I recollect no excitement, nothing more than a mild wonder whether this was the real thing or not. It was not.

* * * * * * *

Oxford done with and Athens in view, and the first of my youthful ambitions were by way of being accomplished. The close of 1911 seemed to postpone the war indefinitely. Occasional scares of a minor kind, fierce speeches by Lloyd George, and the danger seemed to have vanished. But in keeping with the times we were not allowed to forget that a war was impending. A strange play, *The Englishman's Home*, kept up our anticipations. Some hailed it as unadulterated nonsense, others as the great Apocalyptic warning. In fact it was the very first example of propaganda which was ever launched in our country. To me and to my elders, in our life up till then, propaganda was unknown. The Press published its news as news, rarely as anything else, and I have always taken it as axiomatic that the essence of propaganda is to say one thing and mean another, which shows how near to casuistry all propaganda must be. *The Englishman's Home* was the best propaganda I have seen then or since. It showed the simple suburban family at its daily pursuits, frivolities and stupidities. Then a sudden war placed that simple home in the forefront of battle with the waves of invaders rapidly approaching its inviolate threshold. From an atmosphere of cricket, billiards and charity concerts, the small red-brick villa characteristic of those early Georgian days became a pivotal point in a battle. Shells screamed over it, around it and, by degrees, into it. Dust covered the stalls and fear gripped the pit. Papa Englishman, fool-hero of the piece, driven to madness by the incredible insult of an enemy invasion of his very garden, seized a trophy rifle that conveniently hung upon his walls, loaded it with trophy bullets, that as conveniently were also there suspended, and, after a few futile attempts to find out how the damned thing worked, at last discovered how to pull the bolt, loaded the magazine, and blazed wildly away through the battered window of the drawing-room, while son and daughter and mother sat dumb with terror on the settee. By luck he killed an enemy officer, to the joy of himself and the audience. The triumph was almost immediately followed by the entry of a squad of the uniformed enemy. Their uniforms somehow brought me a tremendous thrill, partly by their strangeness, partly by the fact that they chanced to be Serbian uniforms! A few brief orders and Papa was led out bound and blindfolded to be shot. A fusillade and the play was over.

Extreme crudity, no dialogue worth the name, bad acting and a whole skinful of slushy sentiment—and yet the play was dramatic, it was moving and it was, somehow, remarkably real. I laughed at it: I damned it with my friends as mere conscription-mongering and yet, at the end of it all, there remained the plain fact not merely that such a thing *might* happen, but that it *probably would* happen. Five years later, as I walked, when on leave, up towards St Paul's at midnight to watch Zeppelins dropping bombs on Liverpool Street and to admire the searchlights and the reflection of leaping red flames against the dome of the cathedral, the crude realities of *The Englishman's Home* came to my mind. It was propaganda well enough, for it had made one enemy serve for another and one home for a whole nation. I have no idea what the intentions of its writer were. Presumably it was to warn young men like me. If so we were in no need of warning, and I rejoiced that I at least had learned to fire a rifle, if nothing else, during the erratic course of my most ineffectual military training.

2

A few months later I was looking in Belgrade at the very uniforms which had been worn by the enemy in the play. For I returned by way of Serbia from Athens. There too I had seen my first war, that of the Balkan Allies against the tyrant Turk. For me and for many of my age it seemed at first that this was the war we had been waiting for. It looked as if at last the conflagration we had all been expecting was happily confined, as the fire-brigadiers say, to the outhouses, and rapidly got under control. A nice satisfactory little war that would work it all off at the expense of a few thousand Balkan corpses. Young Gaudier the sculptor, whose work I saw for the first time in 1911 at a rebel artist exhibition in London, wrote in October 1912: [1]

> 'Turkey is in the hands of the Slavs who say quite openly that they will divide it among themselves, and Austria accepts. This is all very good news, because after this war, there can be no further excuse for another.'

Poor lad, exactly two years later he wrote:

> 'We crept through a wood as dark as pitch, fixed bayonets, and pushed some five hundred yards amid fields until we came to a wood. There we opened fire and in a bound we were along the bank of the road where the Prussians stood. We shot at each other some quarter of an hour at a distance of twelve to fifteen yards and the work was deadly. I brought down two great giants who stood against a burning heap of straw, my corporal accounted for four more, and so on all along the line.' [2]

He was killed, shot through the head in a charge in June 1915, and with him ended our pleasant delusion of the war to end war in the Balkans.

I remember, while I was at Athens in 1913, having some faint premonitions of evil. The second Balkan war had then broken out and the Allies, having destroyed Turkey-in-Europe, were at each other's throats over the booty. There

[1] *Savage Messiah*, by H. S. Ede, p. 179, Heinemann, 1931.
[2] *Ibid.*, p. 266.

Greek evzones in the Balkan War of 1912

Crown Prince Constantine and Staff in 1912

was a general feeling that the great Pan-Balkan Federation which had been the aim, at least in European eyes, of the first and popular attempt to remove Turkey from the map, had not developed according to plan. Distant thunders of disapproval from Austria were audible. Serbia, her most hated neighbour, the detestable barbarians across the Danube, was getting too strong. Even I, in the assurance of youth, with a solution to every problem, could not quite see how Austrian diplomats could prevent the now enlarged Serbia from becoming the strongest of the Balkan States in military power. For the Bulgarians had been defeated by Greeks and Serbs by military might. There was no question that the Serbs were the better fighters; indeed, as I was to learn later, they were the finest soldiers in Europe. And Austria had to grin and bear it. But I began to doubt if Austria would grin and bear it for long or with unruffled equanimity.

My first return by way of Belgrade had been just after the close of the first war. Turkish prisoners were in the old fortress at Belgrade, flags and troops were in every street, and there were general rejoicings.

So when I returned to England in April 1914 I again chose the route up from Salonika to Belgrade and Vienna. But this time the prisoners of war in the old fortress at Belgrade were Bulgarians. Things, somehow, were not quite working out as we young optimists had anticipated, nor indeed as anyone else had anticipated. And Austrian diplomats were watching and noting, conferring and planning what to do about this troublesome Balkan State who had defeated Bulgaria, the darling of the Austrians, and Turkey her cat's-paw. International knowledge was in a most elementary condition, and the average Englishman of those insular days scarcely knew the permutations and combinations of European Powers, yet I can say without pride or self-satisfaction that I at least, after a few weeks in Serbia and Austria, conceived the most definite notion that whatever was going to happen would begin either in Austria or in Serbia. Belgrade and Vienna in April 1914 were inflamed, the one with pride of military power, the other with the disapproval of which an old Empire will always feel to a young upstart.

War, my war, the war which Max and I had discussed over our beer at Bonn and Godesberg, was waiting for us round the next corner. I say this, not in the light of subsequent events, but because I smelt the odour of war as it drifted slowly up from the battlefields of Thrace and Macedonia, along the valley of the Vardar to Belgrade, and from that white and shining citadel across the sunny plains of Hungary to the decorous streets of Vienna.

Home in England, I resumed the quiet life of an untroubled spring and summer. The distant fumes had not blown this way yet. Even France was tranquil and unheeding, and Germany, through which I had passed, was the same Germany that I had known six years earlier. Yet Ireland, stormy petrel of our seas, caught the infection from afar. Ulster and Carson and Gough and the Curragh, surely the silliest story ever hatched in our history, made out of mimic war and infantile protestations of faith a vague semblance of the realities that had been produced among the stony Balkans. These Irishmen can at least go down to history as wind-vanes who pointed the direction of the storm. Their antics, devoid of heroism, in themselves meaningless and ridiculous, were symptomatic of that longing to be up and to kill which was spreading slowly but surely through the veins of Europe.

* * * * * * *

I was basking in the sun of a Hertfordshire garden when suddenly the papers told in large headlines of the murder at Serajevo. Then Austria struck. Her ultimatum made it clear that things would happen in rapid sequence. I left for London, for I knew somehow that my summer holiday was at an end. My projected trip to Greece for the autumn seemed to have a whole world of nightmares in between that would keep me back and grasp me with nightmare hands. I was unhappy and yet exhilarated. For here at last were events that led on and on to almost any conclusion.

July drew to a close and I knew that at last my war was upon us. Austria, Germany, Russia and France toppled over the abyss, and then came that dreadful pause as we ourselves tottered, the fateful Sunday, Monday and Tuesday. Continuously in London I watched and listened, and all the time I knew what the result would be.

* * * * * * *

Eleven at night was the time our ultimatum to Germany expired. I and some friends went to the Café Royal for beer. Packed full with talking and gesticulating people the place was tense with excitement. At intervals elderly Jews rose and waved small Union Jacks; stray snatches of the *Marseillaise* came from odd corners, sung by intoxicated schoolboys; after a time I left and wandered down to Whitehall, vaguely under the impression that the War Office was the sort of place where news would be given out. Many thousand people apparently thought the same, and the long street was packed with a rather silent and curious crowd. No one quite knew why anyone was there. I imagined wildly that at the stroke of eleven a mounted Uhlan would canter from the German Embassy to the War Office with extravagant apologies and with a public announcement that German troops were *en route* from Belgium back to Germany. In effect nothing of any sort at all happened and no one was told anything. But at length eleven o'clock struck and silence fell for the fraction of a second. A moment after everyone hurried off, and somehow the news spread that we were at war. How it spread I have no idea at all.

Later in the evening two intoxicated Germans who had been drinking beer at the German Gambrinus near

Piccadilly, detached the mediæval spears from the walls of that admirable but Olde Worlde hostelry and marched in step down Piccadilly singing *Deutschland über Alles.* In due course they were shepherded into Vine Street Police Station and *their* war was over for good and all.

Some few patriots broke the windows of Appenrodt's delicatessen shops and gradually we all went home to bed. My war had started.

The next day I went to Oxford and entered my name on the lists of those dutiful young patriots of the Officers Training Corps, and was told that in due course I should be gazetted as an officer. All was, as we learned to say later, going according to plan.

CHAPTER II

ACTUALITIES

As the war developed and spread I waited patiently for my country to answer the request which I had so dutifully made to it. But nobody seemed to be in a hurry, so for some weeks I was left with nothing to do but to read newspapers and to invent theories to rival those of Mr Belloc, who was for a few fleeting moments the oracle of war—at least until he was found out. And what newspapers they were. In the letters to *The Times* you can see revealed in perfect clarity the simple lunacy of those queer weeks. Young men like myself were not in the least disturbed that the world had toppled over; we had no brief for it as it was, and we were not interested that it had passed so swiftly. But our parents and elders saw ruin everywhere. They exhibited every sort and kind of emotional reaction and they suffered deeply and bitterly as they saw the world they had so methodically built up crumble and lurch into intolerable ruin. We heartless young paid them no heed at all, for we had been bred to anticipate destruction and ruin and never a thought as yet had entered our heads that we might perhaps be the people who would rebuild it. We never for a moment sat down together and laid down any project for restoring the world by war. To the best of my knowledge we were all just simply negative young people. If there was going to be a general destruction then we wanted to be in it. Heaven knows, I was filled with mortal and deadly fear when I signed the fatal document that promised me unlimited hopes of slaughter for King and Country. I knew exactly what I was in for, and I decided then and there that no false heroics would ever persuade me to throw my life away except for some most cogent and compelling reason.

I do not think I am more of a coward than most, but I do know most definitely that I was determined with an iron determination to preserve my own skin as far as duty permitted. I was under no illusions whatever as to the nature of war. I had seen the traces of it in the Balkans, and I knew that our war would be far more unpleasant, if only because it would be waged with efficiency above the Balkan standards. And I had known young Frenchmen who had done their service in earlier years and learned from them that war, or at least manœuvres, was largely a matter of lice, vice and exhaustion. I felt no exhilaration except that which comes from launching oneself into an unknown career; I gave up reading serious books and I gave up thinking. During those early weeks while I waited to learn exactly what my country wanted me to do I merely read newspapers and talked war news. To be on the right side, in case I was suddenly summoned, I ordered a uniform and spent many happy hours examining all the wonderful pot-hooks and hangers which enterprising manufacturers invented to make the lot of the subaltern lighter in the trenches. There were map-cases and compasses, large revolvers and small pistols, binoculars, knives and things to extract pebbles from horses' hooves. There were inflational waistcoats to save you if you fell into the sea, swords which neither cut nor thrust, tin boxes about six inches square which contained tabloided meals for a fortnight. Fully equipped the young subaltern would have sunk in marshy soil like a stone or been picked off at once by snipers. When I did go to the trenches I took a moderate supply of these toys, but found that they served more for entertainment than for use. A brother officer and I consumed the fortnight's meals one day at tea. The unsinkable waistcoat made an admirable mat for the floor of a muddy dugout, and the other treasures soon vanished out of sight. Binoculars and revolver alone stayed with me to the Armistice.

The first four weeks of the war found me rarely separated

from a newspaper. I discovered unbelievable treasures in each daily issue. Heaven forbid that I should give the faintest suggestion that I was a young cynic. Indeed, I was not, and I doubt if I ever even began to see things with cynical eyes until the Armistice. But I read things in the papers that just stuck in my mind and left me gasping. Was this really the world into which I had been born? Was this the civilisation I had been bred in? Of the leaders and the editorial comments I took little notice. Men, I knew, were hired and paid to write these things and, as a rule, they wrote them well. Above all *The Times* gave daily a very fair and just appreciation of things in general. It is only since the war that *The Times* has become conscious of its great position, of its duty to guide civilisation into the proper channels, of its indubitable power to influence the currents of European history. In those days it was innocent and relatively virgin-minded. Now it devotes all its energies to imprinting its footsteps in the sands of time. Now hardly any item of foreign news that it publishes is stated simply as news; it appears rather as an awful warning. However, the genius of Footprintinghouse Square is essentially British, if nothing else.

So amazed was I by the views expressed in that bright summer of August 1914 that some few of them I removed and filed for reference. For I wanted to know whether they were right and I wondered what I should feel about them later on. Then I forgot them, but by great good fortune they turned up again, so that I can now quote at leisure from the sayings of my superiors. Oxford had taught me the value of original documents, and the book in which I had pasted them survived all my wanderings and changings of home.

First and foremost of all the horrors that shocked my elders and betters was the fearful destruction of Liège and Louvain. My *Times* of 30th August 1914 contained a letter which showed me more clearly than any personal explanation of views the fury and horror which had overwhelmed those who had been bred in the belief that the nineteenth century had laid the foundations of civilisation for ever.

'The feelings,' said the writer, 'that such a hideous destruction have called forth are too deep for words. . . . This sin against history and against posterity can never, indeed, be condoned. It cries aloud for what retribution human justice, however slow-footed, can offer. . . . With the fate of sister universities before us, we whose associations are academic can hardly read without a feeling of irony the notices put out in several quarters that our own universities and colleges will reopen as usual for the Michaelmas term. Their decision was probably itself unavoidable. But is it too much to hope that they will set up a warning over their gates that none shall enter who are not physically disqualified to serve their country?'

I felt that Oxford was no safe place for such as me. The lash was already being laid on our backs. I felt some secret satisfaction that I was exempt from any slur: my name was already on the list of *alumni morituri*. It was no affair of mine. I thanked heaven that I was physically fit, for it was clear that the unfits would have a hard time in Oxford—or at least I supposed they might.

Another letter froze me into dumb surprise. Frederic Harrison, one of the great men of the last century, scholar, philosopher and gentleman, wrote an August letter.

'Under an inverted doctrine of right and wrong the German millions,' he wrote, 'are now committing enormities as horrible as those of Dahomey and African savages of old. Let us hear no more whining about German 'culture.' But let us make it known that we will make the world ring with our sense of horror. Be it understood that when the Allies have finally crushed this monstrous brood, the Kaiser—if indeed he choose to survive—shall be submitted to the degradation inflicted upon poor Dreyfus. In presence of Allied troops, let his blood-stained sword be broken across his craven back and the uniform and orders of which he is so childishly proud be stamped in the mire. And if he lives through it, St Helena or the Devil's Island might be his prison and his grave. The German people will then understand what the civilised world feels about the modern Attila—the new "Scourge of God." '

I was stark astonished. Was this really the world I had known? Were these amiable gentlemen I had heard of and seen only a few months ago the shrieking furies of *The Times* correspondence column? Something had clearly happened to cause this strange distemper. So I noted the outcry and filed it patiently in my box. Then I hurried off on another of countless visits to the War Office to see if anyone had done anything about my swift response to my country's call. Of course nobody had done anything, and the list to which my name had been appended had been clearly lost. But I met a friend in a corridor who held another list. He knew my name had gone in and obligingly scribbled it down again then and there in some other list which bore the heading 'East Lancashire Regiment.' That was the first time I met the realities of war. Here was an actual regiment of the line, a real unit, already engaged in France and here was I actually seeing myself incorporated into it. I felt this was more encouraging than walking London wondering exactly how Mr Harrison would trample the Kaiser's decorations in the mire or where or when it would be done. Much though I approved of this hypothetical entertainment I was quite sure that it was a little remote and a trifle hard to achieve. I was tempted to write to Harrison to tell him that I would bear his suggestion in mind and see that it was referred to the proper quarters: meantime I was contemplating a visit abroad to investigate ways and means, and that I was his sincerely Second Lieutenant Casson. But I was not cruel and I could see, as anyone can see who reads these strange utterances, that these unhappy elders were frantic with horror, stricken to the heart and bitter beyond any comprehension, at least beyond the comprehension of youngsters like me. It has become a commonplace to blame the Victorian Age for the war, to say that the old men made a holocaust of their sons by their own stupidity and by their own pride. I did not believe that then and I do not believe it now. To them, as to us, things just happened. They did not make the war any more than do men deliberately make a Black Death. War comes, and when it comes it comes as the great and overwhelming Instructor—at least that was the description given of war by Thucydides, who studied the subject more than most both at first hand and by hearsay. And these elders of ours had been brought up in their youth to believe that *they* were the instructors of the world, that there was little they could learn. So that their hysteria was rather in the nature of the cries of the naughty child who will not learn its lessons and will not profit by its own mistakes.

Who am I to lecture my betters? I have no status of any kind. But I can say with a clear conscience that when the war began, and when we learned gradually of its necessary horrors, that no flicker of anguish touched me, that no frenzy of horror palsied my mind, simply because I had known long ago that it was coming and that, knowing what I did, all the consequences were to be endured without criticism because they were all part of what my youthful eyes had seen to be inevitable.

* * * * * * *

We, the young men, were neither queer nor interesting nor unusual. We said no clever things and we held no strong views. The outcries of our elders left us unconcerned and we hardly even commented on them. I can remember no argument and no discussion about these newspaper ravings. But we were all rather sickened by the slick journalism that the war so rapidly generated; it all seemed like so much ooze collecting by the banks of a swift river. The river ran on and the ooze was left behind, slimy and film-covered. Our job was to cross the river, not to paddle in the slime.

As the days of my waiting went on I felt irritated and bored and dull. I often wonder how we should have endured the bright young men of to-day if we had had them to talk to. We were not earnest, nor were we filled with the fires of crusade or the love of England. We just felt that it was worth while seeing what it was all about and going abroad to do what all our friends were either doing or hoping to do. I may now be speaking more for myself than for my friends, but I honestly believe I do them no injustice when I say that the war to us was rather like getting launched into a career. Whatever had been our education or our plans, the war had, years back, been fitted into them. It came as a kind of apprenticeship and we were articled to it. I recollect that when I was asked officially whether I would serve 'for three years or for the duration' I chose 'duration,' because it seemed that that was the proper thing to do.

The young men of my age with whom I talked and who had been my friends were all perfectly clear in what they were doing. They were not stirred by the moral issues of the war very deeply, nor were they passionately aroused by the evil of war in the abstract. But we were all happy and light-hearted and quite certain that there was nothing heroic about our decision.

Somehow or other we neither taught nor learned lessons. And yet we enjoyed ourselves. Two men of those days stand out as typical of the time; one was H. H. Munro ('Saki'), the other Denis Garstin. Munro I never met, but his books had given me a permanent capacity to chuckle at simple things. Garstin, with whom I spent many amusing evenings when he or I was on leave, and one evening before either of us went out, was the embodiment of everything that was worth knowing and doing in those early weeks. His slim figure and keen blue eyes, and his wit and charm stayed long in my mind. Both these men were killed, and both of them had qualities of humour and agility of mind that seem to-day to be replaced by sombre witticisms and androgyne asperities.

I know that every generation believes in its own superiority: there is a detestable team-spirit in each of the seven ages of man. But I am not holding up my own generation as better than any other, but merely suggesting that they were a good deal happier than most that have occurred since. For we were all perfectly happy in that first year of the war, not with the slushy joy of 'the happy warrior' but rather content with our lot. It was the sort of happiness that comes to a man who hears that a house is on fire and is fortunate enough to contrive to get there before the fire is over and see the 'effects.' Admittedly that was a stupid and a rather short-sighted view, but then I have no brief of any kind for the *intelligence* of my generation. If we had been intelligent we should, years before the war began, have organised such General Strikes and sabotages and 'direct actions' among the proletariat of Europe that the militarists would never have been able to get their long-cherished plans going. That kind of preparation against war never entered our minds. To-day a play like *The Englishman's Home* would lead to a vast increase in the ranks of Communism and Pacifism. Then it merely encouraged the Conscription-mongers, the Territorials, and the Navy League. Yes, we were a stupid generation all right. But, thank God, we were not didactic or avuncular and we saw the funny side of most things, though not of the panic of our elders, which struck us as stark tragedy.

Denis Garstin was particularly intrigued by the hysterical outbreak of patriotism which took the form of women giving white feathers to civilians. He longed to be offered one. In the end his wish came true. One day in September 1914 in a bus in Oxford Street an exceedingly pretty girl suddenly leaned across to him and whispered 'Coward,' for he was then in mufti and back wounded from France. When she left the bus he left too. Raising his hat he asked politely for an explanation. Confused but adamant, the girl replied, 'Here are you, doing nothing, while all my brothers and my father are out at the Front!' 'I have a very good reason, madam,' replied Denis with a pained and haughty air. 'What is it?' asked the girl, intrigued. 'I am secretary of the London Eugenics Society,' replied Denis, 'and at our last general meeting it was decided that some of us, the healthier and the better-looking, should stay at home in order to propagate the race and keep up the standard. I am one of the selected.' Then he turned to her abruptly, 'Will *you* be the mother of my next child?' and she fled down the street.

It has always seemed to me ridiculous that those who study history, ancient or mediæval or recent, should not leap at the chance of seeing it made at high pressure. The prospect of being in the biggest upheaval the world has ever seen seemed to me to be infinitely more attractive, despite all the alleged discomforts of soul and body, than to sit on the outskirts as a spectator with the certain knowledge that all sources of information would be tainted. We had been educated in a make-believe world, fed on uncertain stories of the past, bred in a world of discontented and tottering perfection, and now at last we could go and see the whole thing in the melting-pot. To see a volcano in eruption is a perpetual lure to men. And they all try to get as near the edge of the lava as they can. That, I think, is why most of us decided to go to war and be soldiers, that and the feeling that it was the concluding part of our education. We were débutants with a taste for excitement.

There are so few of those young men alive now. We were all exactly of an age to take on responsibility, of an age to do what we had for years known we were expected to do. But we hadn't quite expected that what was mainly expected of us was to get killed. I had the luck of the tenth man, for the early years of the war were a decimation in which the nine were killed and the tenth left, a decimation that even

Nero would have shuddered at. On reflection, there are hardly any of the youngsters with whom I had worked at Oxford or met later in London who survived. I doubt if either Max or Alfred or poor little Malbranckelschen ever got through. All my friends now are either older or younger than myself.

No, we hadn't quite expected that. Gaps we knew there would be, losses we knew would occur, but we hadn't counted on being left alone. I had pictured, in my early ruminations in August 1914, reunions after the war when we should all drink to the memory of so-and-so and someone else. But one cannot drink alone to the memory of a crowd!

When I got out to Flanders I met friends everywhere, in woods, in billets, on the road, in canteens and in trenches. I remember every meeting as clearly as if it were yesterday, for each meeting was by chance and so all the more exciting, the more stirring, like meetings in a dream. Every one of those friends I met in Flanders was killed, without a single exception. If I know them, they are laughing at me now.

* * * * * * *

Little depressed us in those days of preparation. One thing alone began to shock us—the gradual spread of a nauseating vulgarity among people in general, in the Press, among people one met and in ordinary conversation. We did not recognise it at first, but it was the first infection of that vile germ, propaganda. Those in power gradually learned that if only you want a thing done you can get it done by calling it something else. Recruiting and its methods, which soon developed, made us sick. As I waited to hear what was to be done with me, I saw the beginnings of that revolting drive which ultimately produced 'Kitchener's Army.' It was all organised like a jumble sale or a charity dance. All the old gambits came into use on a vast and national scale. Posters, gramophones, songs, speeches, blackmail, bullying, intimidation and threats—in fact all the stock-in-trade of the country squire and the vicar's wife combined into one. I thanked heaven that I had done it all quietly and decently. For, after all, there was something intimate and personal about what we had decided; it ranked almost as a kind of proposal of marriage or announcement of a pregnancy. The Greeks compared a man in battle to a woman in childbirth, and I felt that there ought to be some kind of reticence about both. And here were screaming maids and matrons and old men and boys all yelping to see me, and others like me, exhibit our pregnancy to the public to be photographed, drawn, sung about and made into a public festival. No, we had our maiden modesty, strangely enough. From virginity to pregnancy was for us a long step, more particularly since we had no idea of any kind what would be the outcome of our pregnant condition.

Bored and infuriated that I was kept waiting so long, I made several frantic attempts to become something other than a mere time-server. In some queer way I was put into touch with some secret department of the War Office which wanted special officer motor-cycle despatch-riders for urgent service in France. I rushed up and was at once sent to be examined in French and German, two essentials of this strange job. The examination consisted in the polite exchange of compliments for a space of two minutes between me and two examiners at Burlington House, and I was passed with honours. But on returning to the War Office triumphantly I was asked if I could do all the running repairs of a motor-bicycle. I admitted that I was willing to do my best, but I let it incautiously slip out that I had in fact not as yet ridden a motor-cycle. I was ploughed ignominiously, and returned to my civilian status abashed.

Later I enrolled myself, I have no idea how, in some strange battalion of youngsters who were being drilled in the desolate courts of the White City. I did a few days' drill, with pagodas and palm-courts around me, when suddenly to my astonishment a telegram reached my lodgings which read: 'Rejoin unit at once: 3rd battalion East Lancashire Regiment, Laira Battery, Plymouth: Officer commanding.'

Panic struck me. Was I a deserter? how long had I belonged to this unit? when had I joined it? or had I joined it at all? there was something stern and forbidding about this, my very first order, to *rejoin* what I had not consciously joined at all!

A friend in uniform soon calmed me. I learned my first lesson in Army English. 'Rejoin means join,' he said tersely. 'Then why the hell call it rejoin?' I retorted. 'Ah,' he sighed, 'you will be issued with many an order like that before you have done. The King's Regulations and the King's English are in no way connected.'

So I deserted flagrantly from the anonymous battalion at the White City and leaped into my waiting uniform. The very same night I left by the night train for Plymouth, a soldier at last.

Of those friends of mine who were killed, Denis Garstin saw more clearly than any, after a brief experience of war, that unless we learned the first, and in some ways the only lesson for good which the war had to teach, we should have done better never to join up at all. 'You are fond of your men,' he said, 'and they of you. You do the best you can for them and they return the compliment. That's not Socialism is it? Oh no, because it's something that's regulation. It's done by all the best regiments. But, my God, man, don't you see that it's an ideal? sound practical common sense. If only I thought you'd stick together afterwards as you do now I'd die happy. And you could, so jolly easily, if only you thought. But you'll lose confidence when you get home and start class wars again.' [1]

Denis Garstin, who believed in a drastic renewal of the social order, was shot at Murmansk by men of a race in which

[1] Denis Garstin, *The Shilling Soldiers* (with a preface by Hugh Walpole), p. 282. Posthumously published.

he never lost confidence. He had seen the worst of the fighting in France and was sent to Russia in 1916. His words bring an unpleasant taste to the mouth now. He knew the ruling classes were as weak as water, but had he seen them in panic, as I have in 1926 and 1931, he would have despaired of the world. We never suspected then that the lessons we learned should have been so thoroughly forgotten or so deliberately neglected and made so utterly futile.

CHAPTER III

PREPARATION

Of arms we had in fact none. Day after day streams of patient men came into the depot from Burnley and Accrington and Preston and Manchester, some in mufti, some in strange blue uniforms like those of the Church Lads' Brigade, and all we could do for them was to give them imitation rifles, teach them to drill and march them endlessly about the roads that ran from the outskirts of Plymouth to the lovely hills and woods at the foot of Dartmoor.

Slowly we armed them, taught them to shoot, kept them cheerful and gave them all the comfort we could. They lived at first in houses near by; there they were fed and kept and allowed to sleep in droves on the floors, wrapped up in army blankets. For these slight services the official recompense to the landladies for each man was 24s. a week! what they got was worth about five shillings, so the eagerness and patriotic fervour of the citizens of Plymouth knew no bounds. Some houses took in as many as ten men. Imagine the wealth they must have pocketed! We were besieged by prospective landladies who begged us to let them take the 'dear boys' in and cherish them. Cherishing was a popular entertainment in those days.

As the autumn wore on we began to realise the enormous wastage going on in France. Drafts were called for in increasing numbers. Fragments of earlier drafts began to come back, wounded or mended, to serve on light duty. From them we learned what the war was really like. Those of us who had not been out were a heterogeneous lot. About half were regular officers, the rest oddments like myself. But we all got on together and found that there were common interests in a common mode of life.

One grey windy day in November a large batch of drafts was being sent off to the two battalions in France. The padre, in a white surplice, gave them a service before they left to hearten them on their journey. 'I look around me,' he said in his address, 'and see all these fine soldiers, now shortly to leave for the Front to fight for their King and Country. As I look at them a grief comes over me to think that within a year so few of them will still be in the land of the living'—at this point the Colonel, a gentle kindly soul, stepped quietly forward, tapped the padre on the shoulder, and announced a hymn. We young officers took the cue and started singing lustily. All was well again and the padre took no further part in the proceedings. The next day he left for some other destination to do good cheer for some other regiment! Never once in the war did I meet a padre who had the smallest sense of the realities of the times, but this was certainly my prize padre of the war. Talking to the men afterwards I found that they were genuinely sorry for him and felt he had been badly treated.

Time passed almost unnoticed. I felt now that I was well out of that odious civilian life where everything was make-believe, trumpery and tinsel. To my pleasure I found that by accident I had joined the very regiment to which I was ancestrally entitled to belong. My surname is a rare one in most parts of England, but it was common enough in the East Lancashire Regiment. Cassons of all shapes, sizes and hues were in the ranks. Then I remembered that my family was of Huguenot origin and that we had started life as refugees in Lancashire, engaged in spinning and weaving, away back in the seventeenth century. This was apparently the first family reunion since then!

Plymouth in those days was more English than most places. It was delightful to wander round the old Tudor streets near the Hamoaze and see houses that had been built before the Armada, and streets down which Drake had walked, or to stand on the jetty from which the *Mayflower* had sailed. Naval comings and goings made it always an excitement to walk on Plymouth Hoe, and the searchlights on the boom were a sight that never palled at nights.

Winter came and January passed. News from France did not change much. We all waited patiently, unflurried and unalarmed, neither anxious to go nor unwilling to leave. Slowly the casualty lists showed me depletions in the ranks of my friends, but as yet gave no inkling of the greater destruction that was to come.

At the close of February 1915, as a cheerful party of us were enjoying a dinner-party at a restaurant, an orderly knocked at the door and handed me a pink army telegraphic form. My orders to leave the following day for France with a draft. The manner of my going was as dramatic as *The Englishman's Home*, though less futile. My friends chaffed me on the way it had been staged and accused me of having given the party a nice dramatic finish.

I felt that another milestone had been passed, but how slowly they came along on this road which was to lead me to some strange destination of which I knew less than nothing.

The next afternoon I was sent across the river into Cornwall to an isolated and wind-blown camp where a contingent of Argyll and Sutherland Highlanders were stationed. I had orders to convey a contingent of a hundred and ten of these men to France and had to march them a few miles from their camp, take them across the river to Saltash and entrain direct for Southampton.

Before dawn the next day we were marching along down to the ferry and when, at the ferry, I lined them up and read through their names I found we had six too many! others had joined in unasked, for in those early days we really did want to get out of England. It was not so much that we were anxious to get to France, as that we were all heartily tired of endless waiting and time-wasting. Better to get it over as soon as possible and know what we were in for.

Southampton at last after a riotous journey, buns and

bananas at every station, as though we were the Zoological Gardens being moved to another home. At Southampton things began to look more like business and we marched in fine fettle to the Docks. Arrived there we were told that we were not wanted. So we marched all the way back to a rest camp, from which the men got leave to go into the town. As a result almost the whole contingent spent the evening drunk. I was billeted at a hotel and wandered miserably about the streets feeling dejected and lonely. The anti-climax had made us all excessively dispirited.

Another day of idleness followed and at last, rejoicing, we embarked at night on a small paddle-steamer, of the type that had plied between the Isle of Wight and Southampton.

My quarters were in the ladies' latrine. The men slept wherever they could find a flat and unoccupied place. A peaceful night, a little rolling, a good deal of sea-sickness, and at last we entered the Seine just as dawn broke.

The sun came out in a lovely clear sky and we paddled jauntily between rows of trees and small villages. The Scotsmen crowded the decks and waved hilariously at everyone they saw. After a time villages ahead of us woke up and were soon aware of this strange craft. Girls came to their bedroom windows and waved their nightdresses at us, old men waved their nightcaps, and children shouted. It was like a procession in a dream when everyone does odd and unaccountable things. We were all extremely happy.

At last the lovely spires of Rouen came in sight. We disembarked, marched up a hill to a camp, and I prepared for my final inspection of the men. I found on going through their kit that every single man had at Southampton sold or otherwise disposed of his razor, his jack-knife, his woolly waistcoat, and any other oddment of kit which he had possessed. On starting I had verified that they all had these necessities. I asked the Sergeant-Major if he could explain the wholesale loss. 'Yes, sir,' he replied. 'In every pub in Southampton are men who give the soldiers a drink in exchange for these articles of kit. Then they collect them and sell them to the Government as War Stores. There's many a war-profiteer making his fortune now in Southampton!'

My orders came to go to another camp and collect a draft of my own regiment and to leave for the Front the following day. But I spent a night in Rouen, dined at the best restaurant I could find, and hugely enjoyed seeing the endless streams of soldiers passing by, French, British, Indian, and an occasional sailor. There was something pulsating and vivid about Rouen at that time, and I began to feel that life was really worth living and extremely worth preserving. Everyone was nice to everyone else, there was a tremendous vitality and movement in cafés and restaurants, and one felt that here at least was neither vulgarity nor pretence nor nervous strain. One could at moments hear the guns, and the Front seemed very near. There was none of the make-believe that one had seen in England: none of that courageous 'carrying on' and 'business as usual' note that struck so utterly falsely, and usually was merely a cover to greed or cowardice. I suppose it was really much the same in every country, but somehow or other it was wholly nauseating in England. Then how unspeakably vulgar it was to see our elders asking, commanding, and even threatening us that we should go and fight for them. There were even posts created for old men to serve as 'Recruiting Officers.' They wore full uniform and red tabs of the Staff, and in the country districts were nothing more nor less than official bullies. One such I met six months later at a quiet seaside town where I was resting after leaving hospital. He had nothing whatever to do except to prowl and prowl, looking, like some elderly pimp, for his prey. It was all he could do to keep his hands off me—for I was in mufti—and he paused time and time again to pounce. But his discretion served him well for he was not quite sure that I was the sort of thing he was looking for or not, and he never accosted me. But it was pathetic to think that the country was paying hard cash to hired bullies, the Press Gang in disguise. And not one of these bullies, who all, after all, belonged to the class generally known as gentlemen, ever had the faintest inkling of the indecent and vulgar sight which they presented to youngsters like myself. I honestly believe that, if I had not in fact already decided my own fate, all the blustering and bullying of these pimps would not have persuaded me to apply even for the job of latrine man at a rest camp. I should have become a raging pacifist at once and gone cheerfully to prison. Poor pimps, they were the slimiest of all the slime that the great river of war cast up. Prostitutes at least gave one something in return. These merely drove you to the abattoir, by suggesting insidious thoughts of duty and grandeur of patriotism. I simply cannot conceive how any sane or intelligent man could ever dream of asking another, still less of ordering him, to fight, while he himself was not prepared to do so, or could not in fact do so. That development of the human spirit struck me as the most noisome that the war produced at any time in any place. We, in our tenuous training as officers, had been taught that an officer should never in any circumstances order a man to do what he was not prepared to do himself if necessity called. Yet here were commissioned officers, many of them retired from the regular army, who were delighted to break the soundest tradition and the safest rule of all warfare. I can see no excuse of any kind for this organised procuring.

CHAPTER IV

WARFARE

'Je hais tellement la guerre que je ne suis pas fâché de la subir tout entière.' Le Soldat (In 'Le tombeau sous l'arc de Triomphe'). *A. Raynal.*

THE long train wound its way through the tunnels outside Rouen and stopped on the outskirts. In a moment soldiers had jumped from their carriages and were feverishly hacking off fragments of railway sleepers, making small fires of them and hopefully boiling water to make tea. After some five minutes the train started on. One persistent tea-maker at the front end of the train waited till his water began to boil and jumped neatly on to the last carriage as it reached him.

It was a cold sunny day, and we passed through endless flat fields and open stretches of delightful country. At length we reached a region where everything looked rather sour and neglected and desolate. There was the same village life, the same ploughed fields, the same occasional lines of convoy and groups of British soldiers, but somehow the sun was not on it, it was drab and a trifle fly-blown.

At length we stopped at a small dreary red station from whose name we gathered we were in Flanders rather than in France. I had a draft of about a dozen men of various units of the 4th Division, and we were met by a guide. We set off along a muddy road and at length came in sight of ruined houses, broken trees, and an expanse of neglected fields and broken walls. We passed a cross-roads through a very dull and sombre village that the guide said was Plugstreet, and ahead of us within a mile was the Front. The steady pounding of guns was audible everywhere, but there was no sight of war except the aeroplanes. At length I came to a small farm on the right of the road, with the fringe of a large wood opposite. 'Battalion 'Eadquarters,' said the guide, saluted and left. I entered and found a cheerful party of the Colonel, Adjutant and some others at tea. I was greeted with kindness, shown where to sleep, and invited to tea.

The next morning the Colonel, a peculiar man of little charm but some kindness, gave me a few hints as to what to do in the trenches, and then said, 'Come out for a stroll, young man.' Affected by this camaraderie I joined him, and we turned out at the back gate of the farm into what at first I took to be a garden. It was, but not the kind I was thinking of. 'I managed to get the gravestones cut at Armentières,' said the Colonel. 'Don't you think it looks charming?' and there was a group of some dozen neat small headstones. 'W. H. Hoare: killed in action Feb. 25th 1915,' I read. Why, heavens, I thought, I was dining with him in Plymouth ten days ago. Another and another name followed, men with whom I had laughed and drunk a moment back. I felt slightly sick. But the Colonel was smiling with the smile of the fervent horticulturist. He really admired that burial-ground of his. He thought he was 'doing his officers proud.' It never occurred to him that to initiate a young officer in that peculiar way might not be kind or considerate. Remember, up to that moment I had seen no trace of death, and now suddenly I met my friends disguised as garden ornaments. I often have wondered where men like that colonel were brought up that they should have been so wholly devoid of sensibility. Corpses I was ready for, fresh or ancient; sudden death I was preparing myself for. But for death disguised in the shape of elegant adornment of gardens I was wholly unprepared. It was a set-back. I no longer felt that there was anything fatherly in that colonel. The whole thing was too like an episode in a nightmare—the genial old man whose face suddenly suffuses with a strange green light as he leads you to a cemetery and points with a sinister hand to a gaping tomb. That was how it struck me at the time, for I had not quite yet accustomed myself to the realities of this new dream-world, that had its own perfectly rational inconsequence and inconsequent rationality. I was yet to learn.

The same afternoon I went forward to join my company, which was resting in some battered farm-houses in support to the Front line. In effect I was in action already for at any moment we stood to be called on to fill up the front trenches. But we could walk about and enjoy the faint yellow sun and look at the stray flowers and pretend that we had nothing to do. There was always something to amuse and entertain, so that we were not dull.

A letter to my sister written at this time gives, with a simplicity which is entirely natural, a better idea of the war at this stage than any 'literary effects' which I might now conceive.

'Just a line. As you see, I am here at last. Imagine a stretch of flat country reminiscent of the outskirts of Twickenham, with red farms plentifully scattered around and long rows of "continental" trees everywhere. About 800 yards away are our trenches and, of course, in front the Germans. My company goes in to-night, but so far I have only been in a farm at the back. Every day about lunch and tea-time our guns shell the Germans up a bit and, even as I write, the shells are whizzing overhead on the way.

'Do you notice, by the way, how I have dropped into the "Letters from the Front" style? clichés at every turn (and do you remember that epigram "I always thought 'cliché' meant a suburb of Paris until I learned that it stood for a back-street in Oxford"?).

'At night all the line is lit up by star rockets and so forth, and there are occasional bursts of rifle-fire. Believe me, it is all as you have read.

'But it is really very fine and impressive and one feels really in amongst things at last. Groups of the men sitting round open fires, ourselves sleeping in our clothes on straw, occasional aeroplanes and last, but not least, the regimental graveyard, bring it all home rather forcibly to one.

'There is a grim place called Burnt Out Farm, which some of us have to garrison to-night. It is very near the enemy and surrounded by long-dead Germans.

'Yesterday afternoon there was the deuce of a show over at Y—— (unnamed!) and the guns were simply blazing like hell. I hear we were attacked and countered again.

'Write soon, and if there is any special kind of description you want you have only to name it and it is yours.

'Somebody's servant is deflating an air-pillow in the room just opposite and, as I am getting hungry as a result, I will close for tea.

'P.S. I enclose my will in case it is needed.'

I found that letter recently by pure chance. It had been kept. But it brings the entire scene back to me and I think it has some peculiar power of its own to convey that scene to others. That is why I print it here. It shows how entirely acceptive and uncritical I was. Besides a faint hint of dislike of the sort of stuff one read in the Press, and an obvious attempt to avoid doing anything myself to compose a 'letter from the front,' one can find a good deal in that letter. Chiefly I was struck by the *appearance* of everything, by its beauty and its ugliness. That is why that regimental graveyard and the laconic sentence I gave to it stuck in my mind. My immortal soul finds an appropriate tribute in the postscript.

What we young soldiers and officers thought then about the Germans is of far more interest to me now than it was then at the time. It is hard now to reconstruct my frame of mind and outlook, but of one thing I am quite sure: we did most certainly feel that we were willingly collaborating in a gargantuan attempt to right a gargantuan wrong. None of the post-war revelations have in the smallest degree contributed towards any change of view on my part. I was then wholly convinced, and am as convinced now, that Germany had seized the opportunity to develop long-cherished plans. It may be that she had not provoked the occasion, in fact I am sure that she did not. The occasion had provoked itself. But I felt then, as I feel now, that she did as we should have done if we had conceived similar ideas on the subject of European hegemony. I felt then that if England had wanted to control the destinies of Europe as Germany wanted to do then, that she should have acted as swiftly and as ruthlessly as Germany acted. To win hegemony you had to win a war. To win a war you obviously had to stop at nothing: as far back as 1910 at Oxford we undergraduates had often discussed the uselessness of all treaties when they are faced with warlike ambitions. I was then a member of the inoffensive but not unintelligent Palmerston Club, and I remember how we all agreed that any Power aiming at European control would cut right through all treaties and treaty rights, through all humane sanctions, and simply hack straight at its objective. This Germany did in the full light of day, nor did we for a moment think that it was to her discredit, once the premisses of her ambitions were granted. *But* we refused to grant those premisses; we thought her not only immoral but irrational; we were not surprised at the outcome, only shocked that so civilised a nation could lead up to it in that way. We now know that not only Belgian but Dutch and even Swiss neutrality were at stake,[1] so that I think that our belief in internationalism and international morality was fully justified. We were not prigs, nor were we horrified at the so-called atrocities in Belgium. They were all part of the game, and I, at least, had been led to believe that they were normal, for had I not seen them in *The Englishman's Home*!

We knew that the English view was not the German. We knew that England was not seeking the hegemony of Europe, and we believed that Germany was. Everything that had happened during the six years before the war seemed to indicate as much. And so we went to vindicate

[1] *Un prélude a l'invasion de la Belgique. Le Plan Schlieffen,* 1904, by M. Palæologue, 1932.

the alternative view by processes of war. It seemed perfectly normal to go to France, for we were, in a way then, far more fervent internationalists than the young men of to-day. But we had only just realised it at the moment that the guns started. That was the fault of us and of our elders. We had not thought it all out in time, and so we were let in for the crash. The crash was essentially the affair of young men between the ages of twenty and thirty. We were the culprits, because our vision had been so weak, our capacity for averting cataclysms so inadequate, our prescience so feeble. We never felt for a moment that we were the dupes of a bunch of doddering Victorians. We believed rather that we and they had let things slip into an incalculable mess. That I believed then and believe now.

There beyond the vague heaps of sandbags and barbed wire was the strange land that we could not enter, the 'garden over the wall' of the nightmare. There beyond it, was another world, peopled by men whose way of thinking was totally and absolutely distinct from our own. Had we been fighting in our own land against an invader, like the French, we should have felt quite simply that here was something to be exterminated, something resembling a disease that had to be cured. But, coming from a land of peace to one of war, we found ourselves inevitably taking up a moral standpoint. Looking over some of my old letters of this time I find all the way through that I considered the Germans as the enemies of good behaviour. This sounds incredibly priggish, and yet I was no prig. I believed that to make our point clear it was essential to kill as many Germans as possible; and yet I was no militarist and no flag-wagger. I felt that the Germans had decided that force will win and that sheer hacking through will prepare a field from out of a jungle on which all the fair flowers of civilisation will flourish. To me this was either lunatic rubbish or sheer hypocrisy, and the only answer was to meet force with more force and more successful force.

Deeper than that I did not think, nor indeed was it necessary. In later years I have met individual men whose philosophy is identical with that of the Germans, men who believe in smashing to win. Sometimes they have been men of the academic world, sometimes men of the less violent world of ordinary life. If I have come into conflict with them I inevitably use their own weapons, for they understand them.

So the Germans to me were not men and brothers whom I was asked to slay for the benefit of a national policy of dubious antecedents. I believed that it was my war as much as anyone else's, and cheerfully became part of it. I think we all felt much the same: some of us had thought it out more, some less. But the Germans were our enemies right enough, though we bore them no malice. In these post-war days I think that the outlook of the young men of 1914 requires some explanation, partly because so few of those young men have survived to explain, and partly because the young men of 1916 and 1917 and 1918 had wholly different problems to face and none of our pre-war knowledge to help them to face them. The reasons for becoming a soldier in 1917 or 1918 were totally different from the reasons that made us into soldiers. In those later years the whole safety of England was at stake and with it the fortunes and futures of the young men who then were ripe for killing or to kill. 1914 for us was the end of a period, not a beginning.

I was sent up to the trenches the second night after my arrival. I was neither very frightened nor very satisfied. As I wound my way along a communication trench in pitch darkness a stray bullet suddenly hit a tree not far off with a crack like that of a whip. I had always imagined that bullets were silent things that hit you or vanished quietly elsewhere. I had never marked at rifle-butts and so never knew that a bullet makes a crack no matter what it hits, whether it be mud or steel. That first crack made me jump. My first shell on the other hand left me unmoved, for it made so very little noise. True it was a small shell, but I had heard such bloodcurdling stories and felt pleasantly relieved.

The trenches themselves were more or less what I had expected. They were, in brief, just trenches, sandbagged and traversed. Behind them stood the gaunt ruin of a convent in whose watery cellars the company officers had their meals. Dinner in the evening was a pleasant diversion. The cook managed to produce, as a rule, four courses out of army rations and any extras we had managed to pick up in the villages at the back. I always remember with gratitude an excellent savoury consisting of a French prune enwrapped in a papery slice of bacon. The floor of the cellar held some foot or so of water, and we sat on boxes with our feet piled on heaps of bricks, fortuitously collected by the batman.

Night in the trenches was the most enduring experience of all. I can remember every detail with stark clarity. It was early March, and when I first arrived there was a spell of cold frosty weather. The relief of being able to stand up at full height without dyspeptic stoopings, the joy of being able to climb on the parapet or look undeterred over at the Germans, and wonder what was stirring in that alien land, made the nights worth waiting for. At intervals along the trench came the discreet glow of coal braziers, well screened. Round them sat the misty figures of men off duty. One in every three men stood at the parapet on sentry duty. My task was intermittent—usually three hours on duty and three off, for sleep.

Those nights had a beauty of their own which will never be repeated. Our trenches stood on a faint slope, just overlooking German ground, with a vista of vague plainland below. Away to right and left stretched the great lines of defence as far as eye and imagination could stretch them. I used to wonder how long it would take me to walk from the beaches of the North Sea to that curious end of all fighting against the Swiss boundary; to try to guess what each end looked like; to imagine what would happen if I passed a verbal message, in the manner of the parlour game, along to the next man on my right to be delivered to the end man of all up against the Alps. Would anything intelligible at all emerge?

The two lines and their no-man's-land were clear and distinct, made obvious by the intermittent star-shells that never ceased being shot into the air. Sometimes for re-assurance that nothing was brewing out in front, sometimes for my own sheer pleasure, I would take one of the great verey-light pistols that lay handy at intervals on the parapet and fire it into the sky. The lovely fireworks that resulted were a continual joy. Their penetrating stellar light lit up everything for a square hundred yards. There were those ancient corpses that we all knew, askew and unhuman; there were the sticks and shrubs that looked in the half light of dawn like creeping enemies; there were the tangled heaps of wire and the decaying cows and oddments of war, all lit with the ghastly glare that illuminates the faces of guests at a public dinner-party when the camera-man fires his baneful powders.

For the first time in my life I learnt the stars. I could sit by the hour and watch the Great Bear circling round the Pole, a thing I knew that happened but had never seen actually happening. That alone made the stars into a coherent scheme for me instead of a mere jumbled mass of pin-points.

Here I was, clean out of the world I had known, and set down in another. We all lived behind the Looking Glass. Our standards of action and behaviour, our mode of life, our friendships, and our pastimes were created anew to suit this new world. Our nerves were sound and the nervousness of our peace-time existence had vanished and been replaced by an erratic psychology more suited to this unusual life. The first experience of the new psychology came as a surprise until I had myself adopted it. Suddenly one night, far away in the distance, came a rushing rattling noise, that spread nearer and nearer horizontally extending itself along the line. 'Wind up,' said someone briefly, to my mystification. The noise grew louder and louder until I realised that it was rifle-fire from our own lines coming from the unit on our left. It raged and stormed and I could see the flash and sparkle of a hundred rifles and hear the whistle of bullets. Suddenly my own men ran to the parapet, seized their rifles and fired madly and recklessly into space over the top. The firing spread to the right and the whole battalion was soon repelling an imaginary attack. Slowly the men stopped firing and we heard the concert taken up by the unit on our right and so sweep along the line until it died out. Once the men had started firing it was impossible at first to stop them. Slowly the officers persuaded them that there had been no order to fire, and they ceased. Laughter followed and all was quiet again.

There was nothing of panic, no stampeding, no fear of alarm in it all. It was simply mass-suggestion. Firing, said the men to themselves, means attack by the enemy. The battalion on our left has been attacked and we must help them by firing obliquely at their attackers. And so it had spread. Partly serious, partly treated as a game, it was merely the night-fears of children in the dark. But the sound of this great wave of bullets, the rattle of the rifles, and the sudden humming of activity where previously had been relative silence, was as strange a thing to hear on a starry night as can well be imagined. Sometimes it was the Germans who started. Then we sat tight and did nothing at all: we merely listened to the crackling of thousands of bullets against our sandbags, laughed and said 'Wind up among the Bosches!'

One learned strange things. The habits of bullets naturally interested us all equally. The more we learned the more we felt safe. The continuous whining of bullets fired at a high angle and heard from a flank was our continuous music. The sound was like that of small mosquitoes flying in arcs and humming as they flew. At intervals came the sound of ricochets, more like angry hornets whisking off at sharp angles.

The habits of the bullet when it meets the sandbag are curious. When first I took on the job of controlling parties of men filling sandbags to repair the ravages which shell-fire had made in the parapets during the day, I made them fill the bags tightly and well with the friendly earth and mud. But I soon ceased doing this when I learned from those wiser than myself that the tighter the packing of a sandbag the easier for a bullet to penetrate. A sandbag filled with loose earth loosely packed and relatively dry, is a perfect stopper of bullets, for when they hit the bag they have to penetrate alternate layers or nuclei of earth and air. Meeting the surface of a bag packed like cheese they merely cut one swift hole right throught it. It is like trying to stab a knife through an eiderdown quilt on the one hand, or through a lump of soap on the other. The quilt will win every time.

Many lives were lost through bullets cutting through the upper sandbags of parapets, and the lesson was soon learned.

Our lines cut straight through the ruins of a village called Le Gheer. I cannot say why, but that was exactly the sort of name, I thought, which such a death-surrounded, mud-bedrabbled ruin would have. It was the perfect dream-name. Surely there could not possibly ever have been really a village called that before the war! Among its ruins was the inevitable crucifix, damaged but still bravely standing among the chaotic heaps. But we had long back learned from the daily papers that every crucifix miraculously stood unbroken in a world where God was fighting for the Allies. I have no doubt that all the crucifixes on the German side behaved in an equally accommodating way. Anyhow we took it and its behaviour for granted as all inevitable. Near the crucifix was a broken inn-sign. 'Estaminet de la Paix,' it read. My village was better and better. It did all the comic turns. Still less did I believe in its pre-war existence.

Incidentally I was always delighted to hear the men refer to an estaminet as an 'estanimate,' a charming metathesis that gave the institution an extra halo.

Against the ruined village was Ploegsteert Wood, the Plugstreet of fame. Then almost all of it was intact, except at the fringes. Our trenches in the wood became mere breastworks, with redoubts and small forts. A score of yards behind these breastworks one could, when off duty, walk about among the early flowers and hear the lark, that most Martian of all war-birds, carolling his enthusiastic response to the drum-beats. We all hated larks, and would have eaten them all in lark-pies with delight. Their insensate singing in the very heart of war made them perhaps the most unpopular of all Nature's creations. I never hear a lark now without disliking it.

Plugstreet Wood was virtually a marsh. We could pass along its paths only on duck-boards and faggots, for the water oozed out of the ground. I believe that the water-level was only about a foot deep.

We were told, with what authority I cannot say, that early in 1915 the Corps Commander had received a letter from a well-known French financier, who owned Plugstreet and its wood, requesting him to see that the British troops did not disturb the game in his preserve. There was of course no living thing in it. Instead there was a neat cemetery of Saxon soldiers killed earlier on, some scattered graves of men killed before our lines had been consolidated, and a large number of unexploded shells that had dropped into the soft ground without their noses meeting with anything sufficiently hard to detonate. There were also a few shells neatly embedded in trees, also unexploded. One day

I actually saw a soldier, cigarette in mouth, cap on one side, hacking at a shell, like the famous 'Fuse Collector' of Bruce Bairnsfather, to get it out and take it home. I withdrew to a considerable distance and ordered him to desist.

Just on the edge of the wood was the grim and noisome spot known as Burnt Out Farm. It lay exactly midway between the lines. To get to it you had to cross only at dusk, dawn or night, for there was no communicating trench. It had to be held continuously, day and night, for it gave us an advantage over the Germans in case of their attack. We manned it with machine guns so that if they attacked we should *enfilade* their advance from the very outset. Those who went into it at dawn had to stay there till dusk. No one could help them or communicate with them by day except by telephone.

The farm itself was a mere shell, about six feet in height, of buildings which had originally stood around a courtyard. Just enough of the shell remained for efficient protection against bullet fire, though a few guns would have demolished it in half an hour, and any fugitives who sought to escape in daylight could have been picked off at leisure. Why the Germans never shelled us out of it and massacred the garrison I cannot imagine. At the time I put it down to their sheer gentility, for we had a sneaking affection for our Saxon opponents: they seldom did nasty things to us, and they took life as they found it.

On my second night in the trenches I was sent at dawn with a handful of men to Burnt Out Farm. We strolled across the open in the dim light and, relieving the previous occupants, settled in for the day. Just after the sun came up we heard a scuffle and two men flopped into the trench, with much laughter and noise bringing with them our tea and rations for the day. This was the morning's sport. Although the farm was practically unapproachable in daylight, the men used to enjoy the fun of crawling along below a heap of earth that led to the farm, and then dashing across about ten yards of open ground in full view of the enemy. The Germans responded with a spatter of bullets that did no harm. It was our morning sport—and presumably theirs. The men never considered it as a deadly risk, which it was, but rather as a game of catch-as-catch-can. A few fatalities and it would have ceased to be an entertainment. But so often in these days there were games which remained games until they had a fatal ending.

Once settled in the farm, I took my place behind the outer wall facing the Germans, which had one loose brick, which at intervals I removed, in order to scan the enemy horizon for trouble. After a few surveys suddenly, with a crack, the brick was shot clean out of place on to the ground. I replaced it, now less anxious to use the spy-hole, which the Germans had evidently handed over to their marksman as a target. The feeling of being continually watched made the place less pleasant. But the spy-hole game continued and the brick was knocked out several times again.

After a day spent without movement, and crouching, we were glad to get back to the friendly trenches where we could stretch and walk. At our departure the officer who relieved me suddenly vanished up to his waist in the courtyard of the farm. 'What are you doing?' I asked hoarsely. 'I've found the family cess-pit,' he replied tersely. And he had. Poor man, he had twelve hours to spend in the farm without a wash.

I used to entertain myself in the trenches when off duty in studying the large-scale maps of Flanders which we used. The place seemed to have been hag-ridden by war for centuries, to judge from the names of the places alone. 'Allée d'Enfer,' 'Rue des Canons,' and strange names of farms, exactly equivalent to those which we had coined all around us, seemed to be the traditional names of scores of places where warfare of the past had surged and battered. 'Burnt Out Farm' was a name translated in a dozen ways into Flemish and French. We were indeed on an ancient battle-ground. I have never been back, but I have little doubt that many of the names we coined have stuck.

Occasionally I used to say to myself 'Well, here I am in the war at last. It doesn't seem so bad.' Nor was it. Dawn and dusk, those favourite calling-hours of death, alone brought us face to face with realities of a more sombre kind. For during the first week of my sojourn in the trenches I had seen no death and only a few cases of wounds had occurred. There had been no bombardments, no attacks, no patrol-fights at night and no slaughter. But at dawn and at dusk all good soldiers stand to their posts and await events until the increase of darkness or of light has brought uncertainty to an end in one way or another. And strange things seemed always to happen at dawn and dusk. In civilian life the setting or the rising of the sun bring with them nothing sinister, except to the ill and sick. To us, full of health and spirit, they brought always some uncertain prospect of evil. Those dawns were very lovely. Slowly the rows of sandbags would take shape and substance, the debris and wreckage of war emerged as lovely patterns against the fumes of mist that rose from the damp earth. Rows of bayonets showed above our own and the German trenches. Machine-guns were manned and held ready, but forbidden to disclose themselves unless attack came. Then up came the sun, touched the bayonets, lit the scene with the light of certainty and sanity. We no longer talked in whispers: bayonets were unfixed, sentries placed and the surplus population, a moment before straining to see if action was called for, relaxed, stood down, and all was quiet again. Fumes of tea and fried bacon replaced the mists of dawn. Men and officers not on duty resumed the patient waiting, with nothing to do; that made the substance of a day's warfare.

I began to feel almost a veteran. But I was not, for I had not seen as yet any man's life suddenly brought to an abrupt end. I could not visualise what would happen, and how it would occur. But one thing I knew for certain, that someone, as time went on, myself or another, would be suddenly swept into eternity. For steadily and patiently, riflemen and gunners on both sides were waiting for chances and seeking for targets. The almost complete silence, broken only by occasional stray shots, hardly justified one in believing this. Yet the certainty of death for someone was there. Our battalion had spent no single visit to the trenches so far without losing one or more men or officers. I prayed that my first experience of death should not be of my own. Heaven knows this was as selfish a prayer as was ever devised, but perhaps the only prayer that was being prayed by every man simultaneously along the mighty line of battle. If ever there was a 'soldier's prayer' that is it!

My prayer was certainly granted. One morning as I walked along the trench I heard an exclamation. Rounding a traverse I saw a figure lying at the bottom of the trench, the figure of my most excellent and courageous sergeant. 'Shot through the head, sir, all sudden like,' said a neighbouring sentry impassively. ''E looked up too 'igh, sir, over the parapet and caught it straight.' We covered him with a coat and sent for the stretcher-bearers, for he was stone dead, he with whom I had talked a moment before. It is almost impossible now to recover and write down the feelings I had. I suddenly felt that it was all absurd and wrong. I felt bitter and angry. And as quickly I realised that I was in another world from that which I had left, which had a logic and a method of its own, a world in which certain processes, certain causes and effects were at work which had no connection at all with my other existence. The dream-world in a few moments re-established itself. I had let myself wake, and now I had to get myself back again into the inconsequent, but logically inconsequent world across the border, that fantastic world of war. It reminded me of a film I had seen as a boy—one of the first fantastic films ever made, called 'A Voyage to the Moon.' In that film a band of courageous scientists projected themselves on to the moon and on arrival were furiously attacked by Selenites. But their powers of defence were enormous. As each strange, odd Selenite, shown on the film as a spidery caricature of humans, rushed at the invader, all the invader had to do was to smite the Selenite with a large stick, at which the Selenite vanished in a flash of flame and a puff of white smoke! we were the Selenites now right enough.

Shocks soon pass when the body is healthy and the mind unoccupied. I had forgotten my poor sergeant in a day. I wrote the conventional letter to his wife, had his kit packed up and resumed my labours, mildly wondering whether someone would be doing the same for me an hour later.

A few days later, as I was walking along the trenches, one of my snipers, waiting his chance at a loophole, suddenly fell backwards with a crash, and a loud shout of 'I'm hit: I'm dead.' Death I felt was not so undignified in its manner of arrival, and this was too much. I prodded the man and slowly he arose, rubbing his head, feeling himself all over and grinning sheepishly. After a few moments he discovered that a bullet, from his more alert brother-sniper opposite, had passed right across the top of his head, without breaking the skin. But it had ploughed a neat parting in his hair. From a victim he became a hero, to himself. Roars of laughter greeted his recovery and we all made appropriate remarks. Escape from obvious death always provoked rollicking laughter, I know not why. It rather looks as if Bergson was right. Laughter in such cases indicates the disapproval of the community for a non-social act, in this case attempted suicide. But it also rather looks as if Bergson was wrong, for the victim also laughed, and heartily too: that needs more elucidation than the mere glib solution of Gallic logic can give it!

* * * * * * *

It was curious how unsentimental we all were. One day the post brought me of all strange gifts a bunch of lovely primroses, sent me by my sister. May she receive an eternal reward for sending me a gift such as, I am sure, no other soldier in France or Flanders received. Had we then shown a fraction of the sentimentality which we show in ordinary life I should have been moved to ecstasy by the thought of England in March, of the Old Home, of innocent flowers in the midst of carnage. But this was what in fact I wrote in reply:

> 'Thanks ever so much for the primroses, which arrived quite safely: they have served to decorate the table in our hut in the wood. As there are no primroses here in Plugstreet Wood they are much appreciated.'

Wise and loving sister to send me such a gift: she sent them, I know, simply on the spur of the moment and I received them in the same spirit of completely detached and unspoiled appreciation in which they were sent. Neither she nor I had time for sentiment. But we knew the advantages of primroses and how exquisite is their colour in any setting.

* * * * * * *

One luminous evening a roar of artillery sounded from away in the north and within the hour great wreathes of smoke twisted up into the sky and darkened the sunset. Battle or bombardment we wondered? News soon reached us that heavy shelling was falling on Ypres, that the town was burning and that things were developing. But still our area was quiet: the same routine still prevailed and nothing happened. But our pulses quickened, for things were moving. Would this at last be the beginning of the final battle which we were all waiting for; in which we had indeed been sent out to take part? the roar of guns rose and sank, a sound as mighty and impressive and, in its way, as beautiful as any I know. Great doors endlessly slamming, deep drums and small light drums, insistent thumpings and great crashes—a mighty chorus.

But another day and night passed and we did not move or alter our routine.

Then at last came our turn for relief and a rest in billets at the back. We withdrew, as we had done before, to our particular group of farms and houses for baths, clean clothes, tables, chairs, and relaxation. Then, after a day of ease, orders came to get ready to march.

With a certain regret we left the battered region with which we had become so familiar, and set out on a journey whose destination we did not know. The battalion, neat, fully equipped, and in high spirits set out northwards on a fine day in April, with a hot sun and spring in the air. After some hours' march we reached a magnificent farm set in a lovely piece of green Flemish scenery. There was no sign of war, save for a lonely grave of a French cavalry officer which was by now incorporated in the garden of the farm and covered with flowers. In this fine old farm, with its immense barns and huge courtyard, we spent the night, and the next morning marched off to Bailleul. That night still remains in my memory as one of the loveliest of spring nights I have known. The moon was full and clear, the air free of mist. There was an atmosphere of complete peace and rest: the farmer and his family sat in a room together while we, the officers, had a comfortable meal in a white-tiled room and the men sat in groups in the barns on heaps of hay eating a solid and satisfying dinner. Cigarettes lit up the dusk as we strolled round the fields and among the trees. It was a better rest than any we had had in the frowsy mining towns and villages near Armentières. Here was good rich country, and no sign of war save ourselves and that lonely grave in the garden. The old life of the time before I had entered this new world came back for a few fleeting instants.

The next evening we were off and marching to Bailleul. A lazy morning, with perfunctory duties only, had refreshed us, so that we felt like young lions. We had no talk of the future, but one thing we knew, and that was that in a very few hours we should be in a strange new setting which was nothing but war. In the back of every man's mind was the thought that perhaps this was the last time he would see the soft and lovely countryside. For it is not what soldiers say but what they think that is reality to them.

At Bailleul a fleet of old London buses awaited us, and soon we were bumping along towards Vlamertinghe. It brought London back again for a moment to me, for the driver to whom I talked was in real life a London driver.

From Vlamertinghe we marched east, and soon night was on us, but night lit by the same vivid and lovely moon. In a short time we were in the outskirts of Ypres, a shattered ruin of houses. We halted, formed into single file and began to cross the town. It was a strange and uncanny sight, this corpse of a city that had just died. The smooth cobbled streets and squares were pitted with enormous holes and great pools of blood lay here and there. Dead horses from scurrying guns and limbers lay in swollen heaps, putrefying the very air itself. The moon made every line clear and stark, and every shadow a patch of sepia. Almost every moment, here or there, a violent flash of orange marked the burst of a shell. The continuous booming of the German guns, which seemed so very near, was broken only at intervals and those intervals formed shocked silences as eerie as the moonlight. Once or twice a sound like that of an electric train rushing through the air made us pause, fearstruck. An immense explosion and a blinding flash told us that here were the projectiles of the largest German gun of all. In one place we threaded our way past a vast crater in the road which was one of the holes made by this famous gun. The night was hot and airless and we dripped with sweat. Pervading everything was the reeking stench of dead horses and dead men. Once only did we see a living thing in this murdered city, when a dark ambulance came tearing through the streets picking its way with incredible skill and never pausing for a second, almost as if the furies were pursuing it. At length we emerged from this nightmare land, crossed the old battered moat through what was once the Menin gate and we were out in the open country once more. Here at last we were back again in the sort of setting that we knew. But it was grimmer than any we had seen. Great streamers of smoke from the smouldering city covered the sky, but away east was the Line that we knew, clear to us as on any map, by the long row of constant star-shells. Behind us was the crash of intermittent shells falling on Ypres, in front the crackle of infantry-fire. We paused by the roadside and formed up into column. A few hundred yards on we had an hour's rest and most of us slept coldly but solidly in the moonlight by the hedges. At length we moved into a battered row of half-dug trenches that formed a reserve position in the very centre of the Salient, which it was clear enough by now was the spear-head of a defence, and the main objective of attack in a prolonged battle. Here were no quiet times where we and the Germans could snipe and stand-to and sleep and patrol. This was a battle for a purpose and the only purpose of the Germans must be to break through. In a way we were fortified, for we thought that if we could only hold them and stop them, that they might give up the war as a bad job! poor innocents that we were. But we were on our mettle, and it never occurred to any of us that the Germans would really break through. We had the sublime confidence of the soldier in his own strength. And the Germans were every bit as confident, for every battle in the war was the battle to end it to those who fought. I found a German letter from this very time, written by a soldier of the 51st German Division:

> 'We are going back to the trenches this evening,' he wrote. 'To-day or to-morrow will decide the fate of Ypres and we riflemen will do our best to carry it through. From our trenches one sees the whole country as far as Ypres and we had to-day a magnificent spectacle. Our artillery, that is here located in tremendous numbers, was going strong.'

When dawn broke in our battered support trench it was

evident enough that we were all in the hollow of a great bowl, with the Germans sitting on the rim and shooting at us. We spent three days here continuously on the alert, for we had orders to stand by to be sent in support in any direction. Our little battalion was serving the purpose of reserve for a whole Army Corps, for we were short of men and the line was thinly held. But we had a superb view of the long line of battle. In effect it was an isosceles triangle which was being attacked along the whole length of its long sides. The short base was Ypres itself. At night we could see the flares and star-shells running almost all round us. The main-road, along which all the traffic of reinforcement and supply went, bisected the base of the triangle and ended at its point. Some cynic remarked, truly enough, that if you walked from Ypres along this road you could be hit from almost every possible angle except from directly behind, so that the only invulnerable part of your body would be a long thin line down the spine.

Around us at intervals strange things happened. A small farm barely two hundred yards away sheltered some guns. Suddenly the German observers found the target and in a trice great salvoes of heavy shells came swirling over, and the farm in a few minutes was a waving forest of red smokeless flame. It burned for an hour and what happened to the gunners there I do not know. It was in any case none of our business, and we watched it with the detachment that only infantry can show for gunners, or gunners for infantry.

We were on a small eminence and away towards the village of St Julien we could look down over our own and the German lines. Just about sunset on a calm evening I was looking in this direction when slowly the brown line of trenches and earth began to change to a dull luminous green. Looking intently I saw great clouds of greenish yellow vapour creeping across from the German lines, and all clearly issuing from one or two fixed points. We had heard talk of gas, and we had once or twice detected the smell of strange chemical odours, but here was a gas attack, a mile away, which I could see in action with my own eyes. It was, in fact, one of the last attempts of the Germans at this time to use chlorine and, like its predecessors, which had occurred before we moved up, it failed.

The men had already shown signs of nervousness of gas, a nervousness based only on the wild stories that runners had brought. But here it was for me to see without breathing, to look at impartially so that I could be prepared when I met it. The other signs of battle had filled me with a curious elation. The shells that burst so close, the line ahead of us that we might fill at any moment, gave me a strange pleasure. The gas, with its green paralysis, changed my mood. I was angry rather than frightened, angry as the dog that snaps at the unaccustomed.

Our seniors were alarmed and waited for advice, for they saw that at any moment we might be called upon to deal with a situation that neither they nor we had ever been trained to meet. Unexpectedly help came. A parcel was delivered for each company labelled, 'Gas Masks, Type I.' Unpacked, the parcel revealed bundles of small squares of blue flannel, just large enough to cover the mouth, with a tape on each side to tie round behind the head. Whatever benign personage contrived these amiable death-traps I do not know. But anything more futile could never have been devised by the simplicity of man. On the whole we preferred to resort to the face-towels dipped in our own urine, which an earlier order had suggested would be a temporary palliative. Nor was our confidence restored a day later by the arrival of 'Gas Masks, Type II,' which was to replace the first. On unpacking my particular bundle I found that the new masks consisted of large pieces of hairy Harris tweed about three feet long and one in width, again with tapes nattily fixed to the sides. With much laughter the men tried to don their new masks. But at the bottom of the parcel I found a small printed label briefly entitled 'BODY BELTS.' So without further enquiries I ordered my men to put them to whatever use seemed best to them. To a man they placed them round their long-suffering stomachs.

I have often wondered what inspired genius was at work away back in England to give us these gifts. I have been told since that Gas Mask, Type I, was invented by the fertile brain of a Cabinet Minister. I feel tempted to attribute Type II to the Archbishop of Canterbury.

But local genius did more. The authorities on the spot with incredible and commendable speed bought up hundreds of vine-growers' sprays. These we had for use in the trenches, and filled them with chemicals fitted to neutralise chlorine.

At last our time for action came. On the final day in our trenches the fire along the line became intense. As we waited and watched suddenly over the sky-line ahead of us ran two distraught figures. They flopped into our trenches exhausted, without rifles or equipment. 'We are the last of the Buffs, sir,' cried one. 'The Germans have attacked and the regiment is wiped out.' I gave them some rum and found them rifles and equipment, comforted them and told them to get ready for more fighting. A moment later a signaller came running madly down to us: 'The Germans are coming over in their thousands, sir,' he said, panting. 'They have broken through.' We all got ready, fixed our bayonets and looked martial, when a group of four more men came tumbling over. 'We are the last of the Buffs, sir,' they cried. This was too much for my witty Lancashiremen, and we all roared with laughter. 'Come and meet some of your friends,' I said and took them along to the first pair. They began to look foolish and then they also laughed. Indeed we all enjoyed ourselves quite a lot. And of Germans 'in their thousands' there was no trace. Actually a small trench had been lost to the enemy and these men had managed to get away. But it was a lesson in how a stampede starts. For the line was as strong as a rock and there was no general attack. I kept the men with me, and in half an hour they were as ready as the rest to move up again when wanted. The dramatic touch amused me. I suppose the title of 'Buffs' leads to clichés. The men had done too much reading of the newspapers in quiet trenches. They could hardly help coining the phrase, for in their ears it must have sounded heroic. There was something distinguished in being 'the last of the Buffs' but the distinction was becoming too popular and their sense of humour saved them at last.

But the battle was being pressed in earnest and the position in the Salient had become impossible, for the long triangle was being whittled down to a thinness almost impossible for habitation. It is one thing to hold the front against the enemy but another to be shot in the back from the enemy on the other side of the triangle—and that was what was happening. Our trenches in some places could be fired at from behind by German artillery south of Ypres. The Higher Command took a wise decision. We were told that day that the Salient was to be abandoned, except for a stump that was to be held around the city of Ypres. The great spearhead was to be cut off. Our part was to go up at night to the trenches and man them, while their occupants withdrew. We were to stay there an hour or so and then leave ourselves, selecting a score of men and officers to stay behind and fire at intervals to disguise the fact that the trenches were abandoned. These in turn were to depart at dawn and find their way back.

Now at last was some kind of positive action which would defeat the aims of the enemy. We rejoiced. No one for a moment felt that, in resigning the ridiculous triangle of battered ground to the Germans, we were retreating or giving away anything to his advantage. That he should have ultimately to cross the area he had destroyed and then come up against a happily consolidated army of soldiers who were, for once, angry and full of hate, seemed to us to be entirely satisfactory. For the temper of the men was roused after the gas attacks: they were amazed that so little had resulted from them, but anxious to prevent any further exploitation of successes of this kind. For the first time I saw the British Army animated as a unity with one single feeling. I have read often enough since the war of the dogged good-will of the men, and their lack of hate of the enemy, of their knowledge that they were pawns in a great game of politics, just waiting to be butchered. However true this may have been of the troops later on, after successive slaughters and failures like Loos and the Somme, it was not so now. We all knew that the Germans were anxious to kill as many of us as possible; that every individual German was animated by the same idea; that Germany had her tail up; and we all to a man felt that we should ourselves kill as many Germans as we could in return. It was war in its simplest form, perhaps in its only attractive form—a battle of wills and a conflict of determination. I felt relieved that the uncertainty was at an end. That strange pursuit in single file through shadowy Ypres where we sought we knew not what, and ended we knew not where, was over. I can still recollect the emptiness of our minds as we halted on the road near Zonnebeke: we had no idea whether we were to attack or defend: whether we were to stay there or go further; as we waited by a ghostly row of shattered elms, I remember how suddenly out of the flat moonlight drifted a long weary column of strange dusky men, broken and drooping, with their tall lank forms hardly perceptible at first, and marching with padded feet like a battalion of exhausted leopards. These were the remnants of the Lahore Division, poor untutored Pathans, transferred from their happy hills to this marshy bog, to be blown slowly to bits by high explosive. Inconsequently they had drifted past us, and we, as inconsequently, drifted forwards to the place they had left.

But now all that uncertainty and vague surmise was over. We formed up at dusk, and marched over broken ground into trenches that led us to a sloping hill with the vague outlines of trees near it. As we neared, silence was ordered, and, unexpectedly, we found ourselves filling a trench that was already crammed with those whom we relieved. But they were battered and broken and, as we filled up the narrow trench that we were to occupy for barely a few hours, we could not help treading as we went on wounded and dying men. To this day I shall remember those cries of the wounded as they begged us not to leave them behind when we went. As I turned a bend I trod unintending on a figure heaped up in a shadow. He cried out in agony. I could think of nothing that could conceivably be said to him, for in such a case there is nothing to say. And I had to press on, for the Germans were hardly seventy yards away, and such was the confusion of the relief that, had they turned machine guns on the trenches, we should have been shot like rabbits. It was a matter of life and death to us all, and the wounded had to give way to the prime consideration of the whole and the living. We did indeed attempt to get back all the wounded we could, but, any hint to the Germans that we were abandoning the Salient, and a storm of artillery would have torn up the roads and caught us all in the open. There was no moon yet, and we finally took up our fire-stations in the trench, firing actively, so as to give no hint of the coming retreat. In due course our orders came, and all but the percentage of officers and men who were to be left behind as a skeleton garrison, moved out into the open ground behind the trenches and formed up into column. There was a deathly silence from the German side, and at any moment we expected attack, or at least to be swept by rifle fire and guns. But nothing happened and, strung up to the highest tension, we marched off towards the spinal road of the Salient that would take us back behind the new lines which, we were told, were already held and manned, ready for the German advance which would take place on the morrow. We reached the road simultaneously with other columns and a pack of men, here and there ten abreast, units confused, companies mixed, and officers searching for their men like lost spirits, filled up the whole surface. At intervals ambulances, packed beyond their capacity, pushed doggedly through the moving column. And over all was a soft and velvety darkness. There was, indeed, confusion, and yet it took but little trouble when at last we crossed the canal at Ypres to get ourselves sorted out. I knew my destination, and at a point about a mile from where we started, I moved my small platoon across open country with the aid of a night-compass. I had never done this before except in barrack-squares and had never dreamed that it would ever come in handy.

Before we had started I had found that two of my men were missing, the two whom I had stationed on the road when we entered the trenches, to keep charge of our priceless rum-jars. After a brief search we found them, with one rum-jar full and the other empty, themselves in a drunken sleep. This was the only occasion in the war when I found men drunk in action, my first and last experience of it, and in this case it was due to sheer temptation, not to loss of nerve, just to sheer devilment. I left the men where they lay when we marched off, for every ambulance was crammed with wounded and every stretcher full. I knew of no military regulations to cope with such a case and had no means of removing such types of casualty. They left me no alternative but to leave them.

We had a long and rough march. For the first night, as if by some providence, the Germans neglected to shell the roads. It was the one night when their harvest would have been a rich one. At last we came to the canal and the outskirts of battered Ypres. We passed through the new lines and heard the cheerful shouts of those who were manning it, and were waiting for the dawn when they would be able to pick off Germans as they advanced to the new position. We shouted back, bandied a joke or two and went on. Belgians near the canal waved to us and at last we reached the village of Elverdinghe. Dawn was now well up and, as the sun rose, we filed into the delightful garden of an old castle, with an ornamental lake. But it was raining hard and we found shelter under trees and hedges. Food appeared in due course, but the Germans were shelling every thicket and every copse, and it was not long before we were moved off to shelter farther back in a wood. There we had a magnificent rest, sprawling in the sun, washing in streams and resting to our hearts' content. Fragments of the armies of our allies appeared among the trees—Moroccans with high turbans, French cuirassiers with brass helmets like London firemen, and coloured Zouaves. The men foregathered with all alike, talking unaffectedly in the *lingua franca* of the Low Countries that all Englishmen have always talked when fighting in Flanders.

That night I slept the solid sleep of the healthily exhausted, wrapped in a blanket under a small oak-tree. At intervals I awoke to watch the stars and was greeted by the singing of a nightingale in wild bursts of song, a music as lovely as was that of the lark repellant. At breakfast among the trees I heard some of the men of the transport column telling a strange tale of a secret gun in the woods near by, said to be kept underground, and fired at night by Germans disguised as Belgian peasants. I never found out the origin of the story, but it was firmly believed. It was asserted that the gun was used to fire upon our own guns from behind, and that the Germans had been deliberately left behind there for that purpose after the original German withdrawal of some months before. That night we did in fact hear every now and then the whistle of a shell from a gun near the suspect wood, and it sounded unlike the whistle of our own shells. This was good enough evidence for the men and they all agreed that there was the secret gun in action. I have often wondered about the origin of that story. There are many like it, and stories of the kind spread through an army like fire.

Our rest was not for long. The next evening we moved back to the now reduced Salient. In column on an inky and misty night we set forth, no man knowing the region that we were in or our ultimate destination. Arrived at an open moorland, blasted beyond recognition, with Ypres now flaming afresh in the spaces behind us, we halted. From the darkness a despatch rider on a motor-bicycle appeared urgently. Word was passed to us that our orders were changed. Away a mile off was the Line, with the crackle of rifle-fire and the eternal star-shells. As we waited suddenly a clamour arose from a patch of woodland, the bursting of hand-bombs and harsh cries of men. It sounded from that distance a murderous clamour and filled with beastliness. I pictured men stabbing, killing, and hurling bombs. It was an attack.

We moved cautiously in its direction across relatively level land, still submerged in inky darkness. As we got nearer the order for silence was given, if indeed one can call silence the combined clashing and clanking of several hundred bayonets against entrenching-tools, of rifles against packs, and of bodies jostling and stumbling against each other. Slowly we pressed forward, opening out at last into two long lines. Then came the order to fix bayonets, which was done with a sound like a thousand tin cans being clashed merrily. Tripping and stumbling, almost prodding one another with the naked bayonets, the two lines, waving and breaking over the rough ground, advanced in a frantic march. We were chattering with cold and excitement and fear, and had not the slightest idea of the whereabouts of the enemy. We halted, and from nowhere appeared two Scottish officers, who assured us that they were from the unit on our flank, which was carrying out the same frantic manœuvre. Somehow we did not like the look of those Scotsmen, nor their rich and guttural accent. Their uniforms were tattered and they had no caps. Sudden suspicion overwhelmed us and I hastily summoned a brother-officer of Glasgow extraction to engage these suspects in conversation and to question them hastily, but carefully, as to the geography of Scotland. 'Spy-fever' had caught us, and to an Englishman, a battered Scot in a murky night is bound to appear even more alien than he is in daylight in Edinburgh. But our Scotties passed the test and we found from other sources that there really was a battalion of Scotsmen on our right. So we moved ahead. Suddenly, in a whisper like a muffled trumpet-call, we were told to halt. There ahead of us were battered trenches and, of all surprising things, the glowing lights of cigarettes. Scouts were sent a few yards on and came back grinning sheepishly. 'They are Northumberland Fusiliers, sir, not Germans!' We entered their trench to find a handful of poor fusiliers and as many lying in agony wounded and dying. But the indomitable remainder, with cool stoicism, were waiting for whatever might occur. The fact that we occurred, for their salvation and comfort, left them still cool and collected and quiet, for they were beyond the emotional effects that release from danger can bring. Their soft north-country accents struck gently on the ear after the harsh Scots of our colleagues of a few moments back. They told us their simple story. Almost all their battalion and trench had been taken by assault, but they had barricaded up the bit of trench that was left. The Germans were in the rest of it, only a few yards ahead round a turn. We packed them off with more cigarettes and rum to warm them, and tended their wounded, whom we could not get removed. One poor devil was shot in the spine and lay in my trench groaning loud and long in agony. I gave him a morphine pill every half-hour, and slowly his cries were subdued. Later I got him sent back.

But we took offensive measures at once against the Germans, so as to suggest to them that new troops had arrived, and that they were not the victors that they thought. We pressed up to the barrier which separated our part of the trench from theirs, and flung plentiful bombs over to keep them busy. It was consolation to know that the nearer we were to them the less likelihood there was of German artillery shelling us. Bombs were child's-play compared with shells, and our new sport became lively and interesting. Their bombs came back quickly enough, but no one was hurt. Probably we hurt none of them either. But in a fight where the enemy appears not and the defender does not set out to look for him, the result becomes of mere academic interest. Daylight came and we then saw glimpses of our foe. We were facing Prussian Jaeger, with their black postman hats and green braid, not unlike the Berlin policemen of to-day. Our trench was a battered slit, so low that one could not stand up at any point. We began to suffer from indigestion from the continual bending double. Heaven knows where our trench led to or how it was planned. It dribbled away into odd twists and turns. Suddenly I saw one of my men with his head right up above the parapet. I shouted to him to get down and he took not the smallest notice. Looking again I saw his head jerk every now and then as if he were nodding to someone. Then I saw that he had been dead some time and that the jerking of his head was caused by the bullets which were still hitting him at intervals in the neck and shoulders. His friends pulled him down and packed him away in a corner, poor devil. He was now mere lumber.

Those were ridiculous trenches and we had no facilities for sniping back at the Germans, who, barely a stone's throw away, sniped us without cessation and killed a dozen men in the day. We lay low, angrily waiting any chance that there might be. But it proved an impossible position to hold, and in due course we were led out and sent on another Odyssey. But before we went we filled in our communication trench, using it as a graveyard. Our dead were packed head to tail in a row and then we shovelled in the earth. We crept out in single file to meet fresh orders that told us to hold the trench again for one night more. This was almost too much for us, but dismally we dug out our graveyard again and pulled out the unoffending dead, leaving them sprawling on the edge of our renovated home. The next night we did in fact leave for good and started on our new journey, harassed and rather shaken by our futile performances.

We were marched back, given a rest, and then off again to another corner of the battle. Here we arrived at dusk, and my company was placed in a support trench below a low rise on which was our Front Line. Our trench was again a mere slit, not nearly long enough, and we cut a new one during the course of the night. At dawn it was clear that we were overlooked, and soon shells came lobbing over in *enfilade*. The Line itself here came to a small abrupt angle in which was a farmhouse of two stories and well-preserved, for this was relatively new battle-ground. It was, at first, hard to see what was happening and I could in no way understand the development of the battle. Away in the front line, some three hundred yards ahead of us, was a continuous rifle-fire and spasmodic shelling, but we could see little, for the ridge hid the trench from our view. Where our other companies were I did not know, except that some part of them were, with two platoons of my own company, in front. Our task, as in the larger salient near Zonnebeke, was to wait until we were wanted. My fate seemed always to be the ultimate reserve. So we sat and waited, able to stand up, since the front line was not too near and only stray shells and bullets came our way. The centre of attack seemed to be the farm; 'Shell Trap Farm' it was called officially! Rumours that the Germans were in it were spread at intervals, but nobody knew.

Behind us Ypres, which had hitherto been merely battered and ruined, had broken into flames, and clouds of smoke from its jagged outline blew over the whole area. The sun came out at dawn, but a drizzle soon started. By seven o'clock the battle took on an increased vigour. The rifle-fire from all along the line rose in a great volume of sound, and machine-guns rattled with spurts of jarring and penetrating noise. Here and there the Germans catapulted over great projectiles from mortars, horrid black things that hit the ground, bounced and then exploded with an ear-splitting crash that bored a great hole in the ground and shook the very roots of the earth. These frankly terrified me, for they landed anywhere without any warning. But by the time the battle was well under way all fear had left me. For here was a clear issue. It was not like the murky crawling about at night in mortal fear of every tuft of grass; it was not the aimless tramping up and down trenches in peaceful sunlight, but with sudden death from a sniper's bullet waiting round every bend. Here we were and there they were. There was no time for the hobbies of sniping and marksmanship, or for the refinements of bomb-throwing and machine-gun experimentation. There was no more sport. This was plain battle, and for me it had a kick in it. I was beginning to enjoy myself. I felt a kind of ecstatic pleasure, and I was buoyed up. If I was to be killed then it were better to be killed in a first-rate fray like this in full action. Any such death were preferable to the sudden extinction that a stray bullet would bring. Here was no question of one's departure being symbolised merely by another empty chair at dinner in some ruined convent. There was little enough chance that any of us would ever dine together again. Better that way I thought.

The crashing of shells around the farm suddenly ceased. We gathered that this was the prelude to a German attack with the bayonet. There was a pause, a lull in the noise. The drizzle increased and we were all soaking. Suddenly out of nowhere we saw two long straight lines of our men appear to the left of the farm and walk slowly but in perfect line towards the trenches by the farm. Here were the manœuvres of open order that we knew so well working by clockwork in battle-action. The first line moved up, reached its goal, and vanished into the front trenches. With equal deliberation the second line followed suit, as coolly as if there were no battle. We all stood up and cheered wildly, for the scene, small and trivial in itself, seemed to tell us that no one was worrying much, and that all was going well. If this was the beginning of a battle, then the rest of it would be worth seeing. It made me feel that life was eminently worth fighting for.

Unexpectedly our turn came. 'Take your platoon up to the front line now,' said my company commander curtly. As he spoke the rifle-fire from the front line increased in intensity. I got my men together into line and off we went up the slope. I had precisely the feeling that comes over one when the curtain goes up at amateur theatricals. Here were we, the performers, until so recently, idly sitting in the wings. There was the audience waiting to give us the reception we deserved. Out in the open we headed at a trot, held up for a moment by a mass of straggling wire. But we were the safe side of the slope, and nothing hit us. As we topped the ridge I saw the line fifty yards below us. There was my old friend 'Machine-Gun' Brown with his head bound in a bloody rag, looking like the traditional soldier of the pictures in *The Illustrated London News*. There were the remnant of the battalion—or of part of it—firing hard at strings of Germans who came slowly over towards them. As I looked and ran it suddenly occurred to me that we were probably being fired at. It had never struck me until that moment. The thought made me pause. The air filled with a soft purring noise and I realised that bullets were passing very close indeed. At the same moment—and all these cogitations happened in a fraction of a second—I thought what a fool I was to be there ahead of my men, palpably an officer to pick off, and running in a straight line towards the enemy. It was obvious that the time I took to run that last fifty yards might as well be spent motionless, as far as the German marksmen were concerned. I was more likely to get hit each yard that I moved on, if I continued in one straight line. Self-preservation makes the brain spin with ingenuity. Just as the hare doubles instinctively so did I, though my instinct had provoked a process of ratiocination that was clear and deliberate. I turned to run in zigzags since it seemed that my chances would be better that way, even if it took a little longer. The men followed at a friendly amble behind. I had a rifle and bayonet, but any German could see that I was the officer, and it was clear that most of them would have a shot at me first before they fired at the men. I even thought of that, knowing that, given a hundred men, firing rifles, and a target consisting of twenty-five men and an officer, human nature will inevitably prefer to hit the officer. Nor was my calculation wrong. Even as I turned on my first zig of my zigzag course, the air was full of viperish rushings and hissings. Then, as I turned again, suddenly I found myself turning a somersault, with my legs in the air. Simultaneously I was conscious of a blow like the blow of an enormous hammer upon my left leg. I sat up to see the men amble safely ahead into the front trench. 'Machine-Gun' Brown waved inconsequently at me, and I saw the men get into the trench. Later I verified the rightness of my decision and the truth of my estimate of human nature by finding that only one of my men was killed, none wounded, and myself the only other casualty. I confess frankly that my antics had both drawn the fire and saved myself.

But as I sat up, more unpleasant swishing noises sounded to right and left.

Self-preservation again whispered to me that a good target is hit often. I got up to find my way down to the trench, realising that I was hit only in the leg below the knee. As I stepped forward with my left foot I flopped down like a winged pheasant. No, I was out of action all right. As I flopped I saw a providential shell-hole and flopped to the bottom of it. I tore off my first-aid bandage and took off my puttee. There was the wound right enough, a hole of large dimensions right through my leg. There was no pain at all, but plenty of blood. I bound myself up and crawled up to the edge of the hole to prospect. But the Germans had marked my decline and fall, and, as I put my head up, a couple of bullets cracked into the ground near me. No, I thought, here I am for the day. If I start being heroic and attempt to crawl on to my men, I shall be mutton in about ten yards. So there I stayed, and tried to make my hole a home away from home. Here Fortune helped me, for there was an excellent army overcoat at the bottom of the hole. I drew it over my soaking clothes and lit a cigarette. The hole was a pool of mud, but a very welcome pool. It was now eight in the morning and I considered the prospects for the day. By evening I could crawl out, but by evening perhaps my hole would be in Germany! The firing rose and fell and once rose to a frenzy of noise. Attack after attack was clearly being stopped. Away to the south was a cavalry brigade made into infantry. They bore the brunt of much hard fighting and from that direction came endless firing. I learned afterwards that it was there that poor Julian Grenfell was shot, on this very day, Grenfell who wrote the one perfect poem that the war produced. When I read the poem, which I did but two weeks later in hospital (for it had been published the very morning of his death), I felt that he had put into words the feelings that had been mine:

'And when the burning moment breaks
And all things else are out of mind,
And only Joy of Battle takes
Him by the throat and makes him blind,

The thundering line of battle stands
And in the air Death moans and sings;
But Day shall clasp him with strong hands,
And Night shall fold him in soft wings.'

So there I lay cooped up by a ring of bullets and kept where I was. After an hour I began to find it not uninteresting, when to my dismay a salvo of four heavy shells burst on the ridge on which I was lying. The German artillery must have seen our reinforcements coming over and had decided that they would make that ridge too hot to be used. This was not a cheering thought, for it was clear that, as I was the only inhabitant of that ridge, I should get the benefit of the whole bombardment. I knew, though the Germans did not, that there was little enough chance of more reinforcements coming again, for the simple fact that there were none to come. So the affair lay between me and the Germans! and I could do nothing but wait my chances and calculate when exactly I was likely to be hit by a shell. As I pondered wretchedly, away behind the German lines came a series of dull flat bangs, then a pause, and then the well-known whistling of large shells. Four terrific explosions on each side of me showed where the next salvo had struck. Bits of shell whanged dismally through the rain and embedded themselves in the mud round me. I hunched myself up in the bottom of my hole and waited. But there was a long wait before the next salvo came. The gunners were clearly ranging up and down along the ridge, almost as if they were determined to drive me, its sole occupant, off or else blow me up. Actually they were merely barraging against the advance of any more of our men. How I longed to crawl out and run down to my friends in front. But I knew that, once out, my progress would be that of a worm and that I should last about ten yards at most before I was hit. My hole was friendly and safe from everything except shells. If only those demoniac German gunners would give up firing, my day would have been a perfect one, with the solitary exception of the rain, which continued unabated. But rain did not worry me, when I had the major interest of high-explosive to distract. Again that distant banging, the whistle and crashing of another salvo. Again my hole was happily between the new holes of the latest shell-bursts. I consoled myself with the thought that no shell ever bursts in a hole made by any of its predecessors, for so we fondly believed. But it seemed of mere philosophic interest to me at the time, like the river of Heracleitos which no one crosses twice, for some of the bursts were so near as to make no difference between their holes and mine.

And so it went on till midday. Then there was a pause for about an hour and soon it began again. By a series of continuously repeated miracles I escaped harm. Not even a fragment of shell lodged itself in me, and the air was thick with singing and buzzing fragments after each explosion.

I wish I could state in plain words what went on in my mind during this mad experience. Actually, I must confess, very little went on at all. I was far too occupied trying to survive to do much cogitation. Were I writing the typical war novel of to-day I should set forth the harrowing ruminations that are supposed to revolve in the bitter minds of disillusioned young men. But I was not harrowed at all, merely harassed, frightened, anxious, and hungry. I was also very, very lonely. To face death in company brings into operation all the comforting elements of gregarious instinct. I had never minded bombardments in the trenches much, because one knew that there was help if one was wounded, always friendly sympathy and, if one was killed, someone who saw it who could tell the sorrowing relatives, which—and I am not being sentimental—counted for a good deal. But to be potted at like a rat in a trap, to be partly blown up or wholly annihilated alone and unobserved was a fate which was forbidding. The one fine feature of warfare is the brotherhood and mutual trust that it breeds: that cannot justify war, but it can palliate it. Here, alone in my mud hole, I had lost the one element which had so far made me happy in my doings. Never before or since have I encountered real friendship and solidarity as I knew them in the war. And here at my most unhappy moment I was deprived of their help.

It left me gloomy and helpless. I had no one to turn to and was certain of one thing, that if I was badly hurt by the shells there was no one to come to my aid.

Yet somehow I derived a queer enjoyment at moments from my predicament. I spent some time reconstructing the intentions and doings of those German batteries. I identified the guns that were firing as a battery of high-velocity guns of high calibre, aided by a variety of smaller weapons that fired some shrapnel and others small high explosive. The only really alarming shells were those that came in salvos from the high-velocity guns. They made heavy massive explosions, and the bodies of the shells were thick, for from the jagged and almost red-hot fragments that sometimes stuck in the edge of my hole I could infer a good deal.

Then I had another worry. If the Germans broke our line, as likely as not I should be bayoneted, and certainly I should be taken prisoner. That of all fates throughout the war filled me with most apprehension; for I wanted bitterly to see the war to an end from inside. As a prisoner one saw nothing, and restraint has always been to me an intolerable thing, if it is a restraint for no reason at all.

My German batteries resumed their work after having had, as I computed, a quiet rest and a good lunch which had lasted them an hour. I, miserable wretch, had nothing at all to eat. When I left my trench I took nothing with me, thinking that in the front trench I should find some stray food. Now I had nothing at all, not even a bar of chocolate. How I hated those German gunners and their leisurely lunch.

After lunch—their lunch—things warmed up again. Not merely did they bombard my ridge with increasing intensity, but there was evidently another attack. The rifle-fire below me rose to a mad fury of rattling. Waves of staccato sound rose and fell. I longed to put my head above the hole and see what was doing, but whenever I made any such attempt, warning bullets told me that every inch of my ridge was watched. The Germans seemed to think that whole battalions of men were lurking in the holes of the ridge. If only they had known it was nothing worse than a wretched subaltern with a hole in his leg they would have saved many hundreds of pounds spent on shells and bullets. Again I comforted myself with statistics. We had been told that learned men on the staff had computed that it takes 6000 bullets to kill one man in trench warfare. Unfortunately no one had elaborated statistics for the number of shells adequate to remove one officer from a ridge a half a mile long. I hoped that the number, in any case, was a good round sum. Certainly it was increasing each minute.

I suppose I ought to have pondered on Eternity, to have said my prayers and resigned myself to the imminent possibility of sudden death. But I did nothing of the sort. True I swore with violence and hatred every time the shells came over. That did me a lot of good. True I ejaculated prayers of a sort, but they were not addressed to any particular divinity, they were merely urgent hopes.

The battle rose and fell, the line seemed to bend and waver and then to hold firm. Later, when I met my wounded friends at the back of the line, they told me that wave after wave of grey Germans had come across against every part of this small salient and that those waves mostly now hung lifeless on our wire or lay in heaps on the ground. Of this I could see nothing. But as I listened I knew that countless men, as good or as bad as myself, were being killed like sheep. Every burst of sustained fire meant the passing of so many souls. It was a queer entertainment. But then, in that unreal world, there seemed nothing queer about it at all. That men should be obliterated in heaps like insects did not strike me as odd or even evil. The war had so enshrouded me that I simply could not think in that sort of way.

The rain did not cease, but slowly a kind of smoky dusk

arose. My watch told me that it was six o'clock. Another hour or two and I could crawl back. But those last hours seemed to stand still. How I longed for them to speed. For I had survived so very successfully and it would be maddening to be killed just at the end, after so fortunate a day.

My wound never worried me for a moment. A small pool of blood had stained the mud, but I was clearly not badly damaged. The leg was quite useless, but only the muscles were cut. Indeed it was a superb wound, the sort that every man longed to get when he was wounded, the sort that took you home and gave you no trouble. I cherished that happy wound and wanted to see it get the results it deserved. It would be infuriating if, at the end, I were blinded, or decapitated, or lost the other leg. I have no idea what the Will to Survive really is. But I had it all right, though unfortunately it was only of a theoretical value, for it could do nothing to defeat that Will to Destroy of the German gunners that seemed aimed solely at me.

My thoughts were never much more profound than I here describe. I can, when I wish, be as introspective as any introvert, but out there on that ridge there really was not much scope for introspection; nor did I belong to an introspective generation. That is why I cannot lay bare for you the inner mutterings of a soul in torture! One has to have been born in about 1910 to be that sort of writer. And I was born in 1889!

At last blessed night came. I emerged from my pit, stretched with the joy of a leopard let out of a cage, and began a slimy descent back down the ridge to the trench which I had originally left. But I had to crawl on all fours. Slow and snail-like was my progress. I was famished and rather faint, but I could crawl well and fast. I advanced, my objective lit from behind by the superb spectacle of Ypres, now a raging furnace of fire, red and vivid. No human was in sight and I felt like an intruder into Dante's Hell. My progress was splendid and I was proud of my achievement. I remember as if I were there now, how the mud seethed up in small waves over my wrists and up my sleeve and then fell back in disappointed slabs. On I ploughed. But as I took a stride forwards of which I was particularly proud, I stopped in alarm. Another figure, silent and on fours like my own, was stalking me. Then the line was breaking after all, I thought. So I loosened my large and exceedingly dangerous automatic, pulled down the safety catch and waited silently. The figure approached. When it was twenty yards away I shouted sternly, 'Who are you?' 'I'm Geoffrey Wade,' shouted back the sinister figure. 'And I'm shot in the leg,' he added. 'Then come and join my party,' I replied, 'because I'm Stanley Casson.' Mutual gulps of joy ensued. But when he came up I noticed that he too was fingering his automatic nervously. Indeed our day nearly ended in mutual destruction.

At a trench, which we reached crawling like two mules, side by side, we found about a dozen men who had collected there; some had drifted back from the front line, others had come up from behind on various tasks. But all were silent and stupid and were just hanging about, devoid of ideas as to what to do or where to go. For the first time I met demoralisation. They were not mutinous, nor were they cowards. But they had reached the point at which their initiative just simply gave out. I saw it often later on. They had no officer, nor even a corporal. It was a strange instance of the military machine stopping for a moment or two. For they were mostly regular soldiers, fully trained, as were then a majority of the men of my battalion; or at least they were trained reservists. I could do little with them, but I managed to get four of them to take Geoffrey off on the remnants of an old door which we found. But I had to do all my ordering about from a seated position, and I did not carry much weight.

I smoked a cigarette and gathered what news I could. The farm had been taken, lost, and retaken I gathered.

Even as they told me a new party came in bearing a form on a stretcher. It was that of my company commander. The men said that he had been shot in the throat while leading a most gallant attack in the open against the farm. As he lay there with his eyes closed, there began an ominous rattling in his chest. He was dying and I could think of nothing to do. We found another door and I had him taken as swiftly as possible back to the casualty station. He was unconscious and the last I saw of him was a figure like that of King Arthur in the pictures, carried slowly by four men, lying on this ancient door, hoisted high on their bent shoulders. And I could see him only by the light of the red glow of Ypres, for the moon had not risen.

Suddenly a visitor came. It was the Colonel. He drifted out of the dark like a wraith and asked me the news. I had nothing to tell him and I believe that he thought that I and the handful of men remaining were the last remnant of the whole battalion! and I am equally sure that he had no idea where the rest of the battalion really was. For we did not see our Colonel much in the front line in those days. I expect he was still thinking of that garden of his at Plugstreet and its grey stones.

Two days later he left us and was sent home. I rather fancy that wise men in high quarters knew of him and his garden.

I felt after an hour or two sitting in this queer corner that I deserved to get myself looked after. Indeed the Colonel had ordered me to get back. Not that I would have done so if I could have been of any use. But I was useless. So I looked for a third door. And in this well-bedoored region I found one. A third party set out. The door was very hard and I lay on top of it like a salmon on a marble slab, slithering and slipping as the bearers heaved and stumbled. I prayed that no shell or bullet would hit me now, for the air was still full of them. That was a memorable journey. Ypres, looming nearer, looked more and more lovely, in its own violent and ghastly way. I had seen Ypres dead in cold moonlight. Now I saw it on its pyre in dark mist. If I ever see the Hell that Christianity of the Middle Ages so artistically imagined in verse and panel, that Hell will at first glance look as Ypres looked then. I felt like a corpse being carried to Hell, just as in those terrifying paintings on Etruscan Tombs in Italy, where the dead is clawed away from the living by demons who drag him off to Hades.

A few stumps of trees, a small shack, and here was the casualty station. Cheerful voices and unbelievable kindness awaited me. I was bandaged and iodined, given a tetanus injection, and put in a chair. Others, lightly wounded like myself, greeted me. 'Why, we all thought you were dead!' shouted one youth. '"Machine-Gun" Brown said he saw you turn turtle like a rabbit, shot through the heart.' 'Well, here I am, anyhow,' I replied. The stuffing was knocked out of me and I had no more power for retort or humour. Soon kindly men took me to an ambulance and off we bumped. A few miles and we were decanted at an old barn and laid in rows in our stretchers. Here for the first and only time in France, I saw a padre. He appeared, neat, well fed and comfortable, and stopped with a word at every bier. We none of us seemed to want him and he drifted towards me. 'Can I write a letter home to your parents about you?' he asked me. 'My dear man,' I replied, 'if my unhappy parents were to receive a letter from a padre about me they would at once assume that I had perished; the more optimistic your remarks about me the more convinced they would be that I was dead: no, thanks, I am quite capable of writing myself in due time. What I want now is FOOD.' Admittedly I was rude and thankless. But I raged to think that this wretched man was paid a comfortable salary for this kind of thing. A neighbour told me that shortly before the padre had found a man in a stretcher, soaked in blood and apparently almost destroyed. In fact he had merely been hit by several hundred pieces of a hand-bomb and had fallen into a happy, if bloody slumber. None of his hurts were more than skin-deep. He woke up to hear the padre muttering a prayer in a monotone. The poor soldier nearly died of fright, and thought that it was his own burial service. Fortunately the doctor arrived in time to send the padre off.

All the same there were men in that barn who needed consolation. All round me were groans and cries. One poor wretch kept on calling in a high wail for his mother. Soldiers do that when they are hurt. He was in a bad way. But I was too exhausted to worry. I dozed.

I woke to find myself in a room in some other place. How and when I had been moved I had no idea. It was morning and sunny. A cheerful doctor came in and gave me without comment a plate of ham and a half-bottle of champagne. Of all the meals I have ever put aside for honourable mention in the books of my memory that heads the list. I had not eaten for forty-eight hours and that particular meal was the perfect meal, at that time and for that occasion.

I was soon bustled into an ambulance and carried into a train. There in an ecstasy of comfort and linen sheets I sped to Boulogne, with nothing to worry about any more and no duties to do, no bullets to dodge, no more trenches to dig.

Boulogne and more snowy beds, more good food and incredible kindness. Never once did I meet man or woman in those days who was not doing his or her utmost to make us all as happy as we could be. I suppose we deserved it.

CHAPTER V

INTERLUDE

I SPED in an ambulance along Whitehall. I was back in the old world again. I craned my neck and caught a fleeting glimpse of the War Office, whose doors I had so short a time ago entered eagerly searching for my commission. Now I felt I could pass it and feel that I had done, for the moment, all that it had called upon me to do. I felt almost as if I could patronise it. I was contented for the first time for a long while.

Hospital meant very little to trouble me. My leg began to mend after a little while. I reclined in a comfortable bed, with the May weather getting sunnier and brighter. I could read the newspapers every day with a feeling that, even if I had abandoned my friends out near Ypres, that I had not abandoned them without good cause. The battle was still raging and lasted to the end of May. I could now understand the news that I read in every detail and add a good deal that the papers did not say. The battle was clearly ours. The Germans had by now reached the stage of frittering away their strength in minor attacks. Every battle ultimately ends that way, unless it is a final battle. And at that time neither I nor anyone else knew how final battles ended, for the simple reason that there had been none. Battles were merely eruptions that swelled, became more and more inflamed, burst and then subsided into minor irritations and pains and troubles, and then all would be 'normal' again. But to read of it all now was like peering into the stray fragments of an almost forgotten dream, like trying to remember what you have just dreamed about when you have just awakened.

My afternoons were cheered by the visits of friends.

Girls whom I adored individually developed the disconcerting habit of arriving collectively. But even that was diverting, more especially since each believed that I was known only to her, or pretended to believe it. Yet we all had a sense of humour. The patients were all entertaining enough. One delightful young Canadian told me that he began the war with the fixed intention of winning the Victoria Cross at all costs. He had been not far from me at Ypres and he described how during the height of the battle he had carried on his shoulders into safety at least six different wounded men, across an open and shell-swept field. He had chosen his moments for this humane task only when there was some senior officer in view. Yet not one of them had recommended him for his Cross, and, as he put it, he had carried his victims with every semblance of courage and fortitude. I suggested to him that he had clearly neglected his duties as an officer and taken on the task of the stretcher-bearers. 'But I wanted to get the Cross, somehow,' he replied. In the end all he got was a shattered arm. And he was really rather lucky.

Soon, after about six weeks, I was let loose and went to live once again, as in those distant days of early 1914, in the flat in Chelsea that I and my sister shared. There I hobbled about with a crutch or a stick and did less than nothing. To feel content, at rest, and idle was all that man could want. And London at this time was deeply interesting. I went to theatres, dinners and, as an onlooker, to dances. There was no very evident worry or hysteria or excitement. Noel Coward must then have been trying to learn his lessons at school. The London of his 'Cavalcade' simply did not exist. There were the usual patriotic songs at the theatres that were invariably greeted with cat-calls and laughter, and there were songs of the type of 'I don't want to lose you, but I think you ought to go,' which were greeted with immense cheers of derision by the soldiers who made up the majority of the audience. Nor did the singers even sing them seriously. But they were capital songs and we all joined in the chorus lustily. Never before or since did the accepted stars of the theatre, George Graves, Elsie Janis, Delysia, Harry Tate and the rest, play with such gusto or delight so many cheerful people. London was a continuous feast, irregularly obscured by Zeppelin Raids. You might be dining at the Savoy or the Berkeley when suddenly warning went round. Lights were put out, everything was quiet for a bit. Then came the crash of guns above and around, and those who were adventurous went out to look. Those who were more adventurous perhaps led their partners into obscure corners. Sometimes the raid did not start before midnight. That meant that you could continue your revels until three or four. I never saw anyone particularly frightened by the raids though I have no doubt that many felt more alarmed than I did. One night I watched the raid from the Chelsea embankment and saw the airships darting along below the clouds, with their under-sides lit with the bright silver of the searchlights. I thought of Max Joerrens at Bonn and his cheerful prophecies about the task of those Zeppelins. In his wildest moments he had not suggested that they might bomb London. And here they were with myself to see them doing it. London lit by searchlight was one of the most beautiful spectacles I have ever seen. There was added to the beauty the tang of the dangerous that, somehow, made the beauty more lovely. Had the searchlights been merely a display I think I could not have liked it as much. But to see London, my own birthplace, attacked by silvery things like enormous shining sharks, lit with all the extravaganza of a ballet, resounding to crashings and sirens and bangings, was an experience which to a Londoner brings a feeling too complex to analyse. I suppose I was filled with a mixture of alarm, admiration, pure sensual appreciation of the colour and pattern of it all, and angry as well that any enemy should penetrate into the place in which I had spent most of my life, and treat it as a potential rubbish heap. Mixed pleasures, like mixed fears, are always more potent. Where you cannot tell precisely whence comes the pleasure or what causes the fear you are the more excited.

At length I returned to my regimental base at Plymouth. Here things had changed a good deal. Beyond the few officers like myself, who had recently returned from sick-leave there was scarcely a face I knew. Streams of fresh recruits came in daily from the mill-towns of Lancashire. The same quiet, humorous, kindly, quick-witted Lancashire-men, with their soft voices and their disarming smiles. There was something dreadful in this constant pouring in of fine men with the certain knowledge that after a time they would all go out to the same kind of life in France, and that then, after a time, some would come back and others not. These elementary sentimentalities were as real as the air I breathed. I cannot pretend that I did not feel them.

But there was a changed outlook. We had all settled down, so to speak, to the war. There was no longer any talk of its being over in a few months, or in a year. We knew it was a long steady grinding away of will-power and man-power and that, sooner or later, one side or the other would give out.

But here I was again, once more engaged on the pursuit of the enemy—at least that was what I was supposed to be there for. But there was something slightly ridiculous in the thought, which often occurred to me, that so far I had seen no pursuer face to face, nor had any of my pursuers seen me. The glint of moonlight on steel helmets; the sparkle of a dawn sun on rows of bayonets above the enemy parapet; fleeting forms in no-man's-land at night; the green of Jaeger uniforms and, finally, the silver of searchlights on long cigar-shaped airships—that was all I had seen of the enemy! Yet one of their bullets had hit me and, I hoped, some of my bullets had perhaps hit them.

Still it was a game of pure hide-and-seek. All those exercises with bayonets and dummies stuffed with straw which had shown us how to disembowel our opponents seemed to presuppose a kind of war quite different from that which I had encountered. Up till then I had not even seen a German prisoner in the flesh, for at Plugstreet we had taken none, and at Ypres I was never near any spot where the Germans fell into our hands, except as corpses.

But, theoretically, the game was on for me once more, and I had soon to set forth again on the pursuit of these phantoms. There was something exciting in wondering exactly what the future had in store. I might end up, if I lived, in almost any part of the globe, for by now the war had extended and spread into various distant climes. Turkey was now included; Bulgaria was showing signs which, to my mind—and I knew a little by now about Balkan politics—indicated that she would soon be among the ranks of our enemies.

I passed the winter at Plymouth, now training others rather than being trained myself, and by the late autumn it was clear that before very long British troops would be wanted in the Balkans. But it seemed entirely outside my own life, and I could think of no reason at all why I should be sent there. For I belonged to one or the other of the first two battalions of my regiment, and both of them were still in the neighbourhood of Ypres.

Then one day an order reached us that any officer who had any personal acquaintance with Greece and the Balkans, and any knowledge of Balkan tongues, was to report to the War Office. Excited by the prospect of being sent on a new task, of being able to be of more use than the ordinary officer in uniform, I hurried to London. At the War Office a curious little man interviewed me and asked me if I spoke Modern Greek. I replied that I did, up to a point. Thereupon he handed me a piece of paper covered with rather straggling handwriting which had the appearance of Greek.

'Translate that,' he said, abruptly. I read it and re-read it. It made no sort of sense to me at all. I handed it back. 'No,' I replied, 'I cannot: it is written in Greek but that is positively all I can tell you about it.' 'Don't worry,' he answered. 'It is written in Greek all right, but the language is Albanian, and I did not ask you if you knew that.' He passed me, with the usual honours which I had found were accorded to one in War Office linguistic examinations! I returned to my unit at Plymouth and waited. I did not have to wait long. Orders came for me to go to Salonika at once on a transport then in dock at Devonport.

CHAPTER VI

EASTWARDS

THE *Transylvania* was the largest and most luxurious ship I had ever been on. We left the dock on the very same day that the Germans announced to the world that they were commencing their period of 'unrestricted sinking of ships.' But that did not matter to us, for we were a transport in any case and so fair game for submarines at any time since the declaration of war. Still, it made us all feel that things were getting a bit hot. It was a hard day in February 1916 when we moved slowly out of Plymouth Sound, past Drake's Island and into open water. Two smart destroyers accompanied us. We all sat down to lunch feeling the comfort of good companionship both in the ship and outside it. Away behind us Dartmoor, snow-covered, showed up as a steep rise of white ground. Sun and a keen wind made our departure refreshing. In a trice we were once again in contact, perhaps closer than any of us knew, with our hidden enemies. At length, towards sunset, we were out in the open sea. Suddenly the two destroyers turned abruptly and swung round. I imagined that they had seen something suspicious. They headed fast away back to England. We realised at length that our escort had decided to leave us to continue our journey unescorted. Rather wrily we settled down to our fate. For here we were in open Atlantic, defended only by two small guns fore and aft, a ship crammed with troops and munitions, the ideal target, and the most justifiable an enemy could find. If a submarine torpedoed us and then machine-gunned the troops in the water she would be doing nothing more nor less than her duty. For we were to a man potential destroyers of Germans. It would be no use yelping about 'atrocities':

once we were caught, the most sensible course for any German would be to let us all drown and to kill all of us he could. The perfect simplicity of our situation, I know, was some comfort to most of us. After all, it was a good sporting chance.

At intervals we had our practice boat drill and the rest, but for the most part we read, ate, smoked, drank, and played bridge. Here, if anywhere, was a chance for hard drinkers to drink hard. Were I writing a story all about the disastrous effects of war on character; were I Eric Remarcque or Ernest Hemingway I should here have my chance. But it would not, unfortunately, be true. No one on that great liner was drunk at any time from the start to the finish of our trip. We had troops of all kinds and officers of all conditions. But they all were moderate men. And we were all perfectly happy and deeply interested in whatever came to view on the high seas. We had made so wide a circuit into the Atlantic that the clocks had been put back an hour and twenty minutes. We approached Gibraltar at nightfall to see it a dark mass of rock with sparkling lights below it and the streamers of searchlights striking across the strait. But we went on at full speed. We were told that now we were in the 'Danger Zone,' and crews of boats slept by them and in them at nights. But nothing happened beyond occasional scares, and in a few days we passed off Malta. Still we did not stop. It was as if we were running for our lives. At length we sailed slowly into Alexandria.

The winter was forgotten and a brilliant sun gave us all new life. A few days in camp along the shore at Alexandria was like a summer holiday. We bathed in the surf and slept on the sand. But it was a queer camp. It held a handful of officers like myself, bound on special jobs, and besides a concourse of no less than twenty-seven padres—Catholics, Anglicans, Wesleyans—in fact of all persuasions. Here the poor creatures had accumulated like flotsam in a backwater. Nobody wanted them much and nobody sent for them. So there they stayed. Some were dapper, some uncouth, most just untidy, all in the half-mourning uniform of the militant clergy which has so doleful an appearance in a cheerful setting. Like crows they roamed the sands, kept to themselves and waited. I never once in the war met a padre who had sufficient initiative to devise ways of being useful in places where there was not much demand for non-combatants. A general air of depression covered this drab and dispirited assembly. No doubt the thought in the back of their minds that hardly any two of them could agree upon the principal tenets of Christianity had a depressing effect upon their spirits. They never cheered up all the time I was there.

Cairo for two days was a diversion while I waited for a ship to Salonika. Here I encountered Australians for the first time.

* * * * * * *

A smaller transport took me from Alexandria. We passed by Crete, tall, snowy and remote in a glory of its own, then later right through the Greek islands, past Santorin, Paros, Naxos, and with the mainland in view coasted along Eubœa. There were the same little flat-topped white houses in clusters that I had seen not two years ago. The same air and at night the scent of the thyme that blew in gusts from the sun-heated rocks. The smell of Greece, as individual and distinctive a scent as I know, was in my nostrils again. The war was almost forgotten and I felt as if I were out once more on an archæological tour.

Soon Olympus came into view above the low mists and clouds, with its snow brilliant in a cold sun and a steely blue sea, perfectly smooth, to mirror its reflections. We rounded a point to see a large merchant vessel beached on a sandy spit: a recent achievement of Austrian submarines. Then Salonika appeared dimly at the back. That city will always be one of the really lovely places of the world, as long as it is seen from afar. Its complete circuit of walls, the white minarets and red roofs and the compact appearance of the place gave it a rare distinction. Behind it brown hills rose in a framework of quiet colour. Here, though neither I nor the generals in command knew it at the time, was the end of the right wing of the whole of the Allied armies. Here in this gulf at the foot of Olympus was the last armed defence against a westward push. It was made clear enough at the end, when in 1918 the Bulgarian army broke and fled, and there was laid open to our advance the very heart of the enemy lands. No sooner did we begin to push northwards from the Salonika lines than we had all Hungary and Bavaria open to our advance. Indeed we had orders to that effect and, had not Austria surrendered, the Salonika armies would have pressed across the Danube and penetrated into the rear of Germany. But neither the War Offices of Paris and London nor the generals on the spot had fully realised that here was the flank to turn, that here was the weak spot in the defences of encircled Germany. Instead we looked on ourselves and were looked upon by the rest of the world as a mere containing force, sent to check Bulgarian advance and prevent reinforcements being sent to the Western Front. That, in brief, was the difference between the real and the supposed strategy of this forgotten expedition. Events showed the actualities. Surprised ourselves, we suddenly found ourselves in September nearly three years later rolling up a front that extended from the North Sea to the Mediterranean.

At this time, indeed, I began a more cosmopolitan education in arms. I knew nothing about the major purposes of our side-shows. The general strategy of Palestine and Mesopotamia and Macedonia were utterly obscure. I had seen none of the Allies except the French and Belgians. I had hardly realised even that it was a world-war and not merely a war in the Low Countries. America seemed so far off and so completely disengaged from the quarrels at issue and the projects afoot that the mere contingency of her becoming another Ally never entered my head. But War is a harsh teacher, in that famous phrase, and, within a year, most of us out there began to see that there was no limit in either hemisphere to the extension of slaughter and destruction.

We landed now in a country that was believed to be neutral, but which we were told was being protected against aggression. It was hard to make out who was in the wrong. For the Greeks were ready enough to fight Bulgaria, but claimed that their treaty, by which it was said they were bound to help Serbia in the event of war, had not included in the contract the possibility of a general conflagration. I believe the Greeks were right in this. However, there we all were, some hundred thousand French and British troops, Serbians, Russians, and, away in Albania, Italians. We were all said to be there for the purpose of saving Salonika. A Greek army under arms sat on the outskirts and professed the same intention. Consuls of Austria and Germany still functioned in their consulates and their agents counted the Allied troops as they landed and sent swift couriers to Bulgaria with the news. The Greeks looked askance at us and treated French and British with contempt. The reaction of the French to this was characteristic. They forced the Greeks out of all control of the town, although it was a Greek city in Greek territory. Our own reaction was to treat with the Greeks sympathetically but to get them out of any position where they might hinder the progress of military affairs. This is a simple statement: in fact everything was in comparative chaos, and the policies of the various Allies only approximated to the lines I have indicated. One thing alone was clear, that the Greeks were dispossessed of their own city. They looked at us coldly and contemptuously.

Dust everywhere. Troops marching along the tawdry sea-front. Lorries banging and crashing over the uneven

Allied soldiers in Salonika (left to right: Cretan, British, Serb, Italian, Senegalese, Indian, Greek, Annamite, Russian, French, Senegalese)

Turkoman, Russian and British Staff Officers on the Oxus (*see page* 252)

Turkish roadways. Tall powerful Serbians, shoddy French infantrymen and lazy British soldiers thronging the streets. When I saw the Serbians in their stern forbidding uniforms my mind went to those invaders of *The Englishman's Home* and then again to the smart troops in the old white fort at Belgrade in 1913 and the spring of 1914 when I had passed through Serbia on my way home. Now at last I was in uniform too, side by side with them in the same war. From the Balkan wars to this war was a quick step. I remembered how I had looked on all the military movements of Greeks and Serbians and Bulgars as something rather barbaric. I had condescended to examine those two Balkan wars with a patronising glance. And now here I was, no more and no less Balkan than the rest of them, serving in the very heart of the Balkans, fighting in a war which was infinitely more childish and infinitely more cruel than any which Bulgar and Greek and Serb had waged among themselves. This time just a year back I had been lying out on a ridge in the most civilised part of Western Europe, dodging shell-bursts and hiding from bullets, with my leg bound in bloody rags. And yet we, the citizens of the Great Powers, had for years lectured Balkan peoples contemptuously as barbarians. Now rather I felt like a barbarian neophyte myself, humbled before the sterner and more experienced warriors of these snowy mountains and wild forests. Here was I, a wretched expensively educated young puppy, bred in luxury and trained in all the elements of civilisation, sent out here to vie with these experts in the arts of war. Serbians, Greeks, Bulgars, and Turks had already been fighting for four years! Some of these giant Serbian infantrymen had escaped from Austrian prison camps to Russia and had been sent thence *via* Siberia and Vladivostok again to Salonika to attempt to storm their way back into Serbia. For the first few months of the war in England I had felt an amateur. After a few weeks in France I had felt a veteran. Now I felt that I had only learned the lessons of one kind of war. I was again the amateur, and had to start all over again. These Serbs could have taught me more in a week than I had learned altogether. Their patient and immobile faces, their perfect discipline and their punctilious salutes marked them out as real warriors. Later, at the end of the war, they were the spear-head of attack and victory. They remained then, as they remain now for me, the only true and natural soldiers I saw in the whole course of the war. For there was never a Serbian mutiny, never a Serbian failure in attack, and never a Serbian retreat in disorder. Savages and barbarians though they seemed, they were the world's best soldiers. I felt that Balkan fighting for Europeans from the west and north would be something radically different from other fighting. For here we were in a world of experts.

I was sent up country to a lovely plateau in the hills some three thousand feet up. Below us sparkled the walled Byzantine city of Salonika, looking from that distance as it must have looked to barbarians in the hills a thousand years before. I was now a member of the 'Intelligence Corps,' whatever that may have been. My duties were entirely nebulous. At last I reported to my division, the 10th Irish Division, a body of fine Irishmen all drawn from Dublin. This was the first I had ever seen of the famous 'Kitchener's Army.' Every man in the division was an even worse amateur than myself. But they had seen some hard times. They had been at Suvla Bay on Gallipoli and had taken part in that landing which should and could have ended the war. Withdrawn from Gallipoli they had been bundled in haste up to Nish in Serbia—or as near to Nish as it was possible to get. Still bedecked in the sun-helmets and thin shorts of tropical service which they had worn in the blister-ing heat of Gallipoli, they were thrust into battles in the depths of southern Serbia, in the course of which they trudged in three feet of snow and slept in blizzards on rocky moors. They had lost their guns to attacking Bulgars, got frost-bitten and returned precipitously to Salonika. That was all the British Nation ever managed to do to save Serbia from Bulgar and Austrian invasion. But, being Irishmen, they soon recovered their spirits. I saw them not long after on the night of St Patrick's Day. Every single man of the ten odd thousand of the division was completely and absolutely drunk for that memorable night. And I saw them later on when the news of the Easter Rebellion in Dublin came through. They were all as excited as schoolboys at a football match. They argued anxiously as to the merits of both sides in the battles of Dublin, and betted, and cheered the news as it came along. Then, when all was over, they settled down cheerfully to their daily tasks as members of the British Army.

Here among the spring flowers of these Balkan hills I had a hundred different tasks, though none of them seemed very much to concern our Bulgarian enemy. Indeed no one seemed much to know where he was. People would point vaguely to a line of hills, snow-covered, some fifty miles to the north and say that they were 'somewhere there.' The no-man's-land between us was so vast that neither enemy could find the other. Actually in those days we and they alike were biding our time. We were fortifiying lines all round Salonika, so as to prevent any incursion, and they were sitting on their heights wondering if it would be worth while to descend into the plains and join issue with us. Every trench we cut and every reinforcement we received was known to them because there was not the smallest means of preventing information from passing across that vast fifty miles. Afterwards, when I climbed up on to the highest Bulgarian observation posts that they abandoned after their retreat, I found that every ship that entered Salonika harbour could be plainly seen with strong glasses. They must have known everything that we were doing, and their army was stiffened by German generals, technicians and gunners and by a small proportion of good German troops.

For a time, however, we lived as if we were in training in England once again. How we should ever meet our foe and pursue him we had no idea at all. It was inconceivable then that one day we should be chasing him as fast as legs could take us over those white and distant hills right into the heart of his own land. Yet so it turned out in the end.

Weeks passed in the hills. From the door of my tent I could see Olympus every sunrise. I got to learn its habits and moods. Sometimes there would be nothing except a group of scurrying clouds in an otherwise empty sky over where I knew Olympus to be. The home of the gods was veiled. Then another day I could see every detail of the triple peaks standing out clear and unduly sharp like the print from an overexposed negative. At other times all I could see was the slashed lines of snow down the sides.

We marched and counter-marched among the early flowers of summer; we descended to great lakes in plain-lands and bathed; we made roads and dug trenches. Several times I was sent on reconnaissances into what was, for the most part, unknown land. I and another officer went off one day on our horses, to find out the nature of the ground in that great space between us and the enemy. We left our foremost outposts behind and set off into a wild and lovely land. We had no maps that were even approximately accurate. At the end of our first day's ride I found that there was an error of twenty miles on the map. We should have reached our destination twenty miles back and, instead, rode at nightfall into a strange townlet far up in the hills. Here, in this forbidding cluster of houses, we found a place for our horses and ourselves. It was a mountain village peopled with strange, fierce folk. We were the first British officers who had come there, though I feel little doubt that they were well enough acquainted with our enemies. For the village was on the last line of hills above the Struma plains where the Bulgar outposts lurked. The inhabitants were, in fact, mostly Bulgarians, or rather that mongrel version, half

Slav, half Greek, half anything Balkan, that formed the bulk of the populace of those parts. They spoke Greek with difficulty and it was clearly not their language. They greeted us with suspicion and unfriendliness. But I selected the Mayor to be our host and in the Mayor's veranda we slept that spring night, not forgetting to load our revolvers and place them handy. The village, which bore the odd name of Suho, was in fact the centre from which departed all the various scallywags who pretended to be spies for Bulgar or French or British. Here they were all round us, and making little pretence at a welcome. But we were safe enough, for I gave them to understand that we were only the forerunners of a considerable army. Since considerable armies had passed over those hills and through that and every similar village without cessation ever since the time of Alexander the Great, I had no need to elaborate my theme. Bulgars had raped and burned many a village in those hills, provided it was a Greek village, in 1913. Turks had done the same for several centuries, so that the prospect of the approach of a revenging army of my compatriots who would retaliate for anything done to me was a sufficient weapon in my hands. I got all I wanted in the way of food and accommodation and paid for what I got. But I did not much like the atmosphere, and there was no information of any kind to be obtained. Dark men in brown fustian kilts, with caps of fur, and silver knives in their belts, passed and looked at us disdainfully. These were the raw material of which, later on, we made our spies. They were as ignorant of military affairs as of any mode of putting their information into comprehensible language. Of all the reports made by spies in our service who crossed the Bulgar lines not one that I ever saw gave any information which was of the smallest service. Where we wanted to know the numbers of divisions, the calibre and position of guns and the amount of ammunition in dumps, they would tell us, in long-winded accounts, of the quality of the food in the villages, of the intrigues of the Bulgar general with the mayor's wife, and of the high price of petrol. I think that every penny we spent on spies was sheer downright waste. Later, in Athens, I was able even more definitely to confirm this opinion. The good spy must be highly educated, accurate at observation, and quick to make inferences. The Balkan peasant is none of these things. As a spy he was utterly useless, yet we and the Bulgars alike employed many of them; probably the same men served us both! Indeed in some cases we knew this for certain and filled up our spy, who was just leaving for the enemy's lines, with spurious information. No doubt the other side did the same. The spy business simply cancelled out. Both sides were told useless information or fed with nonsense. However, it was a thriving business. Almost everyone in these villages and towns was a potential spy, for it was lucrative. Later on we organised the more active spirits of places like Suho into a band of military brigands. Trained for generations in the brigandage of Macedonian hills, they would, we thought, make a useful body of irregulars. They were formed into a band of a hundred, disciplined after a fashion and sent off on marauding expeditions into Bulgarian supply dumps, or told to drive Bulgarian cattle back to our lines. They did some few exploits of this kind, cut the throats of a few Bulgar sentries and came back. Every exploit they celebrated by an orgy in one of the villages in our lines. Finally, in one orgy, they looted the entire village, raped some of the girls—and the inhabitants by the way were of the same race as themselves—and that was the end of them. We dispersed them and sent them back to their homes, where individually they could do less harm than they did collectively.

From Suho, perched up on the southern face of a mountain, we ascended the ridge over to the northern side. Here, as everywhere in the Balkans, the north face of hills and mountains is always bare rock, for the north winds do not allow anything to survive. I had not as yet had

Rupel Pass seen from the British lines (looking north)

experience of these north winds, for I had arrived in spring. Later I learned them and endured as I could the bitter frost and snow they brought. But now all was sun, and the north slopes of our mountain were warm and bright. Descending by a slippery cobble path, made centuries gone by Turkish masters, we saw spread out before us one of the most exquisite sights in the Balkans—the valley of the Struma, deep and mountain-hemmed on all sides. Away to the north was a cleft in the long razor-ridge of snow that faced us, and there we knew was the notorious Rupel Pass, behind which the Bulgars sat firm, with three great armies, ready to descend upon the valley and drive at Salonika. Rupel Pass has played its part in every Balkan war, and it was northwards along its defiles that the Bulgar army in 1913 had fled pursued by Greeks led by Constantine, then Crown Prince, and with Serbians working along their flanks from the Vardar river. How well I remembered being in Athens when the news came through of the great advance of the popular Crown Prince. And now he sat in Athens, while his army lay encamped near Salonika, sandwiched here and there among Allied troops, mobilised but not yet 'in a state of war.' This was no longer Constantine the Bulgar-Slayer as he had been called. He was Constantine the time-server.

As we rode down to the plain we reached a village completely in ruins, the village of Nigrita, which the Bulgars had sacked and burned in their retreat to Rupel in 1913. Here we found a Greek division. We rode among them. It was just past Easter and they were feasting on lamb roasted at spits in camp fires, while wreaths of flowers and garlanded portraits of Constantine hung above every tent and shack. They looked at us but did not greet us. Here they were doing the very same duty that we were doing, guarding Salonika. They felt confident that they could do their duty. But, had they known, there were nearly three hundred thousand enemies in front of them, and the total Greek army there was not fifty thousand. We rode on and found quarters in a filthy inn. Nobody spoke to us and the officers openly ignored us.

But we got on with our task, rode on up the valley, made our reconnaissance without meeting even a trace of Bulgar outposts, and later on returned by another route over the hills through the wildest and loneliest of country.

Back in our camp near Salonika I began to be aware of movements of our own and of the French troops. Then came the news that the Bulgars had seized the whole of the Rupel Pass, including the Greek fortress at its entrance. The small bodies of Greek troops I had so lately seen in the Struma valley took no action and the Greek garrison of the fort surrendered. The French in Salonika raised the traditional French cry of 'Nous sommes trahis': they drove out the Greeks from all remaining posts they held in the town, railed and raved at Greek governments, royalties and citizens, and began a systematic action against Greeks that laid the seed of a hatred of Frenchmen and all things French that has never died in Greece. The French showed a particular genius for irritating without purpose and for alienating the sympathies of opponents without at any point providing an ultimate basis for reconciliation. Greeks who had been merely indignant were driven to be openly hostile: Greeks who were apathetic became indignant: Greeks who were originally friendly were soon transformed into critics. In a few swift gestures the French made enemies of neutrals and neutrals of friends. Dissatisfied with the tone of the local Press of Salonika, they founded a paper of their own called the *Independant*, cynically enough, and, to ensure it developing a clientèle, they published an ordinance suppressing all the Greek papers of Salonika for a week.

CHAPTER VII

FREE LANCE

It was evident that the opposing armies were moving cautiously down from their distant stations. We and the Bulgarians were sending feelers forward; each was trying to find the other. The very move itself seemed quite futile. Had the Bulgarians suddenly made a descent in full force upon Salonika, or had we pushed our whole armies up into the Bulgarian hills it would have been a major movement of war and strategy. As it was both sides sent out their cavalry to the plains and valleys between them; the cavalry met, clashed and retired. Then came infantry mobile columns who seized positions of importance here and there, dug trenches, established posts and settled down into some semblance of a line. Then up came the lumbering transport, the long columns of troops and the artillery. In a trice the scattered posts first held were linked up and a continuous line of trenches was formed. Both armies sat at last face to face, separated by a distance of perhaps a hundred yards in some places, at others—especially in the marshy Struma valley—by a distance of two or three miles. Away in the mountains to the west the French and Serbians had also moved up and dug positions or blasted rock-trenches along great mountain ridges, some of which were five thousand feet high. Opposite them the Bulgars patiently followed suit.

It was a pitiable spectacle of two great armies, each now about three hundred thousand men strong, deliberately ceasing to function as armies and transforming themselves into fortresses. Had they remained in their original positions, with fifty miles between them, they might have waited events happily for another two or three years without the loss of men. As it was, ten thousand Englishmen, twenty thousand Frenchmen and forty thousand Serbs died in the various operations of this trench-warfare, and an equal number of Bulgars. Both armies lost alike the power as well as the intention of mobility. Hypnotised by war on the Western Front, we all set about sitting down in trenches, as being the latest and most fashionable thing. But, once transformed into fortresses, we still continued to behave as if we were mobile armies. The little moves and battles and scurryings that went on all the time were but protests against immobility. Only in 1918 did we learn that the Bulgar fortress was made to be stormed as a fortress, not scampered round as if it were an army capable of motion.

Our troops were moving, and I was sent without notice, ahead of our division, to take charge of a solitary post on the one and only road that led from Salonika to the right wing of our army. This was the road from Salonika to Seres. Its seventieth kilometre stone was in the middle of the Struma valley; its seventy-fifth inside the Bulgar lines. I and a groom, a horse and a mule loaded with my tent and properties, went ahead and settled down at a spot by the side of this road about half-way between Salonika and the Struma valley. It was now the full heat of a blazing summer and my home, for an indefinite period, was in the very middle of an absolutely flat plain which was entirely devoid of vegetation. The ground was as hard as iron and red as brick. Within reach of a small stream I planted my tent, built a shack by the road to serve as an office, and started business. A curious Greek armed with a camera was sent to join me to serve as official photographer for the control-post which I now commanded, completely my own master and lord of the plain. I had been told to examine every passer by, other than Allied soldiers, to give them passes to go whither they wished, provided I was satisfied by their claims and credentials. I had indeed started out on a new line of business. After a few hours of my first establishing my post business began to come in thick and fast. There before me passed all that was most picturesque in the Balkans. Caravans of heavy carts drawn by huge gentle water-buffaloes, stopped outside my shack. The buffaloes promptly sat down, while their owners explained their claims. They wanted to go to a village just five miles ahead to get melons. Good, they could go, they were informed, and their passes were prepared, their photographs taken rapidly, and developed in the traditional rabbit-hutch that all such photographers carry. With a shade temperature of a hundred and ten I began to feel sorry for that wretched little Greek, with his head buried in a mass of stained velvet, and his hands fuddling about with bottles and trays within the hutch. But he was devoted to his art. His face, sweating and greasy, would emerge from the velvet tabernacle and he would hand to the client a dripping slab of paper on which was an almost unrecognisable splodge of black. The recipient would grunt with pleasure at so superb a portrait, pay his small debt to the photographer, receive his pass stamped and signed by me with the photo stuck on it, ask for a second copy of his photo for family uses and then depart. The buffaloes would be goaded into life, the great carts would creak and trundle into movement, and we sat down to wait for the next.

It was all very simple. There I was, stopping some and turning them back, if I did not like their faces or their excuses, letting others pass and feeling lord and master of a countryside.

But a few days later some of my clients came along on their way back. They presented to me not the beautiful passport which I had sealed, signed, and delivered to them, but something wholly new to me, sealed, signed, and delivered in French. I asked how they got it. 'When we arrived a few miles farther on, sir,' they replied, 'We were stopped by a French officer, seated in a tent like yourself, who took your passport, tore it up and gave us this. We were photographed again by another photographer and paid another fee.' So I was foiled and no longer master of the plainlands. Ahead of me was an odious Frenchman who refused to recognise my authority. What could I do? how could I vindicate the dignity of Great Britain and the Overseas Empire? I tore up the French passports and gave them new British ones, with photographs free of charge. That was the reply of Britain to France! During the ensuing week I spent many happy moments destroying French passes and scattering their fragments scornfully on the road and then, with a benign and gracious inclination of the head handing out the renewed confidence of Britain in the shape of new passes.

The heat was so terrific that I found it cooler to walk about on the hard road in whatever breeze there was than to sit motionless and sweating in the spurious shadow of my tent, where a million flies equally sought shelter from the sun. So, for the midday hours, I walked slowly but regularly up and down like a sentry, certainly cooler this way than meditating on the heat in the tent. In the evenings came my time of relief. At sunset the hideous plain was transformed to fairyland. Instead of the heat haze that hid all distance during the day, there was a luminous horizon that showed up the distant hills in amber and turquoise. There is no land I have ever seen that can equal Macedonia for evening colours. That plain still lives in my visual memory like a clear fresh background of an Italian Primitive. My mind was storing a few rare and lovely pictures into its exclusive gallery. Burning Ypres, Olympus at dawn, Gibraltar at night, and there were others to come, very memorable.

I would untether my poor tired horse, who had whiled away his hot day cropping miserably in the sun at whatever herbage he optimistically considered edible. Alas, I had no sort or kind of shelter for him, and I hoped he would endure it as best he might. He and I after sunset would canter down to the streamlet nearby and bathe and drink and canter back again in the cool air. Every night before I turned to sleep I would take a glass and fill it with hot paraffin, and hold it under the surface of my tent which was velvety black with uncounted sleeping flies. As I passed the glass beneath them, their legs would loosen and they would fall into the paraffin. Solemnly every night I would collect a large black glassful of the odious things and then put a match to it outside the tent. My task was solely one of revenge, for I might as well have hoped to drain the sea. At breakfast, and at every meal, I could only use one hand for eating since, with the other, I had to brush off the flies that tried to settle on my food between the time it left the plate and the time when it reached my mouth. In the evening I felt that I was settling up accounts.

After a time I noticed that business was getting slacker. I had hardly any claimants for passes. Then one evening I noticed a long string of mules and buffalo carts winding along a ridge about a mile off. I jumped on my horse to find that here were potential clients who were evading my fortress on the road by merely making a circuit round it. It was an outrage, and I was scandalised at this refusal to do homage to Great Britain. I rounded up my caravan and brought it in. We were all laughing, for so far from being criminals intent upon carrying urgent secrets to the Bulgar High Command, they were merely melon sellers, and I recognised some old friends among them. 'We were so tired,' they told me, 'of continually getting our photographs made by you or the Frenchman and then having them torn up again, so we thought it best to go on our journeys and not come near you.'

The futility of my task was even more marked. Here I was, anyhow, doing useless work that was doubly stultified by the existence of the Frenchman ahead of me. And even so, admitted that anyone who really wanted to carry information to the enemy would not come near me, my sole clients, whom I knew to be honest men, even they now refused to come to me for passes! I had no executive power and could not garrison the countryside around me. Anyone who wished to dodge me had merely to walk round my post. It was monstrous. I was being put out of commission by my friends. I put it to them in as many words. We all smiled. I let them go and after that stopped no one but French officers, and them I detained on one excuse or another in order to delay them or make them hot or worry them. I felt I was under no debt of friendship to Frenchmen in that hot plain.

One scalding day, just as I was sitting in my tent, for once trying to find out if it was cooler there than outside, my groom, a pleasant but taciturn man, who suffered all I suffered with stoicism, appeared before me. 'I think, sir,' he said, 'that you ought to come and look at your horse.' There was something about him that reminded me of the fatal messenger in a Greek play. His looks were forbidding, his voice calm, his mien stolid. 'Why?' I asked. He repeated his first statement with no additions. Knowing only too well the fatalistic outlook of the British soldier, I went out. My horse was nowhere to be seen. I looked inquiringly at him. He beckoned dolefully and I followed him. Over a low rise of ground I was suddenly aware of four hooves in the air. There was my horse all right, body downwards, firmly wedged in a crevasse in the ground. How on earth he had got there I never found out, nor did the groom know. Poor brute and faithful friend: it was heartrending. I think he had been tottering about in the sun, not looking where he was going and that he had had a sudden vertigo of sunstroke that made him fall and roll over into the gulley. He was kicking feebly with whatever free leg he had. I surveyed the scene and hurried back to the road. By sheer good fortune at that moment a company of sappers with mules was passing, the first of many bodies of men. I stopped them and diverted them without a moment's delay to first aid. They dug heartily, despite the blinding heat, and after an hour the poor horse was less violently wedged in his gulley. A little more digging and we were able to sling a rope round his hind-quarters and, by attaching the rope to two mules, to drag him out into the flat ground. But he was utterly exhausted. I sent for buckets of water and we slung them over his head and poured them down his throat. I emptied my only bottle of brandy down the poor thing's mouth. Then we tried to get him to his feet. But it was a hopeless task. I left him during the cool night, hoping that his strength would be renewed. The next day at dawn I went to see him, but he was weaker and his eyes were dull and hopeless. I gave him an hour and no change came. Then I placed the muzzle of my heavy automatic against the star on his forehead and pulled the trigger. A spasmodic kick and the poor beast was dead.

I longed to get away from this ridiculous post where there was nothing to do of the smallest importance. A messenger came by that afternoon to say that the whole of my brigade would be passing in the evening. Rousing my Greek photographer and my groom, I scoured the village near and purchased several dozen lemons, and a huge earthenware jar. We spent the rest of the hot afternoon making a vast quantity of lemon squash. Then we covered it with damp towels and put it in the sun.

Just before sunset the column hove in sight. At first just a dull cloud of dust, it soon took shape. There were all my friends again, the men, hot and dry and wretched, the officers dirty and ragged and dusty. At their head my little general, General L. L. Nicol, a gallant little man of nearly sixty years of age, one of the truest soldiers I met in the war. The column stopped at my shack. The men were let to go and wash and drink in the very cool and pure stream near by. The General and a select few of my friends I took into my shack and then revealed my secret store of lemonade. That day I was very popular.

I was told to follow the day after and join the Brigade headquarters. The Brigade as a whole was fit, but feeling the effects of the sun. But with tunics in their packs, shirts open, and sleeves rolled up, they did their best to keep cool. Not so the second of the three brigades that passed along my road the following noon. The men were dead-beat. They had been ordered by their general to keep their tunics on and buttoned to the neck. No slipshod marching for him. Up and down the line the general of this brigade rode on his comfortable horse. 'Remember,' he shouted, 'the men of my brigade never fall out on the line of march!' Nor did they: they merely fainted. He was one of the 'spit and polish' generals of the old style, although himself a young man. He and his like caused more casualties to the army than a bombardment. And there was no one to stop him, why I do not know. The lessons of this blazing summer were learned hard and slowly. It took a year before there were standing orders that no troops were to march between the hours of 9 A.M. and 6 P.M. It had simply not occurred to the authorities that marching should best take place at night! and yet any urchin could have told them.

The troops now marching up were the main army that was now taking up its position over against the Bulgars. Our division was to descend the Struma valley and dig itself in. For the moment they were to halt for a day or two on those hills which I had visited in my earlier reconaissance. Then they were to go down to that steaming valley.

So far no one had said a word about malaria or mosquitoes. We had a fully equipped medical service in England. It was their task to investigate the diseases of the country. I imagine that they had forgotten to do this, and that the War Office in London, on looking for Salonika on the map, found that it was in Europe. I can imagine the conversation: 'I say, Ernest, where is this place Salonika

The British war memorial near Lake Doiran

The Struma at its exit from the Rupel Pass (looking north)

where they are sending troops?' 'Haven't the foggiest, old fellow: let's get a map: you never know: it may be in the tropics or something, and the troops may need topees and mosquito nets and all that sort of troublesome gear: I hope not, because then I shall have such a lot of work to do.' 'Here it is, Ernest: it's all right, you needn't worry. It's in Europe, a few inches south of Vienna.' 'Thank heavens, Henry, then I shan't have to get any of that damned tropical equipment for them or have to write any more memos. If it's in Europe, then of course it can't be tropical. Only India is in the tropics.'

It is only kind to presuppose a conversation something on these lines, when our troops first went out. Otherwise I cannot charitably explain the fact that we were given no mosquito nets, no advice, no quinine, and no help of any kind when we first marched up to the Struma and Vardar valleys—two valleys which are notorious for being more infested with malaria of various kinds than most parts of the Far East. We none of us knew that the biting time of the mosquito is the hour before dawn and the hour after sunset. No one was told that heavy exertion in the heat of the day makes one more prone to catch the infection of malaria than anything else. No one told us to keep our bodies covered at nights, however hot it was. And so all these gallant men and officers were marched down into the miasmic swamps of the Macedonian hills, where every peasant was malarial and every pool a breeding-ground of mosquitoes. Later, when I went down, too, to the depths of the valley, I found the mosquitoes in clouds. They were large and tenacious insects that nothing on earth deterred. By the end of that summer we had sixty thousand casualties in a British army of a hundred thousand. There was ordinary malaria. Suddenly a man would feel faint and sick. His temperature would rise and in two hours he was carted off to hospital. Whole battalions vanished in this way. Some I saw could not muster a score of men. The sick men went away to the coast and returned, to go sick again later. Then there was malignant malaria, of which I have never heard elsewhere. This brand seemed to exist only in certain places and at certain breeding-grounds. Malignant malaria killed its man in twenty-four hours. Then there was a mysterious complaint called P.U.O. I would see some poor invalid being taken off: round his neck was a ticket marked 'P.U.O. Urgent.' Some of the victims were rather proud of having a disease so mysterious and so distinguished. 'What have you got?' one would ask, and the other would reply faintly, but with hauteur, 'Oh, I have P.U.O.' But it was only 'Pyrexia of Unknown Origin'—in other words, the doctors hadn't the smallest idea what it was!

Down in the swamps the mosquitoes settled on the faces and hands of the men and bit and bit to their hearts' content. A few weeks later some desperate reformer at Headquarters bought up all the local supplies of netting, and a square yard of netting was given to each man! Some of them used to sleep with the netting over their faces, and the mosquitoes merely sat on the netting and bit through the holes. I tried using it so, and found that it seemed to attract the insects. Others used it to wash with. The most intelligent found in it a most convenient cloth for cleaning rifles. In the officers' mess it was used to put over the food to keep the flies off!

Only the following summer did the Headquarters and the War Office come to their senses. Then they overdid it. There were whole nets for each man, of enormous size. Head covers and gloves for sentries, ointments and greases for the skin: quinine in tons—and in some cases men were given the almost incredible amount of 60 grains a day. The War Office had woken up to the fact that there are tropical lands even in Europe. Actually Macedonia in those days was, in regard to malaria, probably about the same as the Panama region before it was drained.

I was on the point of rejoining my brigade up in the

hills when suddenly a telegram was sent me by messenger ordering me to report to the Divisional Headquarters. I hurried along the road to my rendezvous. I was told that orders had come that I was to be sent at once to Athens with despatches of importance. Here at last was excitement of the first order and something in the nature of a first-class joy-ride. It was due, I knew, to the schemings of friends in Athens. I was in a seventh heaven of delight. Nor did I feel any pangs at leaving my friends for a week, or perhaps two, for there was no fighting, mere manœuvring for position. I was just one of the lucky ones who had a wire to pull and had pulled it.

Off I dashed on the nearest lorry to Salonika, where I was told that I must procure a suit of civilian clothes, since that part of Greece where Athens was, was supposed to be a neutral country. No uniforms allowed.

I had a day before my boat sailed and I spent it in buying an astonishing Greek ready-made suit of lemon-yellow linen, and a dark blue Homburg hat. I tried out a test walk in this strange garb, but even as I descended the steps of my hotel in Salonika, one leg of the trousers detached itself with a loud tearing sound from the other. I withdrew backwards into the hotel, removed the inadequate tubings, and put on instead my ordinary riding-breeches and leather riding-boots. Thus incongruously garbed, I embarked on a nondescript boat bound for Mudros in the island of Lemnos, once the headquarters of the Gallipoli expedition, now only a naval centre for the organisation of naval intelligence and for submarines. Once more I was among the lovely Greek islands on the still and turquoise Aegean. That evening we passed Olympus again, and the distant shape of Mount Athos showed up against the fading sky. The next morning we skirted the superb rock-peak of Samothrace, which protrudes from the sea like a giant's fang, and slowly we wound our way into the vast harbour of Lemnos where a group of small warships and one battleship made up the naval garrison. The anti-submarine boom was opened and we entered and dropped anchor.

Homer calls Lemnos 'smoky Lemnos' and for two thousand years editors have failed to explain why. 'There is no volcano on Lemnos,' they all shout. Nor is there any permanent fog or mist they add. What they do not seem to have troubled to find out is that one large area of the island is, if not a volcano, at least so hot that you cannot sit down on it. I went there and derived a certain pleasure in prodding the ground with a stick and watching the sulphurous fumes rise from the hole. If that is not what Homer means by 'smoky Lemnos,' then what is? Go and see for yourself has always been my guiding rule in learned matters, or indeed in any matter of uncertainty.

At Lemnos my gala costume did not make for confidence. The naval officers whom I met seemed to think that I was some unpleasant kind of Press agent. In vain I protested that I was as much an officer as they. After a time, however, they realised that, whatever my costume, however sinister my intentions, I was in other respects indistinguishable from themselves; they accepted me, and the few days that I spent waiting for a boat to Athens passed happily. Here I encountered a fresh disease, known as sand-fly fever. The sandflies, with unbelievable persistence, bit like small daggers into one's flesh. No net would stop them except a net so thick that it made breathing in the tropic night almost impossible. Immune apparently to malaria, I was also immune to this complaint, and they bit me in vain. But there were many who were perpetually laid low with bouts of fever.

Here I heard at last of the legendary doings of J. L. Myres, who had taught me archæology at Oxford. Unwilling to do office work and intrigue at Athens, he had carried out enterprises of unheard of gallantry among the inlets and islets of the coast of Asia Minor. He had acquired a reputation for ubiquity and invisibility which Homeric deities might well have envied. Later on he actually materialised in the flesh at Athens and succeeded in bringing order into the chaos which his predecessors had designated by the name of an Intelligence Bureau. I had the good fortune to meet him at Plymouth in 1916 and again at Athens in 1918. Otherwise he retained to the end that quality of elusiveness (as far as I was concerned) which made him into the most efficient Intelligence Officer loose on the high seas of the Near East.

Lemnos is a grim and treeless isle, not lovely, and without that grace of the southern islands. But it had a hard and virile character of its own. Its rich brown soil and clear outlines gave it an individuality.

At last I was dumped on a swift sleek warship, and off we sped for Athens. At dawn next day we slipped round the point of Cape Sunium, with its dead-white temple standing right on the cliff, bright and lovely in the slanting sun. Here I was at last in Greece, in the old world, thrown out of a dusty maelstrom into the calm classic outlines of rocky Attica. The war seemed utterly forgotten as we rounded Hymettus and dropped anchor off Phalerum with the Parthenon rising cool and commanding above the flat city. Here was the one place in the world that I had striven to get to, the moment I left Oxford, the one city which had, and has always had for me an allurement beyond that of any city I know. It was impossible to think that this ancient and gracious spot was, even now, drawn into the vortex. Yet at Lemnos I had seen the very telegrams that described how an Allied fleet had just been ordered to demonstrate off Athens, in order to impress the recalcitrant King with the might of the Allies. There had even been talk of bombardment, surely as lunatic an enterprise as ever entered Allied minds. The trouble was that Athens had begun to be thought of as the pivot of this Eastern conflict. In reality Athens never was at any time of the smallest fundamental importance. But, itself the cradle of literature, it had attracted to it the litterateurs of Europe who were drawn automatically to a region where drama might quickly be transmuted to melodrama, or who, for various reasons, were thought by those in authority to be more competent by virtue of their profession to handle this sophisticated capital. The place teemed with nonentities, invested with a little authority. It was the very breeding-ground of adventure and intrigue and to it fled all who found the tedious routine of slaughter in France too exacting or too dull, all who looked for fame or advancement, no matter of what nationality, by making for themselves a name as master-intriguers and master-organisers of spite and counter-spite. All the nations at war vied with each other in producing master-spies and arch-conspirators. There remained the few men, who by age or infirmity were debarred from more active enterprise, or whose knowledge of the place and people was so profound and useful that their presence there was of advantage. To these all honour.

Here I came, a lover of Athens as a city, as a monument of the past, as a place of light and loveliness, sentimental if you like, but sentimental about the one place in the world which moulds sentiment into something finer and greater, and I found it little more than a resort for half the tricksters of Europe, each striving, not to win the war for his own side, still less to contribute military knowledge to the fighting armies; they were rather playing a preposterous game of catch-as-catch-can, over the half-prostrate body of an anæmic Balkan State. The war itself hardly seemed to matter much. All they sought at this time was to score points off each other. French diplomats suborned Greek butlers in German or Austrian Legations. British agents subsidised Greek agents to find out what French agents found out about German agents. Italians intrigued with Greek Royalists to discover what Mr Venizelos was doing, while British attachés danced with Greek princesses to find out how Constantine was going to dodge French demands.

Germans lavished gold on organisations which were supposed to find out what the French and British were finding out about the Germans.

Into this, with the dust of Macedonia still in my mouth, I walked all unsuspecting, never dreaming that Athens could have been reduced to this state. All was as usual in the streets. Athens of 1916 seemed to me much like the Athens of 1913 and 1914. Yet there was something wrong. The atmosphere was tense. I presented my despatches at the Legation and in the evening went up to the lovely groves and avenues of Kephissia. There I dined with friends. No doubt my appearance was odd and my costume sinister. For I found that wherever I went I was followed by odd men who, as I soon found, were the spies of someone. Of whom they were the spies I have no idea, nor did it matter much. One ridiculous creature, ostensibly a sponge-seller, with a dusty bunch of decayed sponges in his hand, followed me for at least a mile, at a distance of about three yards. I went into the garden of some Russian friends. He followed me right in and pretended to sell us his sponges. No doubt he reported the presence of a dangerous character to his employers. I had not the heart to stop him or deter him. It was gratifying that a subaltern of no importance at all should be recorded in some archives as dangerous. Faces peered into our garden, other scallywags followed me and each other in a straggling procession as I went away.

There was no means of getting back to Salonika. The railway at that time barely ran half the way to Salonika. Not even the track was laid. It was not for another year that the line was pushed through. I had to wait for another boat back to Lemnos, and by great good fortune I waited a week. In that week I saw more than enough of this farcical war-time Athens. I saw enemies and allies, neutrals and nondescripts. The place was pure *opera-bouffe*. I felt as if I had walked straight out of a world of hard and well-organised activity into a Fun-Fair. Here at any rate were all the necessary ingredients and characters. There was General Fairholme, British Military Attaché, vast, rotund, eighteen stone and choleric, the type-general of a hundred years of cartoons and comic journals. His breast covered with three closely packed rows of decorations, great yellow riding-boots and a uniform on which every button was desperately doing its duty against heavy odds. He had never seen a shot fired in anger, at least in this war, and he presided over the military affairs of Great Britain in Greece—there were little enough of them—with distinction and a certain ponderous discretion. 'Fairy' to his friends, he did on the whole more good than harm. At least he was a profound student of military history and had lived long in Berlin.

Then there was Prince Demidoff, Russian Minister, again a picture-book type. Irretrievably pledged to support monarchies the world over, his views and his actions were certain in all crises. He and his aides made little or no attempt to play at the Intelligence game. It was all rather childish to them, and they took no interest in the gilded and exciting figures that passed across the stage in this comic world.

Then there was the sinister Baron Schenk, whose name alone was worth a whole intelligence corps. He played the German cards with ability and skill and knew exactly how and when to make the blood of the French creep.

Alone in a wilderness of honest men striving to be dishonest because it was fashionable, of dishonest men in lamb's clothing, of incompetent spies, of blasé secretaries, and of archæologists thrilled to be in the limelight dressed as diplomats, stood the figure of Sir Francis Elliot, the only just man. He, as British Minister of long standing, the doyen of the Diplomatic Corps, knew not only Greece but Constantine like a book. He knew exactly where the Royal family was wrong and exactly how far they were right. A man of immaculate impartiality he tried to do justice to all. But a Foreign Office that would not take his advice and could not in any case understand it, made all his endeavours futile. He was driven in the end to do his best simply to hold the ring and try to get fair play.

For the Greek King's position was essentially reasonable. He had by now estimated fairly correctly the futility of much of the Allied cause and the stupidity of its strategy. He did not want to back the losing side and yet he was by no means sure at this time which was the side destined to defeat. He knew that war would mean ruin anyhow for a small country, for after the peace she would be forgotten, whether she was on the right side or not. He had in addition a good knowledge of German arms and no little sympathy for them. A man who is at the same time a German Field-Marshal and a brother-in-law of the Kaiser should be forgiven for having a certain partiality for things German. On the other hand, he saw that Greece was virtually an island in an Allied lake, and he knew that any attempt to help Germany openly would be frustrated. So he did his best to keep out of it all.

Venizelos was more optimistic. He was convinced of Allied victory, so he naturally did his best to get his country to join in.

And here were all the representatives of the two opposing sides sitting on the doorstep of this small and delightful Balkan State, bribing, cajoling, threatening and bullying, demeaning themselves beyond belief, irritating the Greeks and each other beyond bearing, and generally making Athens the centre of more absurdities and extravagances than the mind of man could conceive.

After a few days I found that my civilian costume was collapsing into rags from sheer bad tailoring. I asked Sir Francis tentatively whether I could wear uniform. 'Greece is strictly neutral,' he replied, 'but I see not the smallest reason why you should not put on your comfortable uniform. All pretence that we are respecting Greek neutrality has long ago vanished, in so far as there are soldiers and officers of all nations all over the place. So put it on whenever you like.' I did so and found that, as a result, the spies did not follow me so openly and so frequently. I had, so to speak, hoisted my colours.

One evening at Kephissia I was taken to dine by some friends at the one large hotel. The tables were out under pine trees: through the pines one could see the vague form of Mount Parnes against the lemon yellow sky of a false sunset. There was a hot scent of turpentine and a dry clearness in the air, exhilarating beyond belief. Every table was filled by comfortable people, very few of whom were Greeks. The manager, with exquisite tact, had placed on each table a small flag of the nationality to which the diners belonged. There was the German flag a few tables off: next to us a Spanish flag: French, Russian, and our own nearby. Everyone talked in low whispers and heads were wagged wisely. This was neutrality with a vengeance. Plots were developed with the hors-d'œuvres and thickened with the soup. Secret notes and twitches of the eyebrow passed from table to table as the entrée was consumed. With the fruit there was a certain thawing of reserve, and I felt a wild desire to throw bananas at the German Attaché or to write bogus notes to the French. I longed to jump on a table and juggle with oranges—anything to break that fantastic tension. If only all those arch-conspirators could have joined their tables, agreed to sack all their spies, and exchange a few jests and after-dinner stories, half the absurdity of Athens might have been punctured. But there they all were, like babies who have quarrelled in a nursery.

I finished my dinner and went back to a moonlight walk along the lower slopes of Pentelicus, with owls flapping past me and faint stirrings of small beasts in the bushes. Attic nights in June! there are no lovelier. Their scent and silence and softness will not go into words.

My time of idleness and waiting soon expired and off I

went again on the ferry-boat to Salonika. Here the difference was that between ancient peace and ultra-modern mechanical turmoil. Athens, with all its psychological disturbance was quiet and fresh and airy. Salonika was a dust cloud and a clattering of guns and lorries and troops. Its narrow streets, ill-adapted to modern warfare, shook and rattled to the enormous engines of war that continually crashed past. The ear was stunned and the eye dust-filmed.

A hurried meal and I was once more on a lorry bound for the hills. In a few hours I was back with my brigade, eating a frugal dinner on a leafy knoll, with the great valley of the Struma steaming beneath us, its miasmatic swamps obscured by mist. No more the clear Attic skies and incredible sharp outlines of marble hills. Here was the mist and heat-haze of the Balkans, not the luminous colours and shapes of a more Mediterranean world.

CHAPTER VIII

ROUTINE

THE Brigade and all the Division descended soon to the valley. For a time my little general had been made commander of a division, since the normal commander had gone home on leave. I accompanied the general and lived at the divisional headquarters, doing a mixture of jobs of all kinds, from the simple intelligence work, that involved estimating the strength of the artillery and trench systems of the enemy, to the less attractive work concerned with the headquarters itself of which I was, for the time being, the Camp Commandant. This impressive but irksome post was in reality rather like that of a butler in a club. I had to make all the arrangements for the moving of the divisional staff, decide on the siting of tents, and the layout of a new camp, arrange for food supplies and the transport of baggage, for a total of some fifteen officers, most of whom bore the rank of colonel. Now, for the first time, I was in direct contact with officers of experience and standing in our own regular army.

This was the staff of the 10th Irish Division. Apart from the staff the officers and men were almost all amateurs like myself. There was a sprinkling of reservists and regular N.C.Os. but in the main the whole body of them were Kitchener's Army. They and their officers and staff had, for the most part, been involved in the bloody failure of Suvla Bay on Gallipoli. In this criminal disaster some thirty thousand British troops had faced three thousand Turks. The cause of their failure was the utter lack of intelligent foresight on the part of the general in charge. The troops had sat idly on the foreshore while twenty thousand Turkish reinforcements hurried up from Bulair. When we attacked in the end we faced large forces. Of all this I heard as I

Morto Bay, Gallipoli

Dismantled Turkish gun at Kilid Bahr on Gallipoli

got to know the officers and men. Yet neither staff nor men seemed to realise that they had been engaged in the most ludicrous failure of the whole war. No one seemed to have an inkling that this had been the worst managed affair since the war began, and what made it more pathetic was the fact that the men were, physically, as fine a body of men as could be found in the army. Irish troubles or no, they were all fine fighters and capable of great endurance, and, as far as I could tell, they were excellently trained. At Suvla they had seen their first action, and, considering the appalling muddle of that affair, they had fought valiantly. But, as a German general who was present with the Turks has since written, 'Fate opened the gates of Constantinople to the British and *they would not enter*.' That is the main tragedy of the battle. The element of surprise does not often succeed as it succeeded at the landing at Suvla. Seldom in the war had thirty thousand men found themselves faced by three thousand. At no other time in the war when such a situation had arisen did a general order his men merely to sit down and think it over. The value of the surprise passed in a day, and the war was prolonged for nearly two years.

Of all this I heard only by inference. Indeed no one then fully realised the completeness of the failure. I was told of men advancing for twenty-four hours with one water-bottle which was emptied in one hour of a torrid August day, I was told of the great zinc tanks of water landed on the beach by the naval authorities, and how the tanks were pierced with bullets in the first half hour; of the men who in a frenzy of thirst ran back to drink of the jets of water that coursed from the bullet-holes. This was how the attack was staged. And even when it began it was too late to succeed.

Much ink has been spilled over Suvla and I do not propose to spill more. But, looking back, I am amazed to realise that neither men nor staff seemed to appreciate that the failure was not merely a military set-back, but a demonstration of the utter inadequacy of the preparations. Even then I wondered what sort of a fool would land water-tanks of thin zinc on an open beach where any Turk could fire at them, without first having made the tanks bullet-proof by sandbag or steel casing. I wondered what sort of organisers were behind the scheme, which any bank-clerk could have prepared with more common sense.

I was shown the maps with which the officers were supposed to work. Even my untrained eye could see that they were almost useless. They were based, not on a complete air survey, but on knowledge compiled from old and inefficient Turkish maps, eked out with stray knowledge provided by Admiralty Charts and recent coastal survey. They were not merely useless but just good enough to be dangerously misleading.

The light-hearted way in which the division looked back on the great disaster of Suvla had the one merit of illustrating the old adage that a British soldier never knows when he is beaten. These certainly did not, and it was one of the few occasions on which it would have been better, most of all for the staff, if they had been informed of the vastness of the disaster. But I doubt if even at London the implications of the defeat at Suvla were realised. Perhaps it has taken all of us twenty years to find out.

On the 29th of August 1916 I was electrified to learn that Rumania had entered the war on the side of the Allies. Here at last was a matter which concerned us more intimately than any event which had occurred so far in the Balkans. But no one was very stirred because it seemed so improbable and so very far away. The Order of the Day read:

> 'Rumania has declared war on Austria-Hungary and crossed the Transylvanian frontier last night. In announcing the entry into the war of our new Ally, the Army Commander hopes that all ranks will realise that one of the most important aims of the military policy adopted in this theatre of operations has been effected.'

This made me feel that at last things were beginning to happen. I pictured us all marching up into the Danube valley to join a horde of victorious Allies in a march on Vienna, with Bulgars retreating on all sides. How it was to be done I had not the faintest idea.

Nobody talked much about it and no one much knew where Transylvania was—nor cared. But it was jolly to think of someone doing something away there behind those oppressive Balkan mountains in that vague unknown land. 'Brave little Rumania,' we all thought, and then got on with our daily tasks.

One of my many tasks, in my temporary post of Travelling Agency, was to arrange for the move of the divisional camp. Once the move was ordered I became the *Deus ex machina* and was able to control the destinies and comforts of some fifteen colonels. Once we were on the move my orders alone were the orders that counted. For the staff were entirely unable to operate as a staff while we were mobile. Once we had camped I immediately resumed my former insignificance. It was enormous fun getting the whole concern under way, arranging for the transport of three or four messes, of endless mules and of countless typewriters and reams of paper. One reluctant mule kicked the entire contents of a huge medical chest into the air and bolted over the horizon. I rode on ahead and selected the site for the new camp. I placed the tents of each of the colonels and always exhibited my favouritism by giving to those colonels who had been kind to me a better site than the others. When the main *cortège* arrived, like tourists at an unknown hotel, then my job was merely that of a reception clerk. One wanted his tent moved here or there, another had lost his favourite chair or his pet typewriter. A third moaned that I had abandoned his lovely table that his batman had made for him. But I held all the aces, for I worked on an official schedule of weights and merely referred each complainant to the schedule and explained that I had been forced to abandon certain things because my transport would have been unequal to the task. No one hates red tape more than myself, but on these occasions it came in extremely handy; not that I abused my power, but I did really take a specific joy in making these kindly men enjoy a few hardships. Not that they weren't as a whole the essence of kindness and consideration. But I adopted an almost Puritanical attitude of mind. I really felt that periodically it would be good for these staff officers to be deprived of some of their exiguous luxuries and harmless hobbies. I was definitely unkind.

My little general always backed me in the face of dispute or complaint. He was of sterner stuff. I worked with him for the best part of a year and I never found a senior officer more competent, more self-denying or more soldierly. I can see his small figure now sitting at mess, occasionally talking, always refusing anything that might smack of undue comfort, always on the spot and ready. His men loved him and respected him, and they feared him too. He had been the last man of his Brigade to leave Gallipoli, at the very rear of the column, with shells bursting every now and then near and round him. He was fifty-nine and he knew that when his sixtieth birthday came he would be sent home to resume life as a civilian. He went a few months later and I have, alas! never seen him since. But he was a true soldier, able, quiet, and determined—and he never fussed or worried or bothered about minor things. One night, when we had been marching late, had no tents, and merely planted our small bivouacs on the slopes of a hill, a torrential downpour of rain began about midnight. The general, who had selected the site for his bivouac himself, had by ill luck chosen an almost imperceptible depression in the hillside for his dwelling. When the rain began that depression became a torrent-gully and we were awakened to hear strange sounds. The water had rushed right through the poor little man's bivouac and literally washed him out.

There he stood in his pyjamas, with all his properties rolling in the flood down the valley. We all turned out and retrieved toothbrushes, razors, and oddments from the sopping valley, made him a new tenement and lent him dry clothes. A few brief and appropriate expletives were all that he let loose.

Soon we were all down in the steaming valley. But autumn was on us, and the nights were cool. In the grass were the lovely blooms of autumn crocus and cyclamen, and at dawn there was a chill in the air blowing across from the distant Balkan peaks, which every now and then were flecked with snow.

We camped near the great rolling Strymon river and pushed troops across to establish bridge-heads. It was like a tropical jungle. Reeds and osiers stood ten feet high: melon patches and maize crops appeared at intervals in the wildness. At nights pontoon bridges were made and slung across the river and in the ghostly gloom we all filed across. The enemy might be anywhere or nowhere. We found his outposts, which withdrew, and we settled down to a river-bank trench-system, with advance bodies out in the plain.

Not long after a battle developed. We advanced to capture a village. The Bulgars advanced in counter-attack. I crossed with the troops, who crept over the bridges at night and massed behind a small group of battered houses. My job was to get as near the front as possible and watch events and get hold of the first prisoners at once in order that they might be interrogated. It was a still coldish night, and I sat at the end of a bridge watching the long files of helmeted men cross. Each carried a few sandbags to use for cover when the attack developed. It was to be open fighting in a flat plainland, where cover was almost non-existent. The lines of infantry were to advance in rushes in the orthodox way, and, at each halt, to fill their scanty sandbags with earth, as bullet stoppers, and make of them a miniature parapet. When the advance reached its objective—a large village in the plain—they were to dig themselves in in proper trenches which would be strengthened in due course. At dawn our guns started, and the plain was dotted for its whole twenty-mile length with the explosions of high-explosive shell. The Bulgar batteries retaliated on our guns. There was something insane in the sight of this lovely valley, with its neat warm villages (now cleared of their inhabitants whom we had sent into camps near Salonika) and the blue hills in a framework all round, being made into an inferno of fire and death for no apparent reason. The battle was forced by us to drive back the advanced Bulgar posts and trenches. It had no other or very necessary reason. Perhaps it was precipitated merely, as generals at all times and in all places have expressed it, 'to put spirit into the men.' How the deliberate killing of some of our own men was to put spirit into the rest I cannot conceive, but the process of thought among military men is hallowed by age. Its absurdity is patinated with a film of valour and sacrifice, its lunacy obscured.

The bombardment went on for some hours and then the men advanced, skirmishing in and round several villages, and drove out the enemy. The Bulgars, true to the military code, then made counter-attacks, though the possession of these now battered villages in the plain was of not the smallest importance to them or us. We could have remained happily enough in the lines from which we started.

On came the long lines of Bulgar infantry. I waited among the ruins of a village, my task not yet due to be carried out. As the Bulgarian infantrymen crossed the open, our guns seized the opportunity for which they were waiting. Row upon row of running and creeping enemies were cut down by a merciless *enfilade* fire of shrapnel. The metallic clang of bursting shrapnel filled the air, and the venomous whistle of the heavy bullets could be clearly heard. Line after line of Bulgars were cut down; the world-old simile of 'falling like corn to a sickle' was the most apt description for a wholesale destruction.

The battle faded, prisoners came in in dirty dusty crowds, sombre and slouching. I spent most of that morning rapidly going through the pockets and packs of the corpses, for no evidence in war is more valuable than the documents of the dead. Later I learned full well that direct information taken from the enemy is of a hundred per cent. more value than that of a score of spies. Letters home which contain indiscreet references to other military units, chance discoveries on the bodies of officers of orders and accounts—all such are what give the best intelligence. By 1917, as I knew well enough later, our intelligence system knew to within a week the position in Europe of every German division: and this knowledge was gained for the most part almost entirely from the documents found on prisoners and dead men.

A battlefield at any period of history is, I suppose, much the same. The ground is covered with the refuse of war. Even in this relatively small battle—for only some ten thousand on each side were involved—the debris was astonishing. In the wake of our advancing troops were endless rags, blood-soaked and filthy, the hasty bandages of the wounded, shell-cases and unexploded bombs, rifles and bandoliers, lost helmets, lost packs, and finally dead men. The Bulgars lay almost in military formation where they had been cut down. I repassed them in the later afternoon and the sun was hot enough to have made the first and most ghastly changes in those dead men. Their heads had swollen to twice their natural size and changed to a vivid blue-black in colour. The swollen flesh had covered the eyes, and there they lay like fantastic horrors with giant heads devoid of feature. I had seen nothing quite like this in France and I hurried on.

The battle over and our objective won, we settled down for the autumn in our new positions, which were more than half-way across the plain in some places. In the ensuing months I used to ride on to the plain as near as a horse could safely take me, then continue warily on foot and spend the day with the outposts, observing what I could with my glasses and adding to the map that I was so carefully filling. Sometimes I would spot a moving convoy in some unscreened road; at another the flashes of a hitherto unlocated battery and a telephone message to the artillery would see my targets enveloped in the bursts of shell or scattering under machine-gun fire. It was big-game hunting with big weapons.

Our hopes of August were damped. Rumania, in the course of a brief month, had done the record retreat of the war. We had lost our new Ally almost as soon as we had found him! Marshal Mackensen (that fierce Scoto-Teuton) had dissipated the poor little Balkan state of Rumania in one swift move. We had been told in the famous Order of the Day that, with the entry of Rumania into the war, one of the main objects of our expedition had been achieved. Now we were one objective the less, while over against us we felt that the Bulgar army was now potentially reinforced by Mackensen's Army.

Rumours were rife. 'Mackensen has arrived at the Rupel Pass with an army of Germans,' said one. 'Mackensen will take command of the Bulgars,' said another. And Rupel Pass, that fatal doorway to the north which we could not enter, frowned down on us all in the plain below. Enigmatical and unknown, it might hold almost any possibility behind its bastions. Our intelligence system told us what was being done immediately behind the front, but at this stage it gave little information about the distant hinterland. Dawn and evening I used to look at the blue hills and the cleft between them, through which went the one straight road to Sofia, and central Europe. I wondered what would happen in the ensuing months and what part that stern gateway would play in our affairs.

Once indeed it had an immediate and amazing interest that outclassed any other sensation at the moment. Intelligence headquarters in Salonika notified us one late autumn day that the Kaiser of all Germany had paid a state visit to Ferdinand of Bulgaria. He was reported to be holding a review not so very far off, near Lake Doiran. A prisoner had reported that the Kaiser was himself expected on a tour of inspection, and that the Bulgar armies in the plain had been told to stand by to prepare all honours for the war-lord.

There was little that we infantrymen could be expected to do, but the heavy artillery were warned to be ready for sniping with high-velocity guns, and the airmen were to stand by with relays of aeroplanes loaded with bombs. I went to the most advanced observation post, where I could get a glimpse of the one and only roadway that debouched from Rupel down to the plain, a mile or so behind the Bulgar lines. We were told the very day of the supposed visit and everyone was cheerfully excited by the prospect of some extensive sharpshooting by bomb and shell. There flickered through my mind that stern figure of the Kaiser, all in white and silver, which I had seen at Windsor behind the *cortège* of King Edward! And now we were, perhaps, to meet again in a Balkan valley!

I waited and watched at my observation post. Suddenly a large white car swung round the bend of the road that I could see with the powerful telescope which we used. Off went the notification by telephone to Brigade headquarters. We heard the distant hum of aeroplanes starting up and soon the bang of guns.

There our part ended, but I went on watching. Nothing else passed through that roadway except normal transport and troops.

A report was sent to us that evening from Salonika to say that our aeroplane had detected, as notified, a large white touring car on the Rupel-Seres road, had bombed it, or as near to it as was possible, and had finally swooped upon it and machine-gunned it with such effect that it fell into a ditch by the roadside. Figures were seen running from it. But Bulgar prisoners, taken the following day in a small raid, declared that they had been told nothing whatever about any visit of the Kaiser and that certainly, as far as they were concerned, there had been no sign of him or even a rumour of his arrival.

Our white touring car was in fact a mare's nest. There had been no Kaiser there at all. But it was some comfort to think that an unsuspecting Bulgar general had been ditched. Still, the whole affair was a good day's entertainment and made us all feel excited and stimulated. Our pursuit of Big Game had made us ambitious to snipe the very biggest of all!

There were, however, other forms of sport. A persistent German air squadron, commanded by a most able and gallant German, had destroyed a large number of our observation balloons, by swooping unexpectedly on them and firing at them from close quarters. The Air Force had been caught napping. But their retaliation was rapidly prepared. They hoisted a balloon one day in the basket of which was placed a dummy observer and a vast bundle of gun-cotton. To the explosive bundle was attached an electric wire which was controlled from the ground. In due course the prey was drawn to the trap. A lone German airman was detected. Our anti-aircraft guns fired madly at him in order to give no hint of a lure. But they fired with deliberate inaccuracy. The airman came on, approached the balloon, which was hurriedly hauled downwards with every indication of panic—but not too fast. Then came the inevitable swoop. As the airman reached the top of the balloon, perhaps only fifty yards above it, the waiting man on the ground pressed the button that released the electricity to detonate the charge in the basket. A thunderous crash, a burst of flame as the balloon exploded, and from the smoke and debris there came falling a heap of wreckage that was the aeroplane and its occupant. Our enemy had been caught in the trap, poor devil. His last balloon had been added to his list. They found the airman in the wreckage. He was a brave man; we had caught the man we wanted, Captain Eschwege, known to us by fame. A sorry trick, but war is no respecter of rules and manners. There was little credit to us in the matter of bravery. But balloons are expensive, and already we had begun to realise that the war would be won by money as well as by men. There was little room for chivalry in these times. By the end of 1916 Great Britain was fighting for her very existence.

A curious sidelight upon methods of war was illustrated by one of the strange jobs allocated to me. At the southern end of the plain was a wide marshy lake which we and the Bulgars shared. Behind it on their bank was their only railway line and along this line was run all the supply trains which brought the supplies for the valley forces. It was possible, by creeping close to the Bulgar side of the lake, to hear the arrival and departure of these trains from a railhead, the whereabouts of which were fixed by aeroplane reconnaissance. The times of arrival and departure of trains was fixed by listening-posts which were always stationed by us here. As long as the trains regularly kept to their time-tables we had some fair estimate of the condition of traffic and a tolerable certainty that there was no increase of supply. We used to tabulate these trains and reconstruct the time-table. When there was any sign of increase of traffic or of the addition of many more trains we should have a hint of possible Bulgarian reinforcement or projected operations. I often used to go down to listen and to check the time-table, and all went well until a wholly unforeseen development made our calculations useless. In the early spring of the next year occurred an event for which no one had estimated. The millions of frogs who made their home in the lake commenced their mating-season. Every night at a certain hour, and the night was the only time at which the trains could move, for in the day they would have been bombed, the frogs began a prodigious concert of croaking, so enormous in its volume that the puffing and rattling of trains was rendered utterly inaudible. Our time-table was upset and our calculations rendered useless! nowhere else, I expect, in the whole area of war did the croaking of frogs interfere with the conduct of high military affairs!

Winter came upon us with a rush. The distant hills and the vast mountains away behind Rupel and Doiran were suddenly covered with snow. The scenery at dawn and sunset was more glorious than ever. The trees—and here in Macedonia the forests were European in character and largely deciduous, unlike the pine-covered lands of Attica and the Peloponnese—showed autumn tints, and the whole colour-scheme of our deep valley changed into something sterner and more forbidding in its promise of harsh discomfort, yet more tenuously lovely and delicate in colour. Snow came and many of the posts held by us and the enemy alike were withdrawn up on to the drier slopes. Warm dugouts replaced tents, and whatever houses were available were lived in. I had quarters in a fine old beamed house in a comfortable village. So far from causing damage to our dwellings we refurnished them and called in sappers to strengthen them. Only the central villages of the plain were destroyed.

Before the inhabitants had been sent away to camps near Salonika, and before the two opposing armies had descended to the plain, I had ridden through most of the villages. They formed a typical Balkan mixture. One was inhabited entirely by Greeks, the next by Turks, and another by Bulgars. You could tell the difference of race the moment you entered the village. If it were Turkish you entered a place of perfect quiet, almost oppressive silence. As you entered the women scuttled away into the houses, drawing

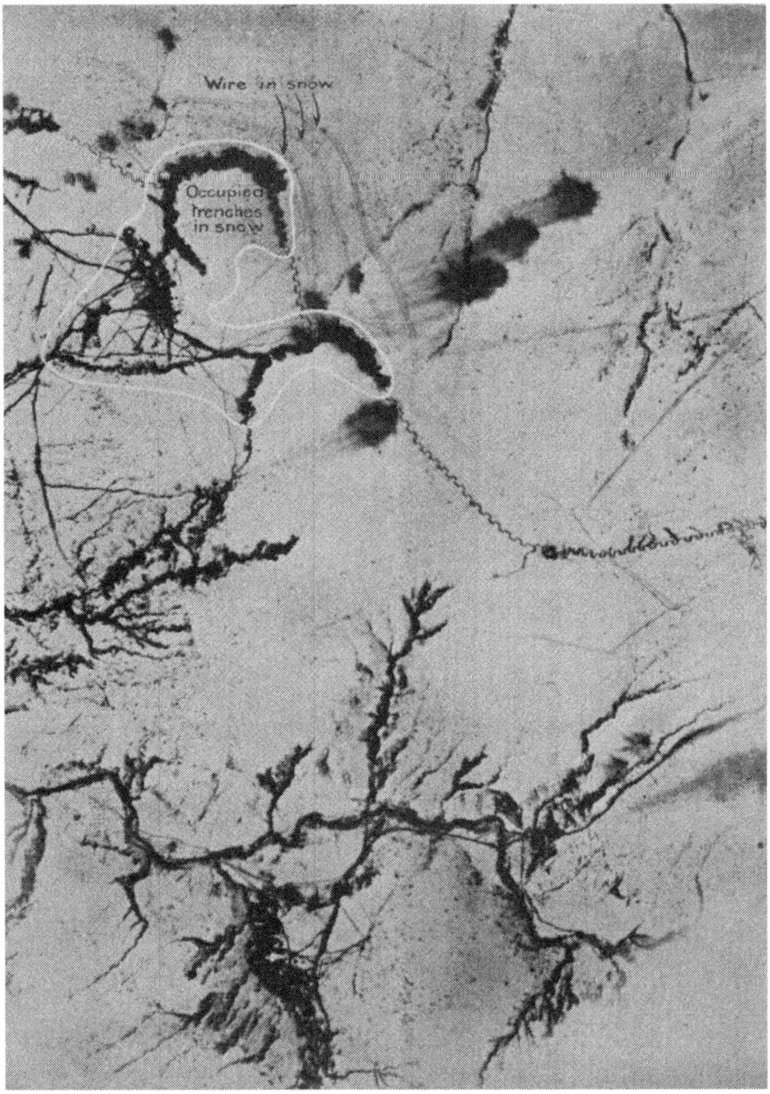

Royal Air Force official—Crown copyright reserved

Bulgarian trenches in the Struma Valley in winter. (A salvo of four shell-bursts is seen in the snow.)

their black veils quickly over their heads. The men remained seated and impassive, smoking and dreaming. No one came near you. No one spoke. Life there was a kind of continuous lethargy.

In the Bulgar village there would be movement. Heavily built men would come up to ask you what you wanted. Women in lovely costumes would look curiously at you. There was a chatter of children and a feeling of movement.

In the Greek village the moment of your arrival was a signal for a general rush to surround you. The inevitable English-speaking native would come forward and converse in English learned evidently in the back streets of New York. The children would redouble their cries, the women come out of their houses with gifts of melons or flowers. You would be unhorsed and seated at whatever small house served as a café. You would be plied with endless questions, told whatever you wanted to know, shown the church and the local school, visited ceremonially by the priest, and sent off again with every indication of welcome and excitement. You were one of the events of their day.

These varied races with totally distinct ideals and aims had lived happily for centuries. War had swept over them time and time again. Every village stood on a mound which was made by the accumulated debris of countless destructions and massacres of the past. Yet they always came back. When we evacuated them, which we were compelled to do, if only for their own safety, they packed up all their household goods and were on the road in a matter of hours, as if by nature they knew exactly how to get moving from the dire training of endless similar experiences of the past. The Turks moved more slowly and painfully.

I remember one lovely hamlet up on the slopes of the hills from which we cleared the unfortunate inhabitants. In a few hours after notice to quit they had assembled the most astonishing caravan. Donkeys, horses, cattle, and carts, almost obscured by strange baggages of richly covered cloth, ancient carpets of lovely colours and small children in vivid dresses. Men and women alike in full baggy trousers marched alongside. The procession wound round a hill-path, appearing and disappearing at the bends. It was like the 'Procession of Protracted Death' in Flecker's *Hassan*, an unforgettable picture of colour and outline.

Life in the valley became stereotyped. I would ride the length and breadth of the plain, getting what information I could, learning slowly where every hostile battery and out-post was placed. As I rode I learned much of the country. What historic land this was! Our valley was the home of the great Pæonian warriors of Homer. The Vardar was the very river which the heroes described as 'the river Axios, than which no fairer stream floweth over the face of the earth.' Next to it, away in the French lines on the west, was the Galliko river, which in antiquity had been famed for the fact that its sand was rich in gold. You just had to lay the fleece of a ram in the bed of the river in the night and at dawn you would find the whole fleece glittering with gold dust which the water had washed into the fleece. This no doubt was the origin of the story of the Golden Fleece. Our sappers did indeed tell me that it was possible to find minute specks of gold in some of these streams, and in idle moments men used to try to wash for gold. But I never heard of any great success, though the villagers near the Vardar told me that they did sometimes try their hand at panning for gold.

South-east of our main positions in the plain was the great peak of Mount Pangæum, the gold-mining centre of Phillip and Alexander of Macedon, from whose mines they and many others, even the historian Thucydides himself, had got rich. But Pangæum was in Bulgar lines and to us a mere distant mountain. On the edge of the Strymon itself, forming one of our most important strong points in the very fore of the front line was the ancient city of Amphipolis. How well I remembered my school-days and the long and stirring story of *Brasidas at Amphipolis*. Here on the summit, perhaps, of our very blockhouse, was the place where Socrates himself had stood. That is a strange and famous story of how Socrates stood sentinel on a hill at Amphipolis, motionless throughout one whole day, gazing at the sun. A little way to the south behind our lines are the ruins of Potidæa, where once Socrates and the young Alcibiades fought before the walls of the city: in the words of North's translation of Plutarch:

> 'Alcibiades was at the jorney of Potidæa, where he lay still with Socrates, who would never let him be from him in all battells and skirmishes he was in: among which there was one, very whotte and bloody, where they both fought valiantly, and Alcibiades was hurte. But Socrates stepped before him, and dyd defend him so valliantly before them all, that he saved him and his weapon out of the enemies handes. So the honour of this fight out of doubt, in equitie and reason, was due unto Socrates.'

Winter enshrouded us all in that Strymonic plain, and we huddled into our dugouts and houses, frozen sometimes, damp at others, seldom dry, and always on the watch. Like to us were the soldiers before Troy of whom the Herald in the *Agamemnon* speaks with the authentic tongue of a campaigner:

> 'For where we couched, close by the foeman's wall
> The river-plain was ever dank with dews,
> Dropped from the sky, exuded from the earth,
> A curse that clung unto our sodden garb,
> And hair as horrent as a wild-beast's fell.
> Why tell the woes of winter, when the birds
> Lay stark and stiff, so stern was Ida's snow?'

The Strymon was filled with jostling cakes of ice washed down in spate from the upper Balkans. Aeroplane photographs showed us the trenches of the enemy outlined in the snow clear and impossible to hide. They and we alike sent bombs and shells to add to the discomforts which Nature had provided. We had indeed settled down for the winter. No advance was possible or even thinkable. A battle might be won, but no forward movement could be made, for what roads there were had by now become almost useless. Sometimes the transport for a whole division had to be carried out by means of thousands of patient mules, passing and repassing along the track that led that seventy kilometres back to Salonika. The heavy guns had to stay where they had been put for they could not move. Great patches of water and half-submerged fields now made up the plain where in late summer we had picked the melons and figs from the orchards. Icy winds swept unceasingly over us from the north. The dogs of the abandoned villages, who had refused to leave with their masters, ran wild, formed into packs and became more dangerous than wolves, famished and savage. It was unsafe for a man on foot to leave his camp and do any journey alone. We organised battues and rode down these poor wild brutes and shot them mercilessly. One of the most hateful tasks I ever remember doing in the whole war.

Traces of the ancient past had emerged as we dug our trenches. Greek vases and Greek inscriptions came to light. Graves were turned up by accident, one or two containing lovely bronze helmets of finest Greek pattern. We were in a land where the fate of many a campaign had been settled. Fierce Thracian battalions had swarmed westwards along the coast in the days of the father of Philip of Macedon. Alexander had pressed up to where Sofia stands, and to the Danube through that very Rupel Pass that frowned over us.

Thucydides had lost his reputation in the gulf at the extreme right of our line where now two monitors at anchor served for heavy artillery to bombard the Bulgars near ancient Eion, once in the dim past a Persian fortress.

There was history in every square yard of this ancient valley.

I have often reflected on the kind of life we led. There we were, hemmed in by hills behind us that rose several thousand feet and cut us off from the world behind. Behind was Salonika, the sea, ships, and ultimately our only way of communication with home. But that background was held to us only by the long thin ribbon of roadway along which streamed endlessly the mules, lorries, guns, troops, and oddments that kept us in touch with an outside world. We lived in the valley, fed and strengthened by that solitary artery that held our very life blood. We could see the white road as it came swinging over the green crests of hills, and we knew that without it we should all starve and die. Before us was the other half of the plain, itself hemmed in at the back by another but more formidable line of hills, behind which loomed the vaster mountains of those inner lands of which we knew nothing. There too was the artery that fed the Bulgars, which slipped unobtrusively through Rupel Pass and down on to the plain. We were like two great beasts, two vast prehistoric monsters, too vast and heavy to get into motion without mountainous efforts of heaving and swaying. There we sat glowering at each other, spitting fire and smoke at intervals, raising a talon here and a tail there, splashing and floundering in the marshes. Like the prehistoric creatures, our bodies were vast and unwieldy, and the poor brain in each body so insignificant and futile as to be incapable of controlling at one and the same moment the whole vast structure of the body.

Our daily life was just what you would expect of such a huge and unmanageable creature. We just lived and ate and stirred at intervals, stretched our vast limbs and then collapsed into uneven sleep. Of the life of the mind or of the spirit, in the sense in which I faintly remembered it, we had almost nothing. With unconquerable persistence the men organised every conceivable kind of entertainment in makeshift theatres adapted from barns and shacks. There we would flock to hear the wit and fun and bawdy nonsense devised by a score of enterprising men. There we saw *Bluebeard*, *The Yeomen of the Guard*, *Robinson Crusoe*, and all the ancient dramas that were most likely to bring us a hint of our earlier lives. But of anything more serious, of any kind of study of the type that belonged to my ardent days of learning, and to the thrills of research, there was none, for none was possible. The stray inscriptions that turned up from time to time in the valley, carved in the clear and lovely scripts of Greece and Rome, for a fleeting moment brought back those long hours at Oxford, when I had listened gravely to the disputes that surrounded the accounts left us by the ancients of their wars and their politics and their intrigues. I used to copy out these inscriptions one by one in a notebook, translate them, and try to find out to what times and events they referred. But this I did more as a kind of pious duty which I owed to some uncertain past. I kept them safely until the war ended. I instinctively recorded and noted them because I had been trained before the war to do that sort of thing. But I could not work up the faintest interest in them. Indeed I could not even read a book of any serious import. We lived our prehistoric life like troglodytes in that deep valley, almost wholly untroubled by the things of the spirit. I have read of earnest civilian soldiers who always carried in their pockets a Horace or a Homer. That they carried them in their pockets I fully believed, but that they ever unaffectedly read them for pleasure in the midst of war and destruction I frankly do not believe. They may have tried to read them, have tried to cultivate the calm atmosphere of detachment which such reading would give: but that they ever succeeded I simply cannot credit. War is a strange master, and he will not let the spirit roam in its own cool realms. There may be no battle, perhaps there has not been a shot fired for days: you may be browsing with nothing to do for weeks on end: here surely was the occasion for the reading of great literature and the calming of the spirit by contemplation. Would that it were true. In fact, war keeps the mind as well as the body at full tension for months and years on end. Whatever may be the condition of affairs at any given moment, it may change into something utterly different a moment after. Our quiet valley might at any second have belched flame and death over us in some unexpected onslaught. Once the mind is attuned to that sort of psychological condition, it is extremely hard to make it respond to a chord struck in a totally different key. There I was in this historic place, whose history I knew fairly well, probably better than most of my fellow-soldiers in that valley. I ought to have been able to read the dialogues of Plato and hear the authentic words of Socrates, who, like me, had fought in this very valley: I might have read the calm clear sentences of Aristotle, whose very birthplace was only a few miles behind those hills at our back. Euripides himself had lived at the court of Archelaus, King of Macedonia, and must have known these valleys and mountains well. But I simply could not bring my mind to accord with any great literature of any age. For it all seemed so utterly remote and out of touch with life as I lived it then. What was the use of finding passages of the Funeral Speech of Pericles, or of the great rhythm of Æschylus, which were in accord with our life? Men of taste and learning in England were seeing parallels and similarities between the epic deeds and martial doings of this war and those of the wars of olden times and of the writings and speeches of men long dead. But to me there was no event in the past which even remotely resembled the events of the present. I could not read, still less could I write. The attuning of the mind to be ready at a moment's notice to devote its whole strength to action did not allow the mind to rove unchecked into the fields of imagination and reflection. It was there chained like a dog to a barrel. True enough the dog can run a little way, he can give every indication of happiness and freedom. But his chain is there, and at the end of it his barrel. So we too were chained in mind and body to this barrel, to this deep hollow in the earth which contained us so neatly within its boundaries.

There was, indeed, something wholly inimical to the

reading and still more to the writing of literature for those at war. Nor was this latent hostility merely due to the state of life in which we lived. Books, writing itself, and all the arts of that other distant world of waking which we had left so long and so far behind us did not belong to our dream-world at all. Some few years ago a German of my acquaintance, who was of an age with myself and who had served on the eastern German front, spoke of this very matter. What he told me I might have told him. He described how his men would enter some new city or townlet in Poland and how they would be quartered in the houses. Once, he described, they were billeted in an ancient castle in which was a small and fine library of books. He found that his men, before he could stop them, had torn the books from the shelves and used them as fuel for their fires. There was much else they could have used for fuel, but they preferred the books. He added that books, as everyone knows, make poor fuel and are in fact extremely hard to burn. But what struck him was the fury and frenzy with which the men tore the pages from the books and rent their leather bindings as if there was something incongruous and rather disgraceful about their very existence in times of war. They did their destruction, until he stopped them, in some strange berserk fury of vengeance, as though to say: 'On books like you we were brought up: in books like you we learned the virtues and the rules of a world of peace: now look to what a pass you have brought us: now you are fuel for the fires that at any moment may consume us as well.'

One winter's day in the valley our mess-cook came to me and held out for my inspection two large wooden panels. 'I thought,' he said, 'that you might like to have a look at these, sir, before I burned them.' The panels were two lovely Greek icons which he had found in the wreckage of some house near by. 'We always likes to use 'em for lighting the fire,' he added apologetically, 'because the wax on 'em burns so nice.' I took them from him and have them still. But he had some faint glimmering of his sin, only it was very faint, and I shudder to think how many breakfasts I had eaten, cooked on fires lit by mediaeval icons! as he gave them to me he smiled apologetically and said, 'I know you take an interest in such things, sir.' Heavens, but my interest was thin and evanescent. Reflecting now, I might have done so much to save destruction; but I was filled with inertia, there was always the feeling at the back of my mind 'Perhaps I shall be dead to-morrow; and what are the arts of peace or the trickings and fancies of culture now?' All such things seemed to belong to a remote and distant youth. I was growing up; indeed, I was now a man of twenty-eight. That the whole of my education and upbringing should have ended by leading me to spend years of my life in this closed cell of a valley in a barbarous land seemed ridiculous. There had been two worlds in my life, and one of them I had left behind.

As though to give point to this severance from the waking world of ancient peace that I had known it seemed so long ago, news that filtered in from England seemed to give point to the fact that I had burned my boats. Almost all the friends I had made in London, and a very heavy proportion of my contemporaries at Oxford, had been killed. Rigby, the barrister who had joined us in many a jovial party in London in 1912, was dead in the hot plains of Mesopotamia: young Norsworthy the painter killed in Flanders: three of my best friends whom I had met in Plugstreet Wood were now forgotten corpses somewhere on that Western front. The generation to which I had belonged was being thinned and whittled down to a mere handful. What use was 'culture' to me now?

> 'Art-magicianis and astrologis,
> Rethoris, logicians and theologis,
> Them helpis no conclusionis slee—
> *Timor Mortis conturbat me.*'

And so the long winter passed. Snow came and went; sleet and slush stayed with us as our daily comrades. Fever ranged here and there among the ranks of men and officers, striking down those who had recovered from their summer bouts. The guns boomed and echoed among those silent hills in a steady volume, and, from afar, Olympus looked down on the scene, aloof but somehow part and parcel of our setting. Here were the barbarians of the twentieth century, learning the lessons of the philosophy and literature of Greece so ill that all they could think to do was to shoot and kill and stalk, bomb and bayonet in hand, through the marshes of the Strymon. What was culture worth if it led to this?

Pedants and high-brows deceive themselves into thinking that they were sustained by the great thinkers of the past to endure the barbarities of the present. They were but pretending. War does not permit of any activity of mind or body except what is immediately applicable to the problems that war itself sets. No single moment does it leave you free. Always is that bugle-call to instant action about to break the silence. False rest, false security, and false contemplation. In a second they are shattered to the winds, and that second may be the next second, or it may come a month hence. The mind cannot function nor the body rest under conditions such as war prescribes.

But as though to prove how war once mastered is as abject a slave as he is unremitting a master, the moment peace was declared and no shell burst and no bullet whined, then in the joy of a certain quiet, we all rushed with a mad intoxication to the arts of peace. Hardly had the bugles of the Armistice sounded than I and everyone else who had ever learned or thought or read or written or wondered about the things of the spirit that matter so deeply and are so easily overthrown, rushed back to books and to pictures and to the whole world of beauty that we had left, frantic to recapture that distant and forgotten world that we had left so long. For it was the Fear of Death, though we never thought of it like that, that controlled every action and thought of our lives as long as there were guns to fire and men to kill and be killed. In that valley one could see the whole epitome of war and a microcosm of all its doings.

By make-believe we made of our valley some semblance of the world we had left. Canteens and concerts, games and horse-shows, took us away from the war that was just round the corner. Often indeed the war insisted and our pretences fled. One day an enthusiast organised a game of football, but it ended ignominiously in our all flying for shelter as a shower of bombs fell on us, dropped by passing aeroplanes.

Away in Greece to the south political confusion reigned supreme. King Constantine and Mr Venizelos had parted mortal enemies for life. Greece was divided into two parts, that part in the north which wished to ally itself with the Entente and that part in the south which preferred neutrality. We had but a vague idea of what it all meant, but we saw the beginnings of the new Greek army organised by the revolutionary party who had made Salonika the headquarters of a revived Greece. Soon detachments of Greeks came among us to learn the new ways of warfare and to prepare to withstand Bulgaria their age-long enemy.

In Athens, as far as I could gather, Frenchmen, Englishmen, and Germans were still playing at spies, still trampling the neutrality of a small Power just because she was small. In Salonika, whither I went on one or two rare occasions on some errand, the band of Allies was becoming more and more diverse. Besides the better known Allies, with whose uniforms most people were by now acquainted, there were the Russians, tall, long-coated and precise, there was a strange contingent of pro-Ally Albanians in red and black coats, organised by an adventurer named Essad Pasha. French Annamite troops wandered listlessly in the streets in their willow-pattern hats and thin khaki, looking for all the world like little toy men from some Chinese shop. We had had some of them in our valley. They had been launched into an attack and had done positive carnage on the Bulgars with their knives and bayonets, hewing their foe into very small pieces with untold valour. But then they had all run very fast back again, disregarding the military advantages of gaining ground. After that they were, like our band of comitadji brigands, sent far back to more congenial tasks. They were largely employed in the commissariat department for the purpose of cutting up meat.

Then there were smart Cretan gendarmes, imported by the Provisional Greek Government to replace the Royalist police. Their spare slim forms and small pill-box caps and baggy trousers made a pleasant relief from the ill-designed uniforms of the French and British. Senegalese and a handful of Indian troops added a touch of variety. Salonika indeed was a menagerie of types. The gods on Olympus must have smiled, when they looked down. So great was the variety of uniforms that the average British soldier or officer had no idea which ally was which. We accepted any uniform and saluted any foreign officer we saw who looked resplendent. Perhaps we were a little too complacent, for one day a Bulgarian officer deserted across the lines in a region where they were thinly held. He looked in vain for someone to whom he might deliver himself. After passing for a mile or so through our lines he offered himself to the soldiers at ammunition dumps, and to transport lines, all without effect. At each he was genially waved on to the next with friendly cries of "Not understand," for he spoke only Bulgarian. Ultimately, tired and footsore, he reached Salonika, where, after much argument, a military policeman on point-duty was at length convinced that he was an enemy. With great persistence he in the end got himself duly interned.

From our daily papers and the sparse official information that was circulated to us we gathered that Greece in the south was in great distress. France followed the one sole policy of *supprimez l'indigène*. Britain merely let things take their own course, which meant no course at all. At intervals the Allied ministers with a blare of trumpets would deliver to King Constantine a Note. Nothing happened and Greece merely became more and more exacerbated. Her very life was now divided into two camps. Families were split up; one son would be serving with Venizelos in Salonika, the other an ardent Royalist. Parties and functions ceased, I was told in rare letters from Athens, because so many erstwhile friends were now at daggers drawn. Between the Old Greece of Constantine and the New Greece of Venizelos there had been established a Neutral Zone, guarded by Allied troops. This zone ran right across the peninsula and was some miles in depth. Movement across it was forbidden. The zone lay along the southern slopes of Olympus. The gods must have found still more to make them smile; could they ever have dreamed of their home with a Neutral Zone drawn round it? It was almost as if we feared that Aphrodite and Zeus and Athena would take sides, just as they did at Troy, and all come rushing down to help us or the Bulgars. So we guarded their passes with Senegalese and with Annamites armed with machine-guns. That would keep them in their place.

At the end of the year matters in Greece had come to a head. The private theatricals organised by the amateur spy-catchers, who had flocked to Athens like vultures to a corpse, had brought confusion, distrust and fury among right-minded Greeks. The French in particular had, by a deliberate policy of goading, driven all Greece to despair. True enough, Constantine, by his own policy of waiting and watching, uncertain which horse to back, had produced an atmosphere of distrust and disloyalty to Greece which made all the Allies equally dissatisfied. True enough, Greece by virtue of being in possession of an army and a navy which were situated in the rear of the Allied armies, had become a potential menace. But, in all the experience I ever had of Frenchmen, they struck me as being constitutionally incapable of distinguishing between the potential and the actual. Everyone knew well enough that, in the wildly improbable event of the Greeks showing signs of direct hostility, their little navy and army would be dispersed like chaff in a day by any of the large forces which we had accessible in different parts of the Mediterranean. But General Sarrail, Commander of the Allied Forces, a man whom the gods of Olympus were even now making mad that they might later destroy him, was determined that Greece was to be humbled to the dust. Nor was there in the armed world of those years anywhere to be found a more disastrous collocation of flagrant opposites than that of Sarrail and Constantine. That two such elements of a detonation should have found themselves in such close proximity was but another of the many pranks Fate had played on us all. Constantine, who had asserted openly a rather infantile belief in the Divine Right of Kings; Sarrail, atheist, socialist, hater of French Royalists, Freemason, virtually dismissed from France to serve in the East by the intrigues of French Royalists. Here he found the cause and root of all that he disliked most in the world. Here, where tact, understanding, friendship and consideration for all points of view, however insane, were the chief requisites of command, there was sent a half-crazy fanatic who could see no view except his own, whose life was controlled by a series of clichés, by that absurd assembly of *choses jugées* which masquerades in France as 'French love of logic.' The French mind works like the clock of a taximeter. It cannot diverge or stop or retrace its steps. It just ticks on. Potential and actual things are to it all the same. If the taximeter records so much money, then that sum recorded is to the French mind an actual sum of money. The traveller in the taxi may have nothing in his pockets. That does not matter. 'The taximeter says five pounds,' says the French logician, 'therefore not only must you pay five pounds but you must also have it in your pocket.'

Thus they treated Greece. Greece, they said, had guns, ships, troops and rifles. They were not fighting for the Allies, therefore those arms were for the sole use of destroying the Allies. They were a potential danger, and so a danger that was a real danger.

In actual fact the Greeks were almost as much embarrassed by their possession of arms as were the French. The Greeks had already seen that their army and navy were useless to prevent the Allies from doing exactly as they wished, and they were far too frightened to dream of using them in any hostile sense.

But the drama was moving to its climax. That Neutral Zone round the home of the Gods had goaded even the Gods. Sarrail struck. He made a demand upon the Greek Government that the Greeks should hand over a large consignment of guns and material of war. This was to serve as their pledge of neutrality. The Greeks were at last moved to open expressions of rage and hostility. Sarrail insisted, and sent a squadron of French and British ships to anchor off Athens. Marines were landed from these ships to seize the guns and material which the Greeks refused to hand over. The Greeks, or rather the hotheads among them, rapidly gathered together military forces in Athens. The French and British marines took up positions in a public park just near the temple of Olympian Zeus. And then at last Olympus thundered. The Greeks suddenly opened fire on the Allied troops, killed a handful of Frenchmen and a few British, and wounded a few more. So inept was the French organisation of the landing that only with difficulty, and with the aid of the Greeks themselves, were the disgruntled troops of the Great Powers able to regain their ships. It was no massacre, or anything approaching it: merely a demonstration, perhaps too violent, by Greeks to make it quite clear that Athens was the capital of a state which was not at war and which was determined to remain free and neutral. But it was a gesture of despair.

At once a blockade was established by Allied ships. Greece was in disgrace. Sarrail raged like a lion smitten with rabies. Constantine grumbled and roared like an infuriated bear. But force counted, and the Greeks were powerless. They were presented with an ultimatum which they accepted. By its terms they agreed to make a public ceremony of apology and to withdraw their army to a point south of the Canal of Corinth. The public ceremony was to consist of a march past of Greek troops headed by the Crown Prince in the presence of the Allied Ministers and the Flags of the Allies. The Greeks were to salute the Allied flags. Here was ignominy of the type that breeds eternal hatred. Here was just sheer lunacy. Olympus thundered again in its clouds. The gods rubbed their hands. The stage was set for a famous tragedy. Nor did that tragedy end till Constantine died in misery and exile in Naples a few years later, and Sarrail, finally demented, bombarded Damascus in 1925, was dismissed from the army, and finally himself died in disgrace. Only then were the gods satisfied. The third party in this queer triangle, Venizelos, has, like the others, crashed to irremediable ruin at last. And his fall is the most tragic of all, the deepest humiliation.

In our valley I read all these things with horror. Athens had even been bombarded. A few shells, which fortunately failed to explode, had been fired at the moment of the Greek attack on our troops. I feel somehow that there was just the same fatal fascination about bombarding Athens that those German soldiers felt, as I described above, when they madly tore up libraries and burned books. Here in Athens was the very core of civilisation of ancient standing: the very wellhead from which the life and thought and art of all Europe had been moulded. In the brain of that insensate French Admiral who ordered this bombardment I feel sure there was that same barbaric upthrust of emotion which stirred in those Teutonic minds. Here, he must have

Lake Doiran

The 'Pip' Ridge from the old front line (1920)

thought, is the wellhead of civilisation. Away in France and Flanders civilisation has rotted away among heaps of stinking corpses and burning towns. If that is all civilisation is worth let us blot out its citadel. I am sure he would have rejoiced to see the columns of the Parthenon crumble and crash into thunderous ruin under the impact of steel shells. I am sure he would have delighted to see the smoke of the burning city consuming its museums and houses and palaces. And yet, after a few furtive and, I believe, deliberately mis-aimed shots he ceased. For even a matricide must feel shame, and, in the end, I still believe that that demented admiral was driven to hold his hand.

I chafed and worried, shamed beyond belief myself that Greece should be so trampled in the mire. Why could we not leave her alone, dismiss all our raving amateur spy-catchers, and abandon Athens to its own devices.

Winter was breaking. Frosts gave way to sun at times. Snow came and went fitfully, and the river mists grew less. Faint hints of spring were in the air. Our battles and stray patrol actions began again. The guns made larger echoes among the hills. The lust to kill was rising with the sap. 1917, another year of war, was opening before us with its incalculable chances and its fears and fantasies.

I have spoken of the momentary life of the soldier on service. How he is always at full tension, waiting and waiting for something that may never happen or which may happen in a sudden flash. But I often used to wonder what the life of the civilian at home was like. In many ways the tension there was worse. For how could men sit down and read or work or cultivate their gardens when so much might happen at any moment? There can hardly have been a family at that time who did not arise each morning with that dreadful feeling of terrible news awaiting them. I envisaged my own family wondering at every knock on the door whether that was to announce the telegram in which 'The War Office regrets to inform you . . .' Thank heavens I was spared all that. I am sure I could not have endured the daily waiting for what might never happen. I think that nothing in war is really more barbarous and unendurable than the waiting of those at home for news of those away. Every day I was grateful that I was here in our valley and not numbered among the waiting. Whatever tension or suspense we soldiers endured, it was an essential part of our life and duty. To be at home, leading the double life of civilisation and barbarism combined would, to me at least, have been intolerable. Give me one or the other. To-day I thank Fortune for having given me a daughter and not a son. For in a future war I could not stand that waiting and waiting to hear if he was numbered among the dead or not.

The rivers in our valley were in flood. Mosquitoes who had survived the winter emerged and bit us. But Nature took little notice of us. One day I would see a pair of pelicans, vast massive creatures, lumbering across the lake in search of new fishing grounds. Sometimes a wolf would be sighted in some distant village. Otters played in the river; storks nested as usual in the house-tops of those villages which survived.

New orders reached me which at once delighted me and grieved me. I was told to transfer myself to Athens, to report there to a General of whom I had never heard and to consider myself as one member of a commission which had been organised by the Salonika army for the purposes of enforcing the ultimatum given to Constantine the previous December. It appeared that in the opinion of General Sarrail the blockade was not achieving its purpose; the Greeks were supposed to be plotting and planning to rise in revolt and with their puny army sweep the vast French and British armies at Salonika out of Greek territory by some fanatic attack from the rear. I was wanted to go to Greece of which I was known to have some knowledge, and to do what was best suited to enforce the ultimatum. Eleven colleagues were to go with me. As far as I could see, our main task was to see that the blockade was being effective—in other words, we were to make a prolonged inspection to satisfy ourselves that the Greeks were being properly starved. Indeed it was a pleasant task for one who loved Greece, an exhibition of the superiority of Western culture which made me gasp. It was incredible that the blockade could ever have been declared, but far more incredible that we should be sent like head-torturers to see that it was being done properly. I had occasion once or twice to supervise the punishment of soldiers who had offended, but I had never dreamed that I was ever to supervise the punishment of a whole people and of a free people for sins which they had never committed. However, I decided that I should at least find out the truth about this preposterous muddle; that I might indeed help to straighten it, and that by seeing our Allies on the spot I might be in a position to find out why things had turned out as they had, and how we might prevent them from getting worse.

CHAPTER IX

SIDE ISSUES

SALONIKA once more. The same dusty streets, dingier than ever. The same movements of troops and guns and traffic. The same dry smell of decay and dirt. I found a boat, and a passage on it, and set off to Athens. Again we passed Olympus and, as we passed, a storm arose at night that sent our small steamer careering up on its end. I groaned in an agony of sickness and waited for the dawn. Again at dawn Sunium came in sight, but now all was calm. In a cold sunny morning, clear as a jewel, coloured like an aquamarine, we swung to anchor in Phalerum Bay. But we could not stay there, and our ship moved again to the larger bay of Salamis. There, just like the ancient fleets on the very spot where Athens saved Europe for all time from Oriental despotism, lay a large fleet of French and British battleships, and a heterogenous group of merchant vessels in which, I was told, lived the legations of the Allied Powers, too frightened to stay in the capital which they had made too hot for them. I reported my presence to the Admiral on the spot and went ashore in a pinnace. The same idle crowds at Peiraeus watched my landing, as I had seen many a time before. The same fuss and scurry and the same curious odours of wine and oil and dust.

I drove up to Athens on one of those mornings which are peculiar to Athens and like no other mornings. The clear crystalline air made the outlines of the hills stark and fresh as if they had just been thrown up from the earth in the first spasms of creation.

In Athens I found the General to whom I was to report for duty. He and a staff of two extremely capable and charming officers were installed at the Hôtel Angleterre.

Here I too was put up, pending definite orders. We all had meals together and I was told the situation. I asked questions. 'Was Greece now to be considered a hostile country?' 'No, not quite.' 'Were we the officers of an occupation or merely officers of inspection and control?' 'We were neither: officially we had the main duty of enforcing the blockade, enforcing the terms of the ultimatum and seeing that things were patched up amicably. Actually (though forget that I have said it) we were there to see that the French did not behave with too serious violence, nor outrage the feelings of the Greeks more ludicrously than was necessary.' Roughly that was what they told me.

However, here was Athens, denuded of foreign diplomats and with only us here to represent general Allied interests. Nearly all the English and French had fled on that fatal bombardment, when the Greeks were firing on our troops. Not even the chaplain of the English church had remained. Just as the Allied representatives had propagated the mad atmosphere of make-believe in the preceding year; just as they had played at spies and spy-catching on the assumption that there were terrible plots brewing and frightful massacres being organised, so now they reaped the rewards of their idiocy. Greeks of all people are least likely to weave hideous plots for the destruction of innocuous diplomats and unimportant charlatans; but when, goaded into desperation, they opened fire on the French and British marines who had actually invaded their land and were sent as a sign of the degradation of Greece, then these wretched diplomats and spy-hunters, and with them all the rag-tag-and-bobtail in their train, and even the level-headed British and French residents of Athens, rushed panic-stricken out of Athens and sought for shelter on ships in the harbour under the guns of Allied battleships. This wholesale scamper of the citizens of the Great Powers from an utterly imaginary danger simply made the Greeks laugh. As I walked along the streets and squares and began to talk to Greeks and to look for old friends, I soon realised that the average citizen of Athens was merely chuckling. However, there it was. The king and his friends lived in the palace, the ministers of the Allies on uncomfortable ships in Salamis Bay, glowering and menacing at the wicked Greek conspiracy. Here were we, together with a similar mission of Italians and Frenchmen, and I soon learned what our job was to be. We had to make quite sure that the Greek army, which was mostly north of Athens, was removed from any proximity to the forces at Salonika, and sent south below the Gulf of Corinth. Once there it would not be able to move northwards, because the only access to the north was either across the Gulf of Corinth by water, and this was prevented by a continuous Allied naval patrol, or else across the one and only bridge that crosses the Corinth Canal, dizzily suspended above the cleft. And this bridge could be held firmly by a mere patrol of Allied troops.

To ensure the removal southwards of the Greek army we junior officers were to be sent to the main strategic points of Greece and there we were to commence the process of removal, or virtual demilitarisation, of the Greek army by despatching from each centre the local garrisons and making certain that they reached Athens and were then sent on to Corinth. I saw before me a prospect of really interesting work, a chance of getting to the bottom of this prodigious mess we had made of everything in Greece and a chance of doing something to straighten matters out. Thank heavens Greece was now for the moment almost free from diplomatic intervention. There were the diplomats safely shanghaied at Salamis, busying themselves ciphering and deciphering telegrams that meant nothing and effected nothing. With them were all the riff-raff of amateur diplomats and amateur spy-hunters and, indeed, all the unwanted elements. Athens was purged and Athenian streets were clean once more. Athens knew more or less where she stood, though where she stood was no pleasant spot.

As people with a purely military intention we were received with extraordinary kindness and grace. We felt like officers of an army of occupation in a conquered land, but the Athenians made us feel more like invited guests. We were known to have nothing whatever to do with the fly-blown politics and childish capers of diplomacy and spy-craft. We were officers in military uniform known to have been detached from fighting regiments. The Greeks gave us credit for doing our duty and for being under orders. We were not disguised journalists or civilians hastily thrown into military garb.

Our colleagues were French and Italian and Russian—for we actually had a couple of Russian captains sent to represent the third of the Protecting Powers of Greece, as those three Powers had been called, in some ancient pre-war treaty.

I learned that already before my arrival a Frenchman and a British and an Italian officer had been sent to Patras, to Chalkis in Eubœa, and to Larissa in Thessaly, right up on the Neutral Zone. I was soon to get my own orders.

Our General was a vast man some six feet five in height, who had served for many years before the war in the International gendarmerie of Albania. That, to the War Office, was sufficient reason for sending him here. They had assumed that once you know one Balkan State you know the lot, as though to say that a man who knows Patagonia must also feel at home in New York.

But he was honest and simple and felt a bitter dislike of all these humiliations which Great Britain had brought on Greece and on herself. He was out to clean the affair up. But he suffered from two defects, one that he could not resist the lure of amateur diplomacy and thought he could put straight what the Foreign Office had muddled, and the other that he knew Albanians well and Greeks not at all: nor did he speak any foreign language of any description. He put the matter before me clearly and caustically. I can see him now, sitting at his table, working his way slowly through a bottle of Greek brandy—he usually had one every evening—and getting more and more lachrymose as he described the tangled and unhappy position of Greece which we were to disentangle.

I went out the next day to see my friends in the Legation on their ship in Salamis Bay. As I went I was just able to see one of those comic-opera episodes which had made up the daily life of the earlier period of Athenian intrigue. Just as I was going down to Piræus a message was sent me telling me to stand by to help in a difficult matter at Piræus. When I got to the quayside I found one of the secretaries of the Legation. He came up to me furtively and whispered that they had got a certain agent, a Greek, who had served us well for the previous year, and that it was essential to get him out of Greece quickly before he was assassinated by Royalists in revenge for all he had done to help the Allies. Always ready to help, I offered my services. The man was lurking somewhere in the background in the crowd and was waiting for a pinnace to take him off to a British ship, which would then deposit him on some Greek island where he would fade into oblivion. The Legation secretary was waiting on the steps of the quay, agitated and fussy, running about like a chicken who had lost its young. The usual crowd of people was waiting by the steps, curious and impassive. Among the crowd was about a dozen stray Greek soldiers. 'The man will come presently,' hissed the secretary. 'He is at the back there with three of our men guarding him. The pinnace from the flagship that is to take him off is ten minutes late in arriving, and I am afraid there may be an attempt on the part of the Greek Secret Police to seize the man before he can be put on the pinnace. Would you mind getting into the crowd with me and these two friends of mine, and then when the pinnace pulls in to the steps try to jostle anyone who looks as if he might be going to grab our man.' I was delighted to help in this ridiculous scene, if only as a way of spending a pleasant quarter of an hour. A cloud of smoke showed the pinnace in the offing tearing through the water that broke in white foam on its bows. It swung neatly into the steps. The crowd surged forward. 'Look out,' hissed my friend the secretary in a truly Lyceum dramatic hiss. At that moment a bedraggled Greek, grey with fear, was pushed through the crowd. The crowd jostled excitedly at the sight of the pinnace with its white ensign and smart sailormen. The man was propelled through the crowd exactly as the pinnace drew in to the steps. I jostled, and the crowd jostled, and we all jostled as per programme. 'Look out,' came that dramatic hiss again. 'Someone may grab him or else put a knife in his ribs.' So I jostled a trifle harder. The secretary suddenly gave the wretched 'secret agent' a violent push in the small of the back and he fell with a crash into the pinnace. He was safe at last on British territory! The soldiers in the crowd gaped and continued to jostle. I jumped into the pinnace myself and went off to the floating Legation. All was well.

That was my one and only experience of Athenian secret service. There had not in fact been the smallest attempt to seize the man. The crowd was perfectly harmless. The secretary was only having the nightmares of a bad conscience. But it was diverting. If Athens had been like this for the last year, I thought, no wonder everyone seemed to have gone mad. The atmosphere of imaginary intrigue and plot had been so fostered that no one was now any longer capable of interpreting anything intelligently. Nothing was any longer what it seemed.

I found the Legation happily engaged in its routine tasks of typing and enciphering, though what they had to type or encipher I could not imagine, seeing that they had no real idea at all what was going on in Athens. They too were surrounded in an atmosphere of make-believe. They felt that there was something heroic about their living out on ships away from the dangerous natives of the mainland.

They seemed to expect that at any moment a fleet of cannibal canoes would set out from Piræus to seize and eat them. I was an object of wonder for living on the mainland among the natives. Was I really safe? they asked: was there still any food to be had, for the blockade was on? Was it dangerous to walk at nights in the streets? and so on.

I returned over the windy Bay of Salamis. A gale had sprung up and it was all I could do to get into the pinnace. We rushed over the waves in clouds of spray. We skirted the little islet where the Greeks landed those many years gone and slaughtered the Persian sailors who were washed up from the Persian wrecks in the famous battle.

Back at Athens I was told that I should leave on the morrow for a tour of inspection in the Peloponnese. What was I to inspect? I asked. 'Oh, just have a look round,' replied the General. 'See if there is anything at all worth note. But I am really sending you so as to keep an eye on the French officer who is going with you, in case he makes a particular fool of himself.'

The next morning I and the Frenchman set off. He was the typical *poilu* of the war, a big man with an enormous Assyrian beard. But he was quiet and intelligent, and evidently sensible. We were to go by train to Tripolitsa in the centre of the Peloponnese, and from thence to Kyparissia on the western coast of Messenia. At Kyparissia the railway stopped, and we were to go thence by road to Navarino. One of our objectives was to see if there was anything to be found about the matter of submarines and illicit supplies of fuel. 'Autrement,' he added, 'nous allons regarder les indigènes mourants de faim et d'inanition!' I welcomed the touch of sarcasm and realised that he was a human being after all.

Our train wound along those lovely hills near Corinth and then plunged into the broken country between Corinth and Argos. The engine snorted and wheezed, for it was being fed mainly on wood and locally mined lignite. This was one of the first effects of the blockade which we were sent to examine. Later I saw engines being fed with fir-cones.

We arrived at Tripolitsa in the early evening. After a hasty meal we wandered together round the little square of this remote hill-town. Suddenly I noticed my companion stiffen like a dog scenting a cat. There, passing us a little way off, were three German sailors in uniform. What on earth were they doing there, I wondered: and what ought an armed Allied officer to do when encountering the enemy in a peaceful city belonging to a neutral, but over which he has virtual control? Should we start a shooting contest or should we punctiliously ignore each other's existence? Two more sailors appeared, passing us almost face to face. We took no notice of them, but I could not help catching the glint of a smile in the eyes of one of them, nor could I resist the hint of a wink in return.

They were, as I soon learned, the crew of a submarine which had been sunk off Navarino. They had swum ashore and been interned in this perfectly safe townlet. But it took some time to soothe my Frenchman down.

From Kyparissia, a lovely coastal town filled with black cypress-trees, as its name suggested, we made a two-day trip down to Navarino. I shall not easily forget that long drive, both of us seated in a rickety old post-carriage that bore the British coat of arms and had been made for some elderly lady years back when the British lived at Corfu. We rocked and plunged over the perilous roads, drawn, or rather dragged, by two miserable and emaciated horses who stumbled and tripped.

We stopped at the towns *en route*, all, like Kyparissia, perched on great ledges of rock several hundred feet above the shore. In the towns the inhabitants flocked to see us, for their life for the last few years had been drab in the extreme and no foreigners had come their way, least of all foreigners in resplendent uniforms. But we were to them the representatives of hostile Powers who were blockading them for no reason that they could understand. People would bring to us their children and hold them up and ask us caustically if we thought they were thin enough to satisfy our requirements. Aged men in the kilts and colours of the Peloponnese, would shake their heads and say that they thought we were being brutal for no cause. Nor had we any sort or kind of an answer to them. The Greeks were shrewd enough and knew in their hearts that the main purpose of that blockade was to make them rise and demand the exile of their king. And they were shrewd enough to realise that we knew well enough that that was the last thing to do to gain our end. Whoever was the maniac who thought that he could compel a democratic people to eject their king by starving them I do not know. So far from making the people hate their king for being responsible for what they were suffering, the blockade only made them think that their king was a hero to stand so firmly against the tyranny of the Allies. They were ready to endure much suffering and starvation to support their king in his attitude. In effect, we merely increased the popularity of Constantine and made ourselves more hated than ever. That in a word was all I had to report to my General when I returned to Athens.

Navarino, where Russia, France, and Britain had once freed Greece from slavery by the total destruction of the Turkish fleet, was now a sombre and dreary little Italianate port. The people looked at us askance and no one gave us any hint of help. There was a Greek who acted as French consul, about whom my Frenchman had received grave reports. His loyalty to France was doubted. He was sent for and arrived, truculent and inhospitable. The Frenchman spoke to him with violence and determination. He was dismissed, he was told, from his high post of consul. La Belle France no longer trusted him. He went, as truculently as he had come.

Navarino was the only rather suspicious place I saw in

all that service in Greece. Many ships had indeed been torpedoed off its shores and there was considerable reason to think that German submarines received help and conceivably fuel from this port. But now that the blockade was on, there was not the smallest chance of their being refuelled, since there was no longer any petrol in the country.

Back in Athens I was given fresh orders. I was to go north to Larissa in Thessaly, the one exciting post in this dreary business. There I had a twofold task, to despatch Greek troops in trains to Athens, to regulate the numbers of the troops allowed to remain there by the ultimatum, and to watch for any organisation of irregulars among the foothills of Olympus that loomed over the Thessalian plain.

So off I went again. Twelve hours in the train brought me at dusk to the half-Turkish, half-Greek town of Larissa, lying flat and uninteresting in the flat lands, with mountains rising away into clouds to the north and the broad river Peneios running swiftly past before it plunged through the Vale of Tempe and so to the sea.

I was met at the station by my French and Italian colleagues, Captain Quenel and Tenente Foladore. The former was a typical Parisian, dapper, friendly and quick-witted: the latter a burly little officer in the uniform of the Alpini, who in civilian life had been a mining engineer at Laurium in Attica at the lead-mines.

The Frenchman had a bodyguard of six Senegalese, and they all lived in a small house that was the Allied Headquarters. The Italian and I took rooms in opposite hotels on the main square of the town. Each Allied officer had his own private cipher with his headquarters in Athens and each worked quite independently of the other. As Allies we had the function of making protests and giving orders to the resident Greek general. And there our alliance ceased.

As private persons we were a very happy family, for we were all congenial, and my arrival was the occasion of a most cheerful dinner-party. Our main task, apparently, was to satisfy General Sarrail, whose name was always spoken by the Frenchman in an awed whisper, that there was no Greek organisation developing to stab the Allied armies at Salonika in the back. How fatuous that delusion was I only found out later. At the time I believed it to be a probability. And even if it had been a fact, we should have fully and richly deserved it.

I set to work in the next few days in getting my bearings. I called on the Greek General in Command and inspected his lists of troops and material. I then notified Athens of what there was there and received orders to send southwards as many trains of troops and guns as would reduce the forces on the spot to the legitimate number. Why I was chosen, and not the Frenchman, for the main task of filling up trains with troops I do not know. But my first fortnight I busied myself with arranging with the Greek general how many troops would leave at a time, and on what days they should go. Then at the due time I would go to the station and see the troops entrained, and, finally, see them despatched.

Here were we three officers, a French captain, and a British and an Italian subaltern, giving orders to a Greek general and a garrison of Greek troops in a country which was not yet at war either with us or with anyone else. It was a situation so preposterous that now it is almost inconceivable.

Once a week I would see a train packed with troops, guns and shells, sent off southwards. A few days later we would ask for the garrison to be paraded and would solemnly count the numbers of men and calculate the amount of material, to see if it agreed with the numbers and the amount allowed to be left for purely formal and police purposes. After our counting we would inspect various barracks and sheds to see if any guns or rifles or material had been hidden. Often the numbers of troops was in excess and soon we found out the reason. The trains we saw off at the station would stop at some roadside station a few miles farther south and scores of the men would get out and walk back to Larissa!

But on the whole our calculations worked out in the long run. I would telegraph to Athens the number of men I had despatched and on arrival at Athens other Allied officers would count them. Then the consignment would be sent farther to Corinth and there left to its own devices and dealt with by the Greeks unhindered. As my trains left the station at Larissa the troops would burst into shouts, fire off their rifles in the air and yell together 'Long live Constantine!' We were doing everything we could to make Greeks rally round their king. But undoubtedly we had control and there was no conceivable danger from the Greek army, nor any hint now of an attack from the rear on General Sarrail.

But the French were dissatisfied. They smelt plots wherever they went. They hired agents and paid them for information. What they learned I can only surmise, but they made elaborate maps of Thessaly and marked crosses at all the places where arms were supposed to be hidden. Later on when, as I shall presently describe, Allied troops invaded Thessaly, I had the satisfaction of seeing those maps put to the acid test of examination on a geographical basis. All the places where arms were said to have been hidden were searched and out of many scores of marked places only one produced hidden arms, and those were fowling-pieces of great and venerable age! I had neither agents nor money with which to pay them, nor indeed the desire to use them. The Frenchmen spoke no language but French and I spoke Greek. So I became my own agent. And I was enormously helped by a splendid addition to my staff of one, in the shape of a soldier servant who had been sent to me from Salonika. He was, by prodigious good fortune, a Lancashireman, who had, somehow, been enrolled in the

Munster Regiment of the Irish Division. His soft northern accent and his unquenchable smile was a perpetual joy to me. What I could not find out for myself he always found out for me. His name, despite his natural Lancashire taciturnity, was Talks, a name I have never encountered before or since. 'Talks,' I said one day, 'I want you to go and get me some information about the views now held by the citizens of Larissa about the general state of affairs.' 'Right, sir,' he replied. 'Leave it to me.' He went into the town and spent the whole evening, far into the small hours, drinking and talking in the cafés. The invariable English-speaking Greeks collected round him in a circle and bombarded him with questions. His replies were, as he related them to me, masterpieces of tact. They had asked him when the British army was coming to occupy Larissa, how many troops would come, whether the British navy was defeated, why the Allies so disliked Constantine, and a hundred and one similar questions. He answered them all, stood them drinks, asked them questions in return and came back. From his account I was able to draw up an excellent report on the condition of Larissa, on the loyalty of its citizens, and on the views they held on current politics. The report, anyhow, was hardly worth the paper on which it was written, but nor were any reports on so insignificant a theme. Yet I knew that my information was first-hand and correct, while that of the French, which probably amounted to much the same sort of material, was highly coloured by the wild reports of their absurd agents and by their own fanatical prepossessions.

Private Talks of the Munster Regiment was a source of perpetual interest to me, and he was my one companion. It was an immense comfort to see his trim tall form and his good-looking face as he presented himself to me each morning and asked for my orders. He thoroughly enjoyed himself, and after a few weeks had learned to speak Greek quite well, sufficiently well, at any rate, to carry on amorous conversations with local beauties. He was, in any case, a far more creditable advertisement for British arms than the six coons in uniform from Senegal who formed the bodyguard of my French colleague.

In the spring evenings I would go and sit on a hill above the town where was a delightful open-air café. Below stretched the brief plain of Thessaly, and behind rose Olympus, overhanging and tremendous, very near at hand. I was now seeing Olympus from its southern and more magnificent side. I was now sitting at the very feet of the gods. But they gave no sign.

Unexpectedly a motor-cycle was delivered to me from Salonika and I now was able to career round to the remotest parts of Thessaly. I had never before ridden a motor-cycle in my life, but I spent some few days teaching myself, and soon became an adept. I visited Trikkala and Kalambaka and many wild and lonely regions. My machine was the joy of all the shepherds' dogs in Thessaly. As I puffed along the bad and beautiful roads of that shining plain, clouds of dust away in the distance on every hand would show me the approach of hungry and infuriated dogs of enormous size. They would snarl and snap and rage and gnash, but the spitting and banging of my engine discouraged them from coming to close quarters. Had I fallen off I have little doubt that my fate would have been unpleasant. Those that came too near I would hit with a length of rubber belting that I carried in my hand; every journey was to run the gauntlet.

My travels on that admirable machine took me to every place where suspicious doings had been reported by my French colleague. By careful conversation and discreet enquiry I was able to confute almost every report he received. There were rumours of the formation of bands of irregulars. So off I would go to the suspected village and descend in a cloud of dust unexpectedly upon it. That, to me, was far and away the best form of intelligence work. Go and look for yourself was my principal rule of conduct. Often I found out that a few brigands, or amateur brigands, had appeared in some town and boasted of how they were going to snipe at Frenchmen, but it seldom proved to be more than braggadocio. And who would not have wanted to boast in such a way when he was certain that in a few hours the story would be related to the French by some hired agent? What fun those brigands must have had, for the French had brigands on the brain. 'Il faut dépister les franc-tireurs!' my colleague would say in the voice of an arch-conspirator. 'Le Général Sarrail insiste pour que nous cherchions partout pour les comitadjis.' It was the old nightmare of attack from behind, though how any intelligent general could have thought that a few hundred shepherds and bootboys from Thessalian villages could have been a menace to Allied might is beyond me.

So we continued into the early summer. Every evening we dined together in the one and only restaurant of Larissa and shared our news. My two colleagues were both charming and entertaining, and we presented outwardly a picture of Allied solidarity. Indeed the Greeks habitually referred to us in their local newspapers as the 'Anglogauls.' One day a peasant in a remote village referred to me alone, during the course of conversation, as an 'Anglogaul.' In vain I protested that I was an Angle and not a Gaul, and that each came from a separate country. But he would have none of it. 'Nonsense,' he replied, 'everyone knows quite well that there is a country called Anglogallia.' And with that I let it be.

We had much time on our hands, and one trip stands out as a most delightful memory. The Frenchman, together with two other French officers who had come for a night, decided to have a picnic in the Gorge of Tempe which we had not as yet visited. Our party consisted of me on the motor-cycle and the French in a Ford. Off we went across the plain towards the vale. The road through that exquisite gorge is a massive rocky path covered with mountainous slabs of rock, impassable for a carriage. But, by careful coaxing and much labour, I persuaded my motor-cycle to get through, and the Ford did as well. We halted at the seaward side and enjoyed a most delicious lunch under the plane trees by the river. I am certain that I am the first man who has ever ridden through Tempe on a motor-cycle.

News began to reach us of stirrings at Salonika. Our orders hinted that Le Général Sarrail was getting more and more dissatisfied with the behaviour of Constantine and his people. Charges of organisation of irregulars began to appear in official communiqués at Salonika. I knew only too well how untrue they were, but I knew also that my French colleague was perpetually sending in absurd rumours and reports of brigands in the hills of Pindus. Sarrail was getting more and more uneasy, or else, as I had already begun to suspect, he was preparing the way for a descent upon Greece in order to eject King Constantine. He was following the age-old rule of warfare of accusing the enemy of what you propose to do yourself. The Germans had accused the French and Belgians in 1914 of the violation of frontiers, and at Ypres in 1915 the German communiqué announced a day before their first gas attack that the French and British had used gas.[1] Here was the same hoary old trick. Nor were the Greeks deceived. They had long suspected a descent by the French, and suddenly it began to develop into something more than a mere suspicion.

I was warned from Athens to expect developments, but was not told what to expect. The Frenchman was mysterious and secretive. Then news began to filter into the Greek newspapers which I watched very closely. People who had managed to cross the forbidden Neutral Zone at Olympus told their friends in southern Greece of movements of French troops on the foothills north of Olympus. Indeed, Olympus

[1] Liddell-Hart: *The Real War*, p. 195. The German wireless of 17th April accused the British of using gas-shells and gas-bombs.

was now the centre of more stirrings and martial comings and goings than when the gods had mobilised to go to Troy.

Suddenly the blow was struck. One evening as we all sat at dinner I saw agitated Greeks dining at other tables gesticulating wildly, and getting every moment more and more excited. 'French troops are at Kozani,' I heard one say. 'They have reached Tyrnavo,' said another—and Tyrnavo was the nearest pass from Olympus, barely fifteen miles off. There was a general uproar, while we sat as if we knew nothing. Indeed we were in a rather ridiculous position. Here we had lived as the accredited representatives of the Allies in a friendly but neutral country, and we and our neutral friends alike were about to be invaded by a French army. We were like spies in a land shortly to be occupied by our employers. Our position had become farcical—or rather more farcical than before.

The next morning we awoke to see a troop of French cavalry halted in the square. Rough dusty soldiers in steel helmets, very warlike. Our town was under military occupation. I dressed hastily and went out.

Away over the plain rumbled guns and transport: aeroplanes hummed overhead and infantry battalions soon appeared and camped in the offing. I went with my colleagues to present myself to the colonel of the French cavalry, who had just entered the town, to place myself at his disposal. He was a most capable and charming officer. 'Good,' he said. 'Since you speak Greek and know the officers of the garrison, come with me and we will occupy the barracks at once.' Off we went in a car followed by a troop of Spahis Marocains at the gallop. Other armaments brought up the rear.

At the barracks I found the wretched Greek garrison in the last stages of despair. I knew all the officers well enough and was on good terms with them. 'Tell us,' they said, 'are we going to be treated as enemies in an occupied country? What do the French want of us? We have carried out our obligations faithfully, and now they send a whole division of troops in fighting array to occupy our country.' 'Don't worry,' I replied, 'I know that well enough, but at the moment the best thing you can do is to obey the French colonel and do exactly as he orders.' Here, indeed, was a situation which amounted to a gross breach of faith. I and my colleagues had been sent here to control the despatch of Greek troops from this region southwards. The garrison had been denuded from about a division to a mere battalion, by agreement with the Greek Government, and here were the French, under Sarrail, now using that situation to their advantage. All this panoply of war, a full French division, could now do what it liked in Thessaly without hindrance. The opposition had been removed. Had the full Greek force been here no French division could have invaded Thessaly without considerable fighting, and the Greeks were good enough soldiers to have been able to hold the Olympus passes against invasion for a long time. And now here were the French about to take the small garrison prisoners although they had shown no opposition.

I tried to pacify the Greek officers. They sent me a request to treat for them with the French colonel. The colonel said to me, 'Tell the Greek officers to come to me and hand over their swords.' I conveyed the message. 'Ask the colonel,' said the Greeks, 'if we may break our swords before giving them up.' Things were moving from melodrama to farce—and rapidly. I began to wonder if farce would give place to tragedy. 'Tell the Greeks,' said the colonel, 'that I don't mind in what condition their swords may be as long as they are given up.' This I told the Greeks, who promptly broke their swords across their knees and heaped them up in a pile in the barrack square. I felt ashamed and sorry. But I must admit that the French colonel was tactful and agreeable and merely carrying out orders. The Spahis were ranged in a row in the courtyard. We stood by conversing. Suddenly a cloud of dust in the offing announced a messenger. A little officer tumbled off his horse at our feet and saluted. He was with one of the patrols that had been sent to surround the barracks, but the movement had been incompetently carried out. He clicked his heels and said, with all the effect a dramatic situation can have, and with a manner and gesture which only a Frenchman can produce for a dramatic and startling moment, 'On nous échappe, mon colonel!' The colonel, a true soldier, rapped out a command. The Spahis unloosed their long hair, like ancient Spartans, loaded their carbines, unhitched their swords and started off at the gallop towards the open downland from which our messenger had come. Further commands brought an armoured car and two ·75 field guns into rapid action. Here was a battle developing before our very eyes. I asked what exactly had happened. A troop of soldiers, led by a Greek colonel bearing the regimental colours, I learned, had been sighted heading southwards as hard as they could go. Poor devils, I thought, they are wise to try to get out of the hands of the French. But the party of pursuit was swift. We waited. The guns and cavalry vanished in a cloud of dust. Soon we saw them open out as they topped the rising ground. Then we heard the crack of rifles and the rattle of machine-guns. The Greek officers with whom I had just been talking shivered in apprehension. They told me that it was probably the colonel of the Evzones and a company of his men who had made the escape. For there were two units at Larissa, a half-battalion of ordinary infantry and a half-battalion of crack troops, the kilted Evzones or highlanders.

The rifle-fire died down. Soon a procession of troops was sighted returning. Here were the Spahis and their prisoners. About two hundred Greek soldiers, dishevelled and exhausted appeared, and ahead of them the colonel, a little plump angry man, lion-hearted and raging. By his side on each hand was a fiery Moroccan trooper, one holding his revolver and the other the regimental standard. It was a humiliating spectacle, as much for me as for him. I asked for further information from the French.

The Greeks, it seemed, like good soldiers, seeing the hostile French force approaching them in battle formation, had themselves taken up a position on an old Turkish fortress on a hill, and had opened fire on the French. They had killed nine French troopers and one French officer. The French had sabred and machine-gunned about fifty Greeks.

This was the famous Battle of Larissa, which I call famous because it was the only engagement during the course of the war that was never mentioned. The French described how *franc-tireurs* in Larissa had fired on the advancing French troops and how in retaliation the French had fired back. In fact it was a battle provoked by the French for no reason of any kind. If the Greeks had escaped, their retreat should have been cut off and then the French should have sent to treat with them. There was no justification for this flagrant attack upon retreating neutral troops. I was the only Englishman there in Larissa, with the exception of a consular representative who had recently arrived. No one saw this battle except myself and the French. Had I not been there no news of it would ever have been divulged.

The troops returned with their captives. The corpses of the French were carried back in state. The Greek dead were hastily buried where they fell so that the Greek inhabitants should never know the number of the killed. We returned to the town. The remaining Greek troops were marched from the barracks by the French and interned in a French camp. As we moved away from the scene a French officer who was standing near said casually, 'On va fusiller tous les prisonniers à six heures ce soir.' I could hardly believe my ears. The French were by now insane enough for any absurdity, but the shooting of nearly two hundred uniformed soldiers seemed to suggest a kind of mania better dealt with at once. I approached the colonel and asked him if it was true. 'General Sarrail has ordered us,' he replied, 'to shoot at once without trial all Greeks found firing on French troops.' 'Does that include uniformed Greek soldiers?' I asked him. 'No distinctions were made,' he replied. 'Then will you allow me, *mon* colonel,' I added, 'to lodge a formal protest against what will certainly be ranked as an atrocity, if it occurs.' The colonel looked at me, blinked, and turned away. One of his subalterns turned to me and said in a furious undertone, 'Moi, si j'étais le colonel, j'aurais répondu "fichez le camp."' 'If you had been the colonel in question,' I replied, 'I should have found it necessary to address myself to someone more intelligent.'

It was clear that this was not a poor French joke. They did at one moment really intend to shoot those Greeks. The orders of General Sarrail specifically entitled them to do so. I mobilised the help of the British Consular representative, an Englishman whom the Legation had recently sent here to observe what was happening. His presence was most fortunate. I notified the Italian of my protest, but he said it was not a matter for him, and he slipped away and I never saw him again.

The townspeople also had now received the story that the garrison was to be shot *en masse*. They assembled excitedly in the square.

They believed firmly that it was going to be done and they were all far too frightened to do anything except to turn out and watch events.

But the French abandoned their hot-tempered project. They merely maltreated their prisoners, as I saw with my own eyes. They knew, however, that within certain limits they were safe to do as they liked. No news of their actions could leak out for a long time, for they had cut the railway line to Athens and stopped all traffic, occupied the post office and got control of the telegraphic lines and seized the only port of Thessaly, Volo, on the great Gulf of Volo.

Except for the presence of myself and the consul, there were no foreigners to observe their actions. Whatever the Greeks might have said afterwards they would have denied. But I fancy that we two were an embarrassment. But they had got us safely shut up in any case. I applied for permission to go to Athens by train, for I knew that they were running certain trains of French troops southwards. I was refused. There was, of course, no wireless, and, even if there had been, I should not have been allowed to use it. It was urgent that I should report the developments to British headquarters at Athens. I was received with exquisite politeness but told that I could not leave. It was vastly entertaining to find myself, an ally, treated as an enemy, but by now I was fairly used to the ways of the French.

They could not, however, restrict my local movements. I went to Volo, with my faithful orderly Talks the Lancashireman, and there started on a new line of inquiry. I found there that there had recently been installed a British port patrol, who had their own wireless. I explained to the young naval officer that it was a matter of urgency that some British representatives of importance should be present to observe developments. We managed to send a wireless message to this effect to Lemnos to the naval headquarters. Meanwhile the French proceeded to a drastic occupation of the town and posted proclamations threatening dire penalties on any who were found in the possession of arms. One such proclamation I still have. It states that the French authorities knew exactly where arms were hidden and proposed to arrest the occupants of the houses where they were hidden unless the arms were voluntarily given up. Nervous peasants came along with antique fowling-pieces and blunderbusses dating from the War of Independence, but hardly anything else appeared. In due course the search was made at all the spots where the French knew there were arms. As I have already described, almost nothing was found in any of the suspect areas. That was one of the best proofs I came across in the war of the futility of information bought from spies.

Within a few hours of our sending our urgent message, to our joy, we saw a small slim cruiser slip quietly into harbour and drop anchor. The commander was a man of considerable seniority and he came at once to visit the French commander. His rank actually made him senior to the Frenchman, who was embarrassed and troubled by the visit. Indeed, the arrival of the ship was most opportune, for it showed the French that we were taking notice of their actions in these parts.

I explained the situation to the commander and he told me to get on board and come back with him to Lemnos.

Tired of being an *embusqué* I was delighted to leave.

Once more we set out under the lee of Olympus, and sped swiftly across the Aegean to Lemnos. There I found a small tug which was leaving for Athens. It was a North Sea trawler, with a small gun mounted aft. Its crew were rough fishermen from Hull and they were glad to see a new face. We bounced over the waves in the summer heat-haze and passed once more all those lovely Greek islands. The crew and skipper, who had uniforms but preferred to wear their civilian clothes, were a cheerful and blasphemous band. We fed at meals in the tiny cabin off huge beefsteaks and Yorkshire pudding, as if we were in the cold winds of the North Sea: I dripped with perspiration, but did my best with this British fare. They told me how they were engaged on mine-sweeping and explained how they worked their gun and how they had an armoury of rifles and bayonets. They were no easy prey for a submarine.

* * * * * * *

The day the French had occupied Larissa, Constantine had announced his abdication, and he was succeeded at once by his son Alexander, that ill-fated youth who, a few years later, was to die of septic poisoning caused by the bite of a pet monkey. In all Greek history there was never a more fateful thing than that monkey-bite, for it led to the return of Constantine from exile, to the ejection of Venizelos, to the open hostility of the French and the non-support of the British in 1922: it led thence to the collapse of the Greek army in Asia Minor, the massacre of Smyrna where 80,000 Greeks were killed, to the Treaty of Lausanne, and to the establishment of the New Turkey under Mustafa Kemal. No monkey could conceivably hope to achieve more. Had Alexander never died the whole course of events would have been different and Greece to-day would probably have held Smyrna, there would have been no Royalist-Venizelos split, and Constantine would never have returned. He had become by now a *bête noire* of the French and Italians, who moulded the whole course of their foreign policy upon his personality. Had Alexander not died, Constantine would never have recovered his throne, only to be ejected by his own people and to die in exile, ruined and disappointed. He would probably have lived in comfort as a distinguished ex-king, along with all the rest that were thrown up after the storms of war, like rubbish on a seashore.

Athens was now fully occupied by French, British, and Russian troops. The Russian troops presented a curious spectacle. The Revolution in Russia had now succeeded beyond even its own hopes, and here were four thousand Russian soldiers, sent from Salonika, supposed to represent Russia in its pre-Revolution guise of Protecting Power of Greece. But the soldiers all knew that their country was now under another régime. They marched in splendid military array through the streets of Athens to their camp and then dismissed their officers, who promptly, and for their own safety, all went to live at the chief hotel in Athens, and did not leave its precincts until the Russian troops finally left. We learnt that the Russian soldiers then elected Councils of Soldiers who controlled discipline. It was the first we saw of the Russian revolution in actual fact. These

Russian troops had been on the Salonika front for a year and a half. They had held a sector away in the west near Albania. There they had fought well, but had later been taken out of the line owing to fears of their loyalty. They were sent to Athens to indicate the solidarity of the Allies to the world. In fact they used their trip to Athens as a means of making their revolution effective, and so got rid of their officers. Their new Councils ruled them with a rule of iron and we had nothing to complain of. They punished insubordination and drunkenness with a severity far greater than that which their old officers had used. They invented one punishment for drunkards which was particularly savage—they merely stripped them of all clothing and put them in barbed wire enclosures to roast in the Athenian June sun! Of course they took no part in the actual occupation of Athens which now occurred, but they were kept isolated in their camp until at last the French transferred them to a ship and sent them off to Algeria, whence after the Armistice they returned to Russia.

Venizelos had descended from Salonika with his Provisional Government. He was Prime Minister once more. Constantine had left hurriedly by night for Italy. Alexander I of Greece, his youngest son, was now King.

French troops bivouacked in the squares and streets of Athens and mounted machine-guns at every corner. French infantrymen camped on the Acropolis, and I watched them cooking their meals by large fires which they built against the fallen columns of the Parthenon. Here was barbarism once more encamped in the City of Light. Greece, after trying so hard to be neutral, had been driven to adopt the guise of an enemy, entirely against her own wishes and for no intelligent reason that I, who had watched so carefully the development of affairs, could detect. The whole thing was sheer lunacy.

The results, however, were soon evident. Greece declared formal war on Germany, Turkey, and Austria, and her statesmen set about mobilising a new army which was to proceed at once to Salonika as reinforcements of the Allies. None of the Greeks really wanted to fight, except a few who had faithfully followed Venizelos from the first, and had formed the three divisions of Crete, the Islands, and Serres, which had already been in action in Macedonia. Six new divisions were now to be formed, and it was definitely certain that the men recruited for them would consist almost entirely of citizens of Greece who had been bullied, blockaded, starved and threatened by the Allies for the past year. No intelligent soldier needed to think for long to realise that out of such lukewarm material you will not easily, at the close of an embittered and devastating war, make military material which will rush upon the enemy with shouts of patriotic fervour.

I was to see these new Greek divisions later, and watch them as they came into action in the Struma valley. We were to gather the fruits of our behaviour and to learn that Greeks of all people will not be driven to fight, though, when they choose to fight, they can be better soldiers than most.

My task in Greece was done in any case. Nor did I wish to stay to see this gross humiliation of a brave people, who were forced to go to war to satisfy mighty nations who were merely looking desperately for new supplies of cannon-fodder.

I hastened back to Salonika by the railway, which had recently been completed, wondering what had been brewing in my valley during my absence from active service on this wild-goose chase. I had been masquerading as a non-combatant too long.

CHAPTER X

FIRE

Returned to Salonika, I bade farewell to my faithful and charming soldier from Lancashire, whom I regret to say I have never seen from that day to this; he went to his regiment, which was immediately sent to Palestine.

I was lodged in a camp and told to await orders. The next day I spent in looking thoroughly at the old city, which I had not yet had time to study in detail. I roamed round its mighty battlements and looked at its lovely Byzantine churches. My camp was far away to the west, on the road to the Vardar river. That evening I walked along the sea-front towards G.H.Q. and noticed that a house almost in the centre of the town had caught fire. No one seemed to be doing anything much, and I imagined that it would soon be burnt out. Some cook, I was told, had upset a frying-pan full of oil, and the blaze had burned the house. As I walked along the front I watched the officers on leave dining with nurses in comfort and luxury in the open windows of the only large hotel. The sun was setting over the great mass of Olympus, a strong summer breeze had sprung up, and the waves of the harbour were breaking over the quay. I went on to General Headquarters to see if orders had come for me. When I returned to walk back to my camp, I saw great sheets of flame rising from the heart of the city, with clouds of black smoke rising high and wide. I reached the hotel on the quay front to find a great wall of flame that barred my advance. The hotel itself, where two hours before I had seen those happy diners, was a sheet of fire. Long flames were licking over to the very boats in the harbour against the quay and I saw several large fishing smacks burst into flame, with their sails afire, and break from their moorings to drift out to sea. The city was burning in its very heart and there was no kind of organisation ready to save it. In another half-hour the whole place was ablaze. It was one of the most stupendous spectacles I have ever seen. I hastened back to Headquarters to be told that every officer was to do what seemed to himself the best thing to help. I and another officer started off for the city, armed with our revolvers, for we knew that there would be heavy looting, with such a rabble as Salonika possessed ready to rob and steal.

I started on my career by attempting to direct traffic along the main roads. My friend went to a point farther on and did the same. After a time I noticed a stupendous jam of traffic, and at length realised that my friend and I had been directing traffic on to each other. With immense difficulty we disentangled it.

About midnight I decided to return to my camp for some sleep. I had to climb right up to the steep upper part of the city and make an enormous detour by way of the walls. From these upper heights I was able to look down on the fire from the battlements. It was like looking into the heart of a glowing volcano. The ancient walls were lit up with a red outline, the harbour reflected the red glare, and there in the centre of all was a vast conflagration spreading slowly and slowly in every direction. I contrived to climb round the upper parts of the city, picking my way through the rows of terrified inhabitants, who, as though accustomed to a hundred sacks and loots and burnings of past ages, had automatically brought out their bedding, and were sleeping in the roadways. They watched, dumb and fascinated, at the slow burning of their ancient home.

I snatched a few hours' sleep at the camp and returned at dawn. Things were at last being done in a half-hearted way to stop the fire. But the actions of the various Allies were not exactly concerted to one useful end. The Italians marched their troops out of the city as soon as possible and camped them on the hills. The few Russians who then remained, marched into the city, piled their arms, found sacks and commenced to loot. The French organised services of lorries who started to collect the refugees—at a rather high charge per refugee—and they sent patrols of cavalry who rode up and down with bared swords among the fleeing people. The British contrived to find a fire-engine, the only one in the city, and with it they started to try to put the fire out! Thus did we all behave according to our lights. We were the great Powers of Europe showing the Greeks what to do! I found the fire-engine up a side street, but so great was the crowd of onlookers that several hundred people were standing on the fire-hose and no water was emerging. Next I found a squad of Greek soldiers, apparently lost and without an officer. I took command of them, which they seemed to like, for they were tired of doing nothing, and told them to clear the street of the crowd and free the fire-hose. They did their task with alacrity. Fixing their bayonets they charged down the street and had it clear in a few seconds. I posted them at different points and told them to go on dispersing any similar crowd that might collect. They smiled, saluted and looked as if they were proud at last to do something which might conceivably save their city. Then I left them, and, for all I know, they may be there still, like the faithful guard at Pompeii!

As I was walking away I saw the great form of General Sarrail. He was walking up to inspect the fire. With his mop of grey hair, his enormous figure (he stood over six feet three) and his quick intelligent face, he gave no sign of the mania that had so long raged in his brain. He looked cynically over the blazing ruins and walked away.

Later the French sent dynamiting parties of sailors to isolate the burning area. But all that they dynamited, as far as I could discover, was the Armenian store, some miles outside the danger zone, which had for three years so grossly overcharged us in our purchases of delicacies and clothes, that it had long been a byword for extortion. On the whole we were all glad to see it dynamited, though the excuse that it was in the danger zone was a thin one.

It was evident that we could really do nothing to stop the fire. It had to run its course like some fell disease. Fortunately, there was little which was of strictly military importance in the burnt or in the threatened area except the post office, which at the outset had been hurriedly cleared of its contents.

That night I and my friend went again into the burning area. We had been told to help the British police in their task of clearing houses of their inhabitants. Most of the people in and near the burning area were the Spanish Jews, for whom Salonika is famous. There they all were dumb and stupid with fear and alarm. There they would sit in their houses until the very walls got hot and the woodwork began to crackle. They seemed spell-bound by some strange Oriental spell. But they had to be saved from being burned alive. I entered one house and tried to persuade the ancient Jew and his concourse of daughters, and his wife and other relatives, to leave. They would not answer a word to my request. There they sat silent and weeping, while the flames were licking the walls of the room in which they sat. There was no time to lose, so I drew my revolver and pointed it at the old man, telling him to start moving at once. This seemed to wake him, and he rose and bustled his family out into the street with wails and strange animal cries of despair. Several other houses I had to clear in this drastic way, but soon the area of my operations was ablaze and I had to leave.

Farther along I found a drunkard, wildly gesticulating and crashing about the street. What he was, Greek, Jew or Turk, I never discovered, for he was too drunk to speak. After a vain attempt to prevent him from walking into the fire, I succeeded in persuading him to lie down and sleep in the courtyard of a small mosque. An hour later I passed near this part again and saw that the whole mosque was burning. I rather fear that my drunken friend must have been wholly consumed.

Some organisation began to emerge. The refugees from the fire were being taken to clean and well-arranged camps far outside the town. There was a serious risk of an outbreak of disease which might spread to the whole army. For Salonika was our one and only base of supplies and our link with home.

In another two days the fire burnt itself out and we were left with the ashes. To have to reorganise the city while we were engaged in a war was added trouble to our already increasing cares.

When the fire was at its height a squadron of German aeroplanes flew over, curious to see what was causing all this vast cloud of smoke. They saw what they wanted, dropped a few bombs just to help things on, and flew back again.

The spectacle of a civilised city, occupied by British and French and Italians, being allowed to burn itself out to ashes, was in itself one of the indications of the way in which destruction had become part and parcel of our lives. We none of us minded much, nor did we think it extraordinary that nothing should have been done to stop the fire at its inception. We were all so used to the burning of cities and villages and farms that it meant little or nothing to see a whole city consumed through sheer carelessness. The love of sheer destruction that grows in all children had been allowed now to grow and flourish again in the minds of grown men all over the world. I was as unmoved by the spectacle of this perishing city as if it were a mere display of fireworks. It was lovely to look at, one of the loveliest sights I have ever seen. But the destruction did not shock me in the least. And I was only faintly regretful when I learned that the church of St Demetrius, one of the most perfect examples of Byzantine architecture, had been burnt down. The destruction of everything was by now so habitual an experience to me that the destruction of the beautiful only caused a faint pang of regret. For the love of beauty, like all other such civilised activities of the mind, had almost left me. I was by now just an automaton, which worked and lived for one single purpose, the carrying out of such military orders as would be likely to bring the war to an end. I had long ago, though then I never knew it, merged my personality in the personality of the war itself. If anyone thinks that it is a literary fancy to attribute a personality to the war, he has not known war. That long war developed after a time a personality of its own. It was like the personality of an unscrupulous blackmailer. Just when you are settling down happily to a quiet life, he launches his preposterous demand which you must obey or perish. You are in his grasp from the very start. No moment of your waking life is free from a thought of him, and at nights you awake only to be recalled to your servitude. If you start to read a book or to enjoy the beauty of a work of art he is there at your side, whispering his obscene threats into your ear. If you pause to breathe in the loveliness of a scene or to respond to the beauty of a human action, his breath taints the air around you. You have no freedom of mind nor any hope of independence. Your soul is his, and your very heart-beats depend upon his charity.

No wonder I could gaze at the exquisite beauty of Greece or of the blue hills of the Balkans and get no refreshment from them. No wonder that I could find no meaning in fine books or in lovely masterpieces of art. No wonder that my spirit had the texture of lead and the quality of dust. War is said by some to be ennobling, but I found it to be merely a crushing weight that slowly squeezed out the essence of existence and left the tasteless pulp. War may have positive merits for some, but I do not know who they are and I never met them in those frantic years.

I am not trying to explain how my soul was seared by

the horrors of war. It was not. What was really happening was that I was, by now, entirely unable to see why there should not be such horrors in the ordinary course of daily life. There seemed nothing unusual to me now in wholesale slaughter and in widespread destruction. My mind and spirit had been levelled down to the level at which civilisation is hardly existent at all. I had come to accept everything as normal, much as the prisoner in the dungeon after a lapse of years takes his life as normal. The only tragedy of the war was that we young men did not even begin to realise the wantonness and hideousness of what was going on. We did not realise it because we had been in the affair from the start and had gradually become accustomed to it all. They say that the human constitution can accustom itself to almost any poison as long as it commences to absorb it by small doses which are gradually increased. That was what had in fact happened to me. I remember with what detachment and calm I observed the total destruction of a great city by fire. There seemed nothing very odd about it and the sufferings of the inhabitants struck me as rather exaggerated. But then at that time I had no property or home of my own to lose. That was the trouble. None of us youngsters had much in England in the way of property, and so we could not learn to respect the property of others, or to sympathise with them in its loss. War is always an affair of young men, and the same consequence will always follow inevitably as long as young men are made into soldiers. If the generals and politicians were made to fight there would be far less destruction.

CHAPTER XI

IMPENDING EVENTS

"As a result of the collapse of the Macedonian front, entailing the weakening of our reserves in the West . . . there exists, according to all human calculation, no further prospect of compelling the enemy to sue for peace."
—Von Hindenburg, 3rd October 1918.

THE summer was ending. Allied fortunes were in process of vast upheaval. The game proceeded with speed. More and more supplies of men were now being sought for to throw into these furnaces of destruction known so euphemistically as Theatres of War. Rumania had gone out like a candle, but now her place was taken by Greece. Russia had, to our astonishment and fear, vanished overnight like a cloud. But these things counted for so little, since in the early summer, in April, America had thrown down the glove and, with all her millions of potential troops, was in for good. The German fortress was more than intact, it was repaired and rearmed, but now we had millions more men to hurl at its walls. For men were by now considered as little more than projectiles. I often wonder if America knew that the Allies and Germans alike were still infected with such madness that they had not yet given up the idea of storming fortresses with man-power instead of with machines. Only at length did the invention, all too late, of tanks show that machines must be used to break walls of steel and concrete. America must have known, but they too believed that men with bayonets will cut through concrete and steel. Hardly had the first American troops come into action than I heard of the death of one of my friends, Robert Bland, of my age, a Rhodes scholar at my college at Oxford, the only American who was President of the Oxford Union. The toll was a heavy one on that group of friends from those distant days. Almost none was left now.

Winter was on us again. I went back to my valley, to find now that large sections of the front had been taken over by Greek troops, all of these newly formed divisions—troops of admirable quality, but troops inspired by no feeling that they were fighting for the preservation of their country. They knew, what we knew well enough, that they were merely more material for the universal slaughter.

At the very end of the year I was sent back to Headquarters and appointed to the General Staff, under that brilliant soldier Colonel Heywood, to be in charge of that section of the Intelligence System that depended upon direct evidence, that is to say, upon the statements of prisoners, upon captured documents, upon aeroplane reconnaissance, and upon direct observation. Other officers dealt with the more obscure forms of intelligence work, such as that which is derived from the deciphering of enemy wireless messages, that which is obtained from spies, and secret means of communication.

I had learned in France, and earlier here, to deride the staff and to look on their life as one of gilded ease, and now I was one of the despised. But I soon learned that efficient staff work means fifteen hours' work a day, and that unless a staff officer is constantly in the front line, finding out what he can, he can do no work worth doing.

What made my work so exciting was that now I knew in advance of every move of our troops along the whole front, and, further, that I was able to learn what was going on in every theatre of war. Telegrams from the War Office and a weekly intelligence summary, that was known only to the army headquarters in each theatre of war, now illuminated me as to the whole of the Allied and German position. No day passed without its scare or its excitement. October had already shown that the Allied front might at any moment collapse into ruin, and 1918 dawned with ominous suggestions of vast German offensives. The collapse of Russia had let loose all Germany upon us, and we had as yet no effective answer until America should intervene in enormous strength. Our policy was to hold on.

Early in the year I was warned that something was brewing on the front and that the Bulgarians were suspected of preparing a spring offensive. I organised a system of photographing all the main centres of importance behind the enemy lines, and of searching for new ones. After a time I was in a position to know every detail of the Bulgarian supply system. What was not made clear from photographs we obtained from prisoners. Then we had each vital spot photographed twice a week regularly to see if there was any increase of supplies or of movement. Railway stations would show new sidings or perhaps large heaps of supplies. Camps would increase or decrease in size. Roads would show more wear and tear and more movement. I was now to unify all the varied information that came from every section of the front. After a week or two it was perfectly evident that the Bulgarians had some great plan afoot. All our evidence suggested it. Railways were immensely active. The tell-tale photographs showed enormous increases of supplies, and prisoners told us of new movements and new orders. Documents captured on the dead showed the presence of new units and newly mobilised classes of soldiers. I visited all the observation posts in the line from the Vardar river, where we joined with the French, to the Struma, and warned observers to redouble their watch. I watched myself at all points where railways and important roads could be seen behind the enemy line.

On one occasion as I was watching, with some gunners in a forward post, the Bulgars opened a heavy bombardment in the small ravine just behind our post. My road back lay through this ravine and I was in a hurry to get on to another job. My gunner friends, as we watched the explosion of heavy shells in the ravine all round the roadway, smiled sardonically to think of a staff officer running such deadly risks. I said I preferred to wait until it was over, having myself none of the heroism that leads to rash risks! But I could not wait indefinitely, and as the bombardment continued I saw little prospect of getting back. However, after a time, the shells ceased for a few minutes. Then they started again and fell at intervals of about three minutes in a less violent bombardment.

Choosing the moment when a salvo had just exploded I jumped into my car and drove at full speed down the road. At the bottom of the ravine was a sharp bend in the road where it turned to ascend the steep side; here I had to slow down almost to walking pace and, as I turned, hoping that the next salvo would not arrive, my hosts waved derisively at me and cheered. I waved back and speeded up the slope to hear the next salvo arrive too late to catch me.

Another of my various tasks was to select from the elaborate intelligence map which we had prepared a weekly list of targets for the bombers of the Air Force. This gave me at the time a source of interest which I should find it difficult now to recapture. For one day I would select a bridge or an ammunition dump, for another a village filled with the billets of the enemy; for another a Headquarters or transport lines. Our greatest success was the destruction of an enormous dump at Hudovo, on the Upper Vardar. Here photographs taken after the dropping of the bombs showed an immense conflagration. This sheer destruction was a source of the greatest satisfaction to me. It all seemed like a genial game of "You drop bombs on me: I drop them on you." To be able to choose the targets for this costly sport made me feel I was getting some return for the innumerable explosives which had been hurled at myself on various occasions.

After some intensive work on the various evidence which had accumulated I was able to come to the conclusion that the Bulgarians were preparing an offensive due to start some time in March 1918. In due course these results were embodied in a full report for the Commander-in-Chief. At the same time we were able to get information through from deserters from the Bulgar lines which more or less confirmed it. But things were moving now rapidly towards a conclusion. The War Office telegrams and reports notified us of the impending German offensive in France. In early March the reports pointed to a tremendous attempt on the part of Germany to break the lines that encircled her. I remember the excitement with which we read the report that notified us and all the British armies on all fronts that a German attack in force was expected about the 20th of March. Here was good intelligence work being used to the best advantage. But we could do nothing but merely wait upon our own events. We strengthened our defences to the utmost and watched. The Bulgar preparations increased.

But March opened and nothing had happened. The days went past, and then came the news of the great German offensive in France. It was agonising to read the daily telegrams of repeated retirement and of persistent German advance. It was like watching our own fate hanging in the balance, for we knew that if the French front broke then we would be left high and dry, marooned in a world of defeat, perhaps unable to get home for years.

Daily we waited for the Bulgarian offensive to develop in sympathy with the German. But nothing happened. The Bulgars, as we found out later, had delayed their move in order to judge whether the German attempt was going to succeed. When at the end of April it was clear that the Germans had not won a smashing victory, the Bulgars decided to sit tight and wait indefinitely. King Ferdinand was too sly a rascal to risk an attack against us until he was assured that his masters had started the ball well rolling. Nor indeed had the Bulgars now that numerical superiority which would have carried them to victory against positions so strong as ours. Now there was the Serbian army, waiting its time, watching for the moment when they could drive the invaders of their land back again and exterminate those who had ruled their country with such a rod of iron. Those Serbians, with their indomitable courage and iron resolution, were the enemies whom the Bulgars feared far more than us or the French. For they had ejected almost an entire nation from Serbia and driven them into exile. Meantime they had embarked on a policy of complete subjugation of the land of Serbia, designed to make it harmless and servile for ever. So grim and cruel had Bulgarian domination of the land they occupied been, that in the autumn of 1917 there had been an insurrection of the Serbians who remained, who could not tolerate any longer the manner of Bulgarian control. This insurrection had been followed by the wholesale massacre of Serbian inhabitants who were thought to be implicated, with every conceivable barbarity. For the Bulgarian, when master, is a savage and uncivilised master. I have with me still evidence of the wholesale hanging and shooting of civilians in Serbian villages in Bulgarian hands. Old men, women, and children alike were killed without mercy. The Bulgars were filled with that madness, now so widespread, which was leading them to their own destruction. The news of the insurrection reached the Serbian army and did more to inspire them with determination to destroy the Bulgarian army for ever than any propaganda which we could have made. The Allied armies at Salonika, instead of being depressed or anxious at the long and weary years of war, began to stir into movement as though, like a tired horse, they had seen the distant goal.

We now had Greek divisions in the Struma valley, which had come to replace our own troops, some of which had gone off to Palestine, and others of whom had been moved into reserve. One of my many tasks was to keep a watch on these Greek troops to see if there were any signs of depreciation. In any case they were bad troops, because they were almost entirely from Southern Greece, conscripts driven against their will once more into a war the purposes of which they either openly disapproved of or did not understand.

There were cases of desertion to the Bulgarian army. One Greek officer went over with a complete set of our most important maps. Ordinary infantrymen, tired to death of the wrangles of the Allies, walked across—and who were we that we should blame them? We had bullied their country out of its neutrality, infringed its sovereign rights, exiled their king, and now we had put them into uniform—for which the Greek people paid—and thrust them into trenches. It was little use after all this to tell them that they were fighting their hereditary enemy. By now they were convinced that the French, and in a less degree ourselves, were far more their enemies than the Bulgar.

Anxiously we watched these raw divisions sitting entrenched among the ruins of the villages which we had demolished, speculating on the advantages of fighting other people's battles.

On the mountainous Doiran front were the other Greek troops, now veterans, who had come in with us when Venizelos first came over to our side on the occasion of the revolution, when Greece had been divided into two parts by the Neutral Zone. These were lion-hearted men, whose main objective was to win back for Greece the lands which Bulgaria had taken from her.

The news improved. Things were moving to victory in Palestine. In France, the Germans were stopped for good. Still, however, the Germans were an unbeaten foe, and we envisaged another two or three years of war. Had we only known it the Germans were already beaten and the Bulgars had now no more idea of launching an offensive. They were determined to stay where they stood, hoping that if the Germans lost the war they could extricate themselves without loss of territory or prestige, so later to attempt a new domination of the Balkans.

The German troops serving with the Bulgar army, now mainly gunners and specialists, began to filter back to Germany, whose man-power had no more reserves. Meantime our allies from America were more than making good our losses. By August it became evident that events had turned in our favour. And yet still no man had the faintest idea how events could conceivably turn out to our advantage, where the first blow would be struck that would bring the war to an end. We were so accustomed now to the daily routine of war that it was inconceivable how it could ever come to an end except by the general agreement of all parties concerned. It never entered my head that it was any longer possible to fight a battle which would end in a retreat of the enemy and the breaking for good of his line. For there we both sat in the hills and valleys of the Balkans immovably fixed in our fortresses, and nothing which had so far occurred seemed to indicate then that one side or the other would ever budge again.

One curious event occurred about this time which, in the light of later discoveries, had no little interest. An officer of the Tank Corps was sent out to us by the War Office, with instructions to examine the ground on our front to see whether it was the sort of setting in which tanks could operate. This excellent man travelled overland, through Italy to Taranto, whence he took ship for Salonika. In conversation I discovered from him (of course by the use of extreme tact) that he had stayed at various hotels in Turin, Rome, and Naples *en route* and that it had been his custom always to enter his name in the hotel registers as 'Captain X, Tank Corps, London. Destination Salonika.' 'What was wrong in that?' he asked, as he detected some look of surprise and possibly of alarm in my face. 'Oh, nothing at all,' I replied. 'Why not, indeed.' But I knew well enough that the damage was done. It was not until

Bulgarian poster issued for the instruction of troops in anti-tank defence. It will be observed that the methods suggested are somewhat elementary

the final advance, when we captured enemy documents of importance, that I found that my fears were verified. A German order to their 11th Air Squadron was then found, which read as follows:—

> 'The arrival of Tanks from the western front is reported. Behind the Vardar-Doiran front is a lorry-park. Characteristic tracks lead one to suppose the presence of a Tank-station. The Squadron is ordered to proceed to take photographs of this. Watch is to be kept on this region.'

Two years after the Armistice a German scholar whom I met in Athens told me that he had been engaged on precisely the same work as myself on that very front, and that he remembered the scare that went round about the presence of tanks on the British front.

The innocent tank officer had done his work better than he supposed, for although, in the end, he had advised London against the use of tanks on our front, the news of his arrival had soon leaked through from Italy to Germany, and the Germans and Bulgars were prepared to identify as a tank almost any broken-down lorry that rattled about our front. For an officer of the Tank Corps to advertise his occupation and to announce his destination so explicitly was, in the end, quite useful propaganda, but it was at this late stage of the war a strange indication of the primeval innocence of those who had not learned the ways in which information leaked through. We had no tanks, but by sheer accident we reaped the benefit that their presence might have conferred. Had we had them and used them there would, of course, have been no surprise for the enemy.

Summer was at its height, and we all waited for developments without knowing in the least from what quarter the next news would come. Gradually the counter-offensive in France developed. The Germans were pushed back here and there, and August saw the beginning of a tremendous and continual pressure on their whole line.

Then at last came orders. We were summoned to secret

conclave by the Commander-in-Chief and told what was shortly to happen on our own front. At the time there seemed nothing sensational in the plan. It had been decided that in mid-September the whole line was to come into action, over three hundred miles of trenches were to become the field of a great battle. Sarrail had, a little while previously, been recalled at last, and the whole band of Allies heaved a sigh of relief. Sarrail had been too much for us and apparently too much for Clemenceau, who was now the soul and spirit of France. He was in disgrace, and no longer grand commander of the Armée d'Orient. In his place we had first, Guillaumat, and next, the splendid little soldier, Franchet d'Esperey, a man of one idea only, to win the war, and a man who understood to the full the value of the allies he was using. His plan, based upon Guillaumat's, which was now communicated to us, was that the Serbians should be the lance-head of attack. Their soldierly qualities coupled with their passionate desire to expel the Bulgars from their land was to be the motive force of our offensive. The French were to support them by an offensive which followed immediately upon the Serbian début. The British were to attack, with the Greeks, in full force on the rocky front of Doiran, while the uncertain Greek troops in the Struma valley sat where they were, and merely contained the forces opposite them. Our main task was to hold firm all the concentration of Bulgar troops on the British front and to make them think that here was coming our main offensive. For our front was geographically the most vulnerable, while the Serbians were entrenched three or four thousand feet up in the mountains in a region where it seemed impossible that any real break-through could be effected. So certain were the Bulgars that that mountainous region was safe that they had not even dug a second line of trenches. They were convinced that no attack could develop in such a wilderness of rock. But war breeds folly even in the most experienced. Only sheer paradox could win such a war as this, and the military mind as a rule will not admit the existence of paradox. But the French commander, and with him the Serbian commander, devised this astonishing scheme whereby the main attack was to come at the most difficult and impracticable part of the line. The Bulgarian trenches were to be overrun in a place where there was scarcely foothold for a goat. In warfare there are so many axioms and most of them are contradictory. One says that you should attack the enemy at his strongest point. Another that surprise is the essence of success. But here, what seemed the strongest point of the enemy's line was really his weakest, though he did not know it. Really what you attack is what the enemy thinks his strongest point and what you know to be his weakest. Surprise is inherent in such a scheme. I must admit that we viewed the offensive with scepticism. Perhaps it was the dreary years of war that had made us disbelieve in military conclusions of any sort, perhaps it was the fact that we could not conceive that the war would ever end at all.

But a month of feverish preparations followed. Troops and guns and ammunition poured unceasingly up to the lines. Guns were registered, reserves of troops formed, and I was able to see a first-class offensive being planned in all its astonishing detail. Where in France and Belgium I had been an unseeing unit in the machine, I could now watch the machine itself working. And it was an enthralling spectacle.

A week before the offensive was timed to start, when every nerve was strained and we hardly had time even for meals, and I slept by a telephone each night, awakened from time to time for fresh duties, one morning an urgent call came through. 'Enemy observation balloon broken loose and drifting over our front line: what shall we do?' 'For God's sake let it drift a bit farther,' I replied, 'and then instruct our gunners to bring it down. Only in no circumstances use high explosive: use shrapnel only.' This I said because we dearly wanted what was in the basket of that balloon. Could ever a gift of the gods be more opportune? I had to prevent those gunners at all costs from making a mere bonfire of that balloon to please the countryside. The maps that might be in the basket would have on them all our own gun positions that the Bulgar observers had spotted. In view of the offensive, it was most urgent that none of our positions should be known. To get those maps might perhaps mean the saving of hundreds of lives of our men, though the gunners who fired at the balloon had little or no idea of its importance.

After twenty minutes another message came through: 'Balloon brought down unburnt: maps in basket are being forwarded to you at once.' Another hour passed and a dusty messenger came in with a bundle of maps. Here they were, with a score of our heavy guns marked upon them, positions which would be inevitably shelled by the enemy, with the loss of men and guns. But then I had to consider whether the whole thing was an elaborate plant. Was the balloon a mere deception deliberately sent over? But I telephoned the gunners and found that they had been correctly fixed on the map. In the course of the afternoon all those guns were moved to new positions, so that when the enemy fired upon them (for duplicate maps probably existed) they would fire upon empty emplacements.

This was but one of many excitements, and my days were passed at full tension. A mistake of any kind would cause untold harm, and I was at every moment ready for the unexpected. But the excitement alone kept me going, and the imminence of events of the first importance gave a zest to life which was incomparable. Even though we felt that the war could never end, yet somehow we smelt the fresh wind of peace in some obscure way. Excitement was abroad like the excitement that swells and grows as the climax of tragedy in a Greek play comes nearer and nearer.

All was now set, and we waited for the events to develop. On our own front our men were to storm the grey row of hills that had watched over our lines so long and so cruelly. They were like the rocky hills of Dartmoor, rising steeply to broken ridges. Each ridge we knew was riddled with concrete posts and machine-gun nests. Each slope was thick with barbed wire. The ravines were already strewn with the bleaching bones of those who had fallen in previous assaults. Against those rocks both we and the Bulgars had our heaviest concentration of troops.

Then, on 15th September 1918, came the first assault far away in the mountains to the west. The hills were awakened at last by the drumming and thunder of a thousand guns. We listened to the sounds of battle and waited, almost incredible of success. But the plan was well and faithfully drawn up. The enemy, as incredible as ourselves, would not believe that this was the major attack. The incomparable bluff of the scheme was that the attack should begin away in these fastnesses of the mountains and then spread slowly eastwards until it reached us. We were due to start on the 18th, three days later. The enemy had assumed that our first and opening attack was a bluff, to draw away his forces. He never dreamed that sometimes a player will play his strongest card first. So he left his mountain positions unstrengthened and waited for the attack that he believed would come on our front, thinking that there would develop the main pressure. The next two days were days of continuous work. We knew every Bulgar battalion opposite our front and watched and waited to see if any of them would be taken away to be sent westwards. From prisoners and from aeroplane observation we satisfied ourselves that not a man was being moved. Indeed troops were being brought up from other points to our front where the enemy was preparing for our break-through.

The evening of the Serbian attack we had full reports. Unbelievable success had followed. The Serbians and

French together had assaulted those rocky eyries and swept over them. There was a vast breach in the Bulgar lines, that slowly widened. But still the Bulgars did not believe that their fate was to be decided there. Still they sent no reinforcements.

Twenty-four hours later we learned the news that Serbian troops, without guns to support them or transport to feed them, had pushed ten miles through the Bulgar lines, and that all was there at last in motion.

Our Commander-in-Chief, and that part of his staff concerned with the immediate conduct of operations and of intelligence, moved up to a point a little over a mile behind the battle front. I went with them. The battle opened at dawn, after a preliminary bombardment. Everyone was now at full strain and one snatched sleep when one could. The grey ridges that our men were to assault sparkled with endless shells during the night, as we bombarded them without cease. The whole air quivered with the sound of guns and the whistle of shells.

Our attack was launched but the Bulgars held firm and shot down our men in hundreds. Their positions were impregnable, but they were taking no risks and now we learned that they were denuding every sector for reserves. They fought like lions. Yet, all that time, the Serbians, far off to the west, were pressing on and on, held up here and there by scattered Bulgar defences, but never for long. The enemy was hypnotised still into thinking that ours was the main attack while, all the time, the line was breaking and the breach widening away in those hills. It seemed as if he would never wake up to the truth.

Our attack continued. Assault after assault was made on those rocky tors, and was as repeatedly repulsed. Yet we knew that our own failure meant the success of the greater scheme.

Exactly a week later the news flashed to us that the Serbs had descended from their hills and reached the valley below.

In that valley was the only railway line the Bulgars possessed and it was used to supply their central army on our own front. What would happen now? the situation was fast becoming unbelievable. We were on the point of rolling up the whole line, and so of opening the road to our greater enemies. Central Europe itself was before our eyes. But still we did not know what would happen. Of one thing only I was certain, that the Bulgars had no troops of any kind behind the lines with which to stop those rushing raging Serbians. I knew every unit in the Bulgar lines and I knew that no troops were available. The end was in sight. And still we could not guess exactly how it would come.

Here was the immensely strong Bulgar position, held against every assault by victorious troops. There away at the back were Serbian columns, now at last astride the line of communications of the enemy. It was a question only of hours.

The next dawn I was called urgently on the telephone by the Corps Headquarters. 'Clouds of smoke observed behind the Bulgar lines: fires burning in many places: our patrols are being sent forward.' An hour later another message: 'Bulgar lines and all strong points evacuated in the night: no opposition to our patrols.' At once our aeroplanes were ordered to make a concentrated reconnaissance of the whole area. Startling news followed. Endless columns of troops and transport were seen streaming along the roads from the front that led to that one main road to Sofia. The famous Kresna Defile up which Greeks had pursued Bulgar armies in 1913, the defile that led into the mountains behind Rupel Pass, was now crammed with the columns of the enemy's troops, so recently immovably entrenched. The pursuit was on at last.

CHAPTER XII

PURSUIT

OUR weary infantry had now no more battles to fight. They were to race ahead and bring the campaign to victory. Slowly, like some vast sleeping monster, the army stirred into movement. Guns were limbered up, lorries plunged ahead, columns formed into array, and the whole army surged over those lines which we had faced so long. But the enemy was racing for his very life.

The Bulgars were in desperate straits. We had startling proof of this in the reply to a frantic demand for German reinforcements which was found in a Bulgarian headquarters. It was a telegram sent by Hindenburg himself, and itself the first confession of defeat that Germany had given. I print a translation of that tragic telegram here in full, for, to the best of my knowledge, we who read this document in G.H.Q. were the first people other than the sender and the recipient to see it.

Copy of the Telegram of the Headquarters, dated 19*th September* 1918, *under No.* 11583, *addressed to the Minister of War.*

Referring to No. 11516 of the 16th instant. Please make the following telegram known to the Government, which was received in answer to the request of the Commander in Chief by telegram No. 11515: To General Todorov. Reference your No. 11515. As Your Excellency is aware Germany is now engaged in a most terrific struggle on the Western Front. All our forces will be required for that purpose. There doubtless the issue of the Great War will be decided. I am therefore compelled to refuse the request of the Scholtz Headquarters that a whole German division be sent to Macedonia. I can put at the disposal of the Army Group only some units of a reinforced infantry brigade which will have to be transported from Sevastopol. I will also try to free further troops, but for the present I cannot definitely say what units. Prior to the receipt of Your Excellency's telegram I had been in communication with the High Command Baden concerning the reinforcement of the Macedonian front by Austro-Hungarian troops, but have not yet received a reply. I am extremely sorry that I am unable to do more to satisfy Your Excellency's request. In the present highly critical military situation the Bulgarian High Command must try to deal with the situation with the forces now at its disposal which are not less numerous than those of the enemy, and must reconcile itself to a possible loss of territory. I think I must leave it thus to Your Excellency, suggesting that you for your part come to some arrangement with the High Command Baden concerning the despatch of help.

Signed for the High Command
General Field Marshalvon Hindenburg.
11583 Chief of the Staff of the Acting Army.
(Sgd.) GENERAL-MAJOR BOURNOFF.

Given out by Captain Lukas.
Received by Captain Pomyanoff.

The old Marshal tells the Bulgarian Commander-in-Chief that the war was at last being decided in the West. Within a few hours of sending his telegram he would know that it had already been decided in the East. The Bulgars asked for a division of German troops, surely the smallest demand they could make—but ten thousand men. Hindenburg offers him 'units of an infantry brigade,' a few hundred men, to be sent from a garrison at Sevastopol! and he encourages the Bulgar general 'to be reconciled to a possible loss of territory,' the most cynical comfort one ally ever offered to another! This telegram is surely one of the most astonishing documents the war could have produced. It shows that callous sacrifice of others, even allies, which is to-day the most characteristic feature of German diplomacy.

Almost as soon as we found this document we had strange confirmation of its contents. While the central army against us were breaking and running, the army on our right flank, facing the Greek troops, still sat firm, not knowing the full danger in which they were. On the third day of the battle astonishing news reached us: it was reported that all the church bells behind the Bulgar lines were being rung and that troops had been seen marching and counter-marching. Patrols were sent forward and captured some *German* infantrymen. The prisoners were at once sent up to me for interrogation. They proved to be poor ancient men of the Landsturm, men too old or too unfit for service in the ordinary way. I can still see one unhappy old man with a walrus moustache as he stood in front of me and told me his story.

They were, he said, infantry from a battalion, not five hundred strong, sent hurriedly from Russia to help the Bulgars. They had been told that they were to give the Bulgars the impression that they were part of a large army of rescue being sent by the Germans. To achieve that purpose they had been ordered to march and counter-march behind the Bulgar lines in the Struma valley, like a revolving stage army, to create the impression of numbers by their repeated appearances! 'It was very tiring,' he said, 'having to march so much after a long train journey.' Then they had been made into patrols to get into touch with the Greek forces opposite them, whose defections were known well enough to the Bulgars. It was hoped that, with the aid of authentic Germans, the Greeks would be encouraged to desert *en masse*. For this purpose the aged Landsturm Germans (known to us in our ribald moments as Land-worms), had been provided with pamphlets printed in Greek. One of these pamphlets was found in my aged friend's pocket. This is what it says:

HELLENIC SOLDIERS!

The German Army has taken over a section of the front opposite you. Behind the Bulgar lines are other German re-

ΕΛΛΗΝΕΣ

ΣΤΡΑΤΙΩΤΑΙ!

Γερμανικὸς στρατὸς κατέλαβε ἕνα μέρος τοῦ μετώπου, ποὺ ἔχετε ἀπέναντί σας.

Πίσω ἀπὸ τὶς βουλγαρικὲς γραμμὲς εἶναι καὶ ἄλλες γερμανικὲς ἐφεδρεῖες.

Καθένας ἀπὸ σᾶς, ποὺ δὲν θέλει νὰ πολεμάῃ πειὰ γιὰ τό συμφέρο τῶν Ἄγγλων καὶ τῶν Γάλλων καὶ νὰ ὑποφέρῃ, ἄς ἔρθῃ σὲ μᾶς. Ἄς παραδοθῇ στοὺς Γερμανούς, οἱ ὁποῖοι θὰ τὸν περιποιηθοῦν σὰν φίλον.

Οἱ Γερμανοὶ στρατιῶται

Manifesto to Greek troops in the Struma Valley captured on German soldiers in September 1918

> inforcements. Each of you who no longer wishes to fight for the benefit of the British and French should come over to us. Give yourselves up to the Germans who will treat you like friends! (Signed) THE SOLDIERS OF GERMANY.

Incredible document! but it had arrived several weeks too late. Our ancient Germans had no idea what was written on it, and, in their attempts to hand it to the Greeks, they had themselves been captured! but what cunning was in those lines. The Greeks, we knew well enough, had no wish to fight for us, but they had a deadly fear of being taken by the Bulgars, for they knew well enough that Bulgars had no love for them, however pro-German they might be. Previous wars had taught them the danger of falling into Bulgarian hands, for there has always been undying hatred between the two. Even so, some Greeks had already preferred the dubious safety of Bulgarian prison-camps for the certainty of serving as Allied cannon-fodder. Yet the stream of deserters was not large enough to satisfy the Bulgars that the Greek forces were disintegrating.

But this final stratagem came too late to be effective. The Greek forces in the Struma valley knew by now that the end had come, and they preferred to stay where they were. Their surprise at capturing Germans instead of Bulgarians was great. It made them feel that they were in the thick of a European war and no longer in a mere Balkan conflict.

A day or so after the capture of these German elders, we knew that the battle had ended in a rout. Up that grim pass behind Rupel streamed a mass of infantry, guns and transport in disorder. Our aeroplanes came and went like birds of prey, now no longer opposed by German airmen, for they too had fled, and left their allies callously in the lurch. This was no time for mercy. Our airmen swooped down upon that lonely road, which, in some places, was so closely hemmed in by the rocky walls that there was no escape off the roadway. Into the crowded mass of troops in those defiles the airmen hurled bombs and fired their machine-guns. Our own troops, who arrived later, said that the ground was littered with endless fragments of men and horses and guns. It was just plain slaughter on a scale we had never dreamed of. Some of the airmen came back sick and full of loathing for the endless murder. But they had to do it, for the enemy had not yet announced that he was beaten, and we could not let remain alive any single infantryman until hostilities ceased. This was war in its most savage aspect, war with the gloves off, war to the ultimate end. The massacre continued, not a massacre of wilful intention, but a massacre which was exactly what we had been sent there to commit. For there can be no peace in war. One side or the other must be exterminated, unless he hands over his arms.

Back flew those squadrons, every hour, to load up with fresh bombs and cartridges. Off they went again, following relentlessly that fleeing rout of soldiers. Farther northwards pushed the rabble in their wild attempt to escape, and the fewer they were in numbers the farther they progressed along that fatal pass.

Prisoners were now streaming over in columns to our lines, and marching to Salonika under guard. At our headquarters feverish activity prevailed as we sent new columns of our men in high fettle northwards to follow on the great pursuit. With the hum of planes in the sky and the rumble of artillery round us, as it galloped past to the north, we worked frantically at the thousand new problems that we had to face. For the enemy was still in being. I was standing looking at a map outside a tent when a cloud of dust a little way off showed a car racing towards us at top speed. The car stopped with a screeching of brakes, and a young infantry officer jumped out. The car was of a make with which I was not familiar, and it was covered with dust as if it had made a long journey. In it sat an officer in the uniform of the Bulgarian army, his eyes blindfolded. The British officer ran to me and said, 'Here is a Bulgarian major who has just come into our lines with an official demand for an armistice!' 'What exactly is an armistice?' I asked him, for I had only the mistiest idea what in fact it was, though I knew that it represented some kind of a demand to cease fighting. 'I haven't the least idea,' replied the officer. 'But he wants to see the Commander-in-Chief.' We telephoned the Commander-in-Chief. 'Tell him to go away and see the French,' came the angry reply of the Commander. 'Tell him there is a war still on and that we don't intend to stop it for him.' No one could really believe that he was genuine. No one could realise that here was the end of the war before our very eyes. The British Commander-in-Chief had no authority to stop this mad pursuit, nor did he want to. So I was told to take the Bulgarian in one of our cars down to Salonika, some fifty miles away, and to deliver him and his demand to the French general, who, after all, was the only man competent to decide any such weighty matter. The Bulgarian was released from his blindfold and given some food and drink. I placed him in a car and off we started for Salonika. I thought it best that he should see as much of our preparations for the pursuit as he could, so I did not cover his eyes until we were leaving the area of concentration and approaching a region that was for some thirty miles almost devoid of troops and guns. But I thought that he would expect to be blindfolded, so as soon as we approached this empty region I covered his eyes, and explained that I did not want him to see our reinforcements. I told the chauffeur to drive slowly at intervals so as to give the impression that he was passing marching columns of men. I have no idea if my poor stratagem succeeded, but the unhappy major looked extremely depressed when we arrived at the French headquarters.

When he presented himself to the French general, he was not a success. 'Do you mean to tell me,' said General Franchet d'Esperey, 'that you, a mere infantry major, have the impertinence to come to the Commander-in-Chief of the Allied forces to demand an armistice? Go back at once and say that we shall treat with no one except Army Commanders. How do I know that any arrangements I made with you would be ratified or kept by the Bulgarian Ministry of War? You are a nobody.' So my wretched major was taken back and hurled once more into Bulgarian territory. Meantime the pursuit continued and the slaughter increased. We were determined that the Bulgarian armies should be utterly broken and their pride humbled in the dust. Not otherwise would they admit defeat. If we treated with them and patched up a premature peace, in after years they would feed the flames of new military ambitions with the legend that they had never been defeated in the field. To countenance and to assist, as I had to do, this continual slaughter was a hideous task, but war can only be stamped out in the minds of those who love it by the direst and uttermost sufferings. We were teaching unborn generations of Bulgarians what war really was, that they might never forget it. To-day Bulgaria is the least bellicose of the states that fought against us in the war. I think our brutal lesson was learned.

The French general had acted wisely. The very next day, on 28th September, but ten days after that great Serbian attack in the hills, the Bulgar Commander-in-Chief accompanied by the Minister of War from Sofia arrived in our camp and were speeded as fast as a car could take them to Salonika. They announced that they were plenipotentiaries, and could agree to any terms that seemed to them suitable. The French general was curt with them. 'We do not propose,' he said, 'to argue about terms. The only terms I propose to discuss are my own terms. You can accept them unconditionally or leave them. If you do not accept you will be sent back to Bulgaria and the pursuit will be continued as far as Sofia, where we shall dictate harder terms still.' 'We accept your terms unconditionally,' replied the Bulgarians. In a few moments the deed of armistice was drawn up, and, as far as we were concerned, the war with Bulgaria was over. Yet, even now, it was almost impossible to believe that in another hour that slaughter would stop, those guns would cease to fire, and that a British soldier could encounter a Bulgarian face to face without attempting to kill or prepare to be killed. But the orders were flashed round the armies and the bugles for the first time blew that unaccustomed call of 'Cease fire,' which we only knew from hearing it on rifle ranges.

This was the end, but of what? Germany, Austria, and Turkey were still in the field. Half our forces were at once directed to advance through Bulgaria to the Danube to turn the whole enemy flank. The other half was sent to Salonika, embarked in ships and mustered up against the Turkish frontier in Thrace, ready to march on Constantinople. A thousand new problems now faced the staff, and we had to prepare for two entirely new campaigns. That mad ten days' battle had ended in as complete a victory as we could imagine. It had something of the fairy story about it and something of the most hideous nightmare. The unexpected had happened almost in a night.

A little time passed, and suddenly Turkey collapsed and claimed an armistice. Austria followed suit almost at once, and our two new wars were left high and dry. I was back in Salonika now, exhausted but filled with an elation that kept me going.

Thousands of British prisoners came back from Bulgaria, and I was able to learn from them much that concerned the German conduct of the war and much that was of the highest importance to the Western front, to whom now all our information was sent. Our British prisoners were all emaciated and worn. They had had all too little to eat and not the best of treatment.

Sofia was now occupied by British and French troops to prevent the Serbians from getting there. Had Serbian troops reached the Bulgar capital there would have been a destruction and carnage beyond belief.

October was now at an end, and a new winter sparkled in the snow on distant Olympus. The news from France showed that there things were coming at last to a conclusion.

On a windy November morning I was working at the new scheme for the full occupation of Constantinople when an orderly laid a telegram before me. 'As from 11 A.M. to-day, 11th November, hostilities will cease on all fronts.' That was all. My head reeled. The sky looked blank and dull. I gazed stupidly at the paper. 'It looks as if we had won the war,' I said to the orderly. He smiled faintly, saluted, and went out. My strength seemed to leave me, and I felt suddenly that here I was, a simple civilian, masquerading in an absurd uniform, just as I had felt in 1914.

An hour later I went shivering to bed. That night I had a raging temperature and was carted to hospital with Spanish influenza.

All interest seemed to have gone out of life. I watched the orderlies in the hospital carrying out from their beds those who had died during the night. I lay and gazed at the roof of the hospital hut, my mind no longer working. One thin determination stuck, that they should not carry me out as well. One could hear at intervals from the hospital cemetery the volley of rifle shots and the bugle-call that denoted that one more soldier had been put in his grave, victim of this scourge of influenza. Somehow those repeated bugle-calls increased my determination to live.

CHAPTER XIII

LIQUIDATION

Who thunders at the Golden Gate?
  Whose is the banner wide unfurled?
Into whose waiting basket falls
  The Crimson Apple of the World?

'As these powerful but taciturn men stood on the decks of their ships as they sailed in and gazed at the exquisite outlines of Byzantium that burst upon their astonished view, their eyes grew dim with tears to see so much beauty': thus the padre, as he gave us an after-lunch lecture in the saloon of the transport as it pitched and rolled in tempestuous Marmara on a grey December day.

'Blimey,' remarked one of two powerful but taciturn Crusaders who stood in front of me on the deck and gazed at the distant prospect; 'looks like Southampton wiv spikes on it.' For anything more depressing or woebegone than the view of Byzantium as you approach it from the west, feeling slightly seasick, I do not know. All you see at first is the dirty tenements of Pera and the barracks and villas of Moda on the Asiatic shore. Only when you are almost at anchor does the lovely skyline of Stamboul appear: and that was never seen by the Latin Crusaders of 1204.

It was nearly Christmas, and I had emerged finally from a succession of hospitals and convalescent homes, thankful to escape alive. Not that the nurses and doctors were not the soul of kindness and efficiency, but here and there one encountered stupidity and staleness. Not easily shall I forget the case of one poor wretch who was borne in with a temperature of 105°. He had not slept for four nights, and at last one evening about 7 o'clock he dozed off into a fitful slumber. We others breathed a sigh of relief—for we had watched him with all that deep sympathy and comradeship that grew up in hospital wards among the invalids. At last he had achieved that life-giving sleep that saves battered bodies from death: that deep sleep whose healing power we all knew so well. But at nine o'clock in bustled a night-nurse, gave one look and shook him roughly by the shoulder. We whispered urgently to her to let him be. 'My orders are,' she replied tartly, 'to give this patient his sleeping draught at nine every night.' He died the following dawn.

Our transport was a small ship, but a merry one. Off we went to assist in the occupation of that long-desired city, Constantinople, whither an advance guard of troops had gone after the Turkish armistice, following on the heels of a mighty contingent of warships. We were the oddments who had been left behind in hospital or who had contrived to get home on short leave immediately after the Armistice. I came under the former category, and I had been home on leave only once since March 1916. The main body of the staff had already installed themselves in the great city. A few only had been left behind. I was on my way to take over my old post with its new and complex duties.

At Galata Quay we disembarked. A screaming mob of the worst riff-raff in the Levant crowded the quay gates, beaten back with difficulty by the military police. A car was waiting to fetch me and we drove through this dirty and depressing throng. Up we went along the grimiest and dirtiest streets I have ever seen, up the long hills to Pera. Here was the city of our dreams, populated with as criminal a set of ragamuffins as I had ever seen, with tattered Turkish policemen here and there; cleaner but less friendly looking Turkish officers strolled along the pavements, and everywhere was the cheerful sight of British soldiers and British lorries. A few German troops still remained, but the major part of them had marched out under escort as we marched in at the moment of the formal occupation of the city. There were no German officers left.

General Headquarters had been established in an old Turkish barrack at Chichli, lice-infested and filthy when first taken over. Now it was spruce enough, and I reported to my colonel in the Intelligence Section. I took over my old job from the officer who had done it in my absence and started to investigate the new tasks that were before me. For living quarters I was placed at first in a grubby little hotel in the Grande Rue de Pera. I found that Intelligence now meant something totally different from what it had meant during the piping times of war. Apparently I had half Asia to supervise. At Salonika I had been the only G.S.O. 3 on the Intelligence staff and now there was need of others, for we had a vast area to control. Indeed I soon found that we were not merely the Army of the Black Sea, as the War Office now named what had originally been the British Salonika Force. We extended our area of interest far beyond the Black Sea. The whole of Asia Minor to Syria—now under French control—the whole of White Russia from Odessa and Ekaterinodar northwards to the Don Cossack country, all the Caucasus and, apparently, a large chunk of North Persia came under our view. For the War Office had seen that to the right flank of the Allied line could now be tied all the odds and ends of small expeditions which had hitherto been more or less in the air. Quickly our lines of communication from England, now safely pouring in food and munitions to us, were hooked up to these stray expeditions. White Russians, fighting ineffectively and incompetently on the Don, were fed and clothed and munitioned as never before. Detachments of troops sent on from our army to the Caucasus joined hands with the lonely Dunsterforce that had pushed slowly and doggedly up from Baghdad to Baku led by General Dunsterville, and there checked by the German and Turkish forces shortly before the Armistice. To them we brought such wealth of good food and clothing as they had hardly hoped for, for they were too far from Baghdad to receive much from there.

Rumours reached us also of some vague British army away out beyond the Caspian. But as yet we heard only rumour and knew that it was a venture run exclusively by the Indian army from Quetta. However, here we were, the fairy godmother to a variety of almost forgotten enterprises, that now grew into renewed strength.

My particular task seemed simple enough. I had to supervise doings in the Caucasus and keep touch with what was going on in South Russia. A few days' study of geography and recent history gave me a faint indication of what was in store. Herodotus, I remembered, had said that there were seventy-two different races in the Caucasus. Apparently what he said two and a half thousand years ago was still true. As I studied the files waiting for me on my table it began to dawn on me that Wilson's Self-Determination of peoples would find a most fertile soil in the Caucasus. Barely a week after this reflection, a bunch of urgent telegrams informed me that my amiable surmise was coming true. I was told, in short, that the military authorities concerned at Batum were forwarding for my inspection during the ensuing fortnight no less than three delegations from the Caucasus representing Republics which had just sprouted, after hearing the good Wilsonian tidings. These delegations were respectively of the Don Cossack Republic, the Daghestan Republic, and the Kuban Republic. Each delegation, I was told, had struck Republican paper money in each republic, recalled all silver and gold, and were bringing their treasure-chests with them to Constantinople. Each delegation announced that it intended to proceed to Paris to state its claims and to render thanks unto Wilson. My informants at Baku added that there was a fourth republic which they had not allowed to send any delegation. It had grown up overnight in a small town not far from Batum, of barely 600 inhabitants, called Kobuleti. It had declared its independence of all other places and announced that it was to be known as the Republic of

Kobuletia. But the British general at Batum declared that the line had to be drawn somewhere, and he drew it at Kobuletia.

It rapidly became apparent that my job had now ceased to be a serious one, from some points of view. I foresaw myself interviewing endless delegates and arranging endless trips to Paris. I was becoming a Cook's Tourist Bureau for nomadic Caucasians.

A few days later an orderly ran in with a look of awe on his face. 'Please, sir,' he said in an agitated voice, 'there are some foreign gentlemen asking for you, sir.' 'Show them in,' I told him. To my stupefaction in there walked six enormous Cossacks, in full war-paint, clanking and clattering with their accumulation of metalwork and medals. Their spokesman, however, who spoke perfect French, was a grubby little man with a wideawake hat and corduroy clothes, looking exactly like a Rive Gauche artist. And that was exactly what he was, for, as he explained to me, a Don Cossack by birth, he had gone to Paris long before the war to paint. There he had stayed until after the Armistice. Wilson had fired him with zeal to save his country: so back he had gone to the Don, and here he was, proposing to take his six Cossacks to Paris. We gave him his passports and off he went. You will see his Cossacks to-day, poor fellows, outside some Parisian Russian restaurant. They all certainly wanted to get to Paris, and I am as certain that none of them intended ever to leave it. Whoever had sent them from the Don had, I imagined, never seriously expected them to return there and found a republic. Russians after all are a highly intelligent race.

The Kuban republicans were more serious: they were fine Circassians dressed also as Cossacks, for the Cossack costume is Circassian in origin. Them also we blithely forwarded to Paris.

The delegates of Daghestan were a more sinister party. They were only two in number and arrived a few hours after the Don Cossacks. All had travelled by the same boat from Batum. Daghestan I had studied in some detail during my first quiet days. It was apparently a region more primitive and essentially Caucasian than any other in the Caucasus. The inhabitants were simple mountaineers, in no way sophisticated. But their two representatives maintained stoutly that they were the President and his secretary, and that they were authorised plenipotentiaries of the citizens of Daghestan (which, incidentally, had no capital). The President was a large, jocose, and obviously able man who claimed to be the owner of most of the oil-wells north of the Caucasus range. These wells were in Bolshevik hands and his titular claims were worthless *de facto*. With his pockets stuffed with title-deeds and with his very efficient secretary armed to the teeth with documents of all kinds, they also departed to Paris. After all, we were in no position to prevent the free movement of men who had been until quite recently our allies, and, unless their aims and qualifications were obviously spurious, we had no business to detain them. But I felt sorry for all those struggling peacemakers in Paris who had ultimately to deal with these commercial travellers in new republics.

A week later a much more serious delegation appeared —that of Armenia, which had at last emerged as a large and promising land, independent for the first time for hundreds of years, backed (so the Armenians then thought) by the might of the Allies and destined for a long era of peace and development. My ideas on Armenians had been largely founded on the stories usually current in the Levant about that unhappy race. But here before me was a set of magnificent fighting men, physically fine, admirably tactful, and very much in earnest. Most of them had served with the Russian army in an Armenian division, and the Turks had learned to fear that division as they feared no other of the Russian forces in the Caucasus.

These, without hesitation or qualms, we forwarded to

Paris. Clearly Paris had by now become the Mecca of the Near East. Many of those wandering delegates would, I expect, to-day be glad to see their native hills again. To ride the grassy Caucasian plains on a shaggy pony would please them now far more than driving a Paris taxi, which is the occupation of many of them.

Still another Caucasian republic had emerged—Georgia. The Georgians are perhaps the only race in the world which can claim to be *sui generis*. No one knows their racial origin: their language has affinities with no other: their temperament is unlike that of any other semi-Asiatic race. Naturally they were the very first to become independent as soon as the Turko-German grip of the Caucasus was loosened and after the Russian control had lapsed. With the great Caucasian city of Tiflis as their capital they had set the fashion of republics. And they above all had the best claim. But their republic wanted to be original. They were neither Bolsheviks nor Capitalists. They made themselves into a Menshevik Republic and flew a purple flag.

Last, and certainly least, was the republic of Azerbaijan, whose delegation was also forwarded to Paris, carriage paid. This was the immediate neighbour on the east of the Georgians, and their most deadly enemy. The Azerbaijanlis were pure Tatars, of the most uncompromising type, and from their ranks were drawn all the workmen of the oil-fields of Baku.

Republics palled after a time, and at length I began to survey this astonishing city of Constantinople. If the Crusaders had wept at its beauty, we wept at its filth. Never before or since have I seen a city which had fallen into such neglect. Whole patches, acres in area, of Old Stamboul had been burned down in various fires which the exigencies of war had not allowed the Turks to deal with (though none of those fires was caused by enemy action). The streets were filled with garbage and dirt that had accumulated during months, perhaps years. The tramways did not work, and the trams lay derelict where they had stopped as the current gave out. The water-supply was unsafe and erratic, and the electricity and gas was so uncertain that candles and lamps were a necessity in every room. Public safety was non-existent, and after dark it was one of our nightly entertainments to stand at the hotel windows and count the number of revolver-shots which we could hear in an hour. We used to have sweepstakes on the results. We were told that for the first few weeks an average of twelve freshly killed corpses, mainly of Greeks and Armenians, were found each morning in the streets and alleys. Lest it be thought that this condition of affairs should never have occurred under an Allied domination, I should say that it was so only for the first few weeks of our occupation. The main purpose of the occupation was to hold the important military posts and see that the city was in a state of defence against the native population on the one hand and against external forces of Turks on the other. For we had by no means interned the armed forces of our late enemy. The occupation was a military move in its first phases, and we were concerned only with the general safety of the city and with the protection of the Allied forces and Allied citizens. What happened to the natives, and the condition of affairs in the city itself, was a matter with which we could deal at leisure. And in due course we dealt with it with the utmost firmness. We found that the Turkish police, in whose keeping was still all that concerned public safety, had not been paid for several months, perhaps a year, and that in order to keep body and soul together they levied a quiet blackmail on most of the citizens who could pay. The various murders at night were mainly due to mere banditry and robbery, though sometimes to the Turkish police who, naturally enough, fired without warning on any suspicious character. After a time our military police took all these problems in hand, our Ordnance Department saw to it that the trams and the electricity and water were made to operate once more, and the suburbs of Pera and Galata at least were got into some semblance of civilisation. Stamboul, with its almost wholly Turkish population and its underworld of criminal elements, always on the wait to rush across the Golden Horn and loot and massacre in the Christian quarter of Pera, we left aside. The naval patrols on the Horn and machine-guns at Galata bridge were sufficient to keep them in hand for the moment. One day, by mere chance, a brand-new British submarine of the latest class, with a great gun mounted beside the conning-tower, hove-to near Galata bridge. The tide swung it round so that its gun pointed towards Stamboul, aimed at the centre of the bridge. For twenty-four hours hardly a soul would cross the bridge. So, for the most part, we felt that there was nothing to fear in Stamboul.

Our position in the city was in many ways paradoxical. Turkish troops still guarded the Turkish War Office and many other principal centres. And they were under the orders of the still existing Sultan. For as yet there was no Mustafa Kemal and no Nationalism. On spare afternoons I would wander over Stamboul, seeking out the lovely old Byzantine churches, or looking for bargains in the bazaar. On my first trip I went to see St Sofia, and was horrified to find that it was garrisoned by a company of the most ragged, lice-ridden, Turkish soldiery imaginable. They were quartered in the entrance hall of the mosque, with their arms piled just beneath the Royal Entrance, above which, two years ago, has been uncovered a superb mosaic of the Saviour. The soldiers were placed there, with our cognisance, by the Turkish Government to prevent any possible seizure of the mosque by Greeks, for the great mosque has always been the objective of every irredentist Christian movement in the East. No Greek or Armenian was allowed to enter and we, the officers of the Army of the Black Sea, were asked by a ragged corporal to show our passports! The lovely church was filthy and neglected, and the entrance where the soldiers had piled their arms was like a stable.

The Turkish Government, as far as we could see, represented nobody and did nothing. It was a mere puppet government, which had been formed when Enver Bey bolted for his life. The Sultan shivered in Dolma Bagtche and his various princely sons and their princesses lurked in the obscurities of immense mansions along the Bosporus between Pera and Therapia. There was hardly anyone with whom we could deal whom we knew to be a proper representative of the Turkish people as a whole. And where, too, were the Allies? We were no longer allied. Instead of one general military headquarters there were three, the British, French, and Italian. And in addition there was a High Commissioner of each nationality sitting in his Embassy, with a full Embassy staff, doing similar but mainly civilian business with the tattered Turkish Government. There were also three armies and three navies, and finally, just to make things more difficult, an American navy and with it an American admiral who was also American High Commissioner. Since America had never been at war with Turkey his occupation was largely that of what, from long experience at Geneva, we now call an Observer. I have often wondered what has happened to all the observations of American Observers. Are they stored up in immense volumes at Washington, and did they consist merely of rude or caustic remarks?

So on the whole the government of Constantinople and its million of inhabitants was largely run on the lines of the control of the Salonika fire. Every officer did what he thought best for the general cause!

But thanks to General Milne, who had so wisely and so brilliantly directed the Salonika Force through its campaign and who was now the Commander-in-Chief of the Army of the Black Sea, some solid semblance of law and order was achieved. Certainly the French and Italians did nothing at all as far as the well-being of the city was concerned. They hastily immured themselves in immense barracks and started intrigues with every disgruntled Turkish official. Their intrigues were in the main designed against us, for the one prospect which the French and Italians alike found intolerable was the growth of British prestige in the Near East. Consequently all the measures we took to control and rule the city, many of them extremely unpleasant for the citizens, were done by us alone because the French and Italians saw that by refusing to help they could throw the *onus* of unpopularity on us. They certainly succeeded, for no one to-day is so unpopular among the rank and file of Turks as an Englishman. The Turks forget that we were a victorious army occupying an enemy city, and that measures taken by such an army in such conditions are bound to be onerous. For never a day for the first two months of the occupation could it be said that the city was safe from disaster, either from plague, from famine or from fire and massacre. That it escaped all these is due solely to the rigid discipline and thoughtful measures of control instituted by General Milne. To-day Turks forget that we finally handed them back their capital as a well-conducted city, while we had taken it over as a mere rubbish heap infested with rats. We bore the brunt of the unpleasantness associated with the occupation because our Allies had decided that it would be good for them if we did so! and the Americans observed continuously.

About this time an entertaining episode occurred in the Naval community. Out in the Bosporus were anchored all the mighty vessels of the Allies and Americans. It happened one day that the American contingent found that they were short of fresh meat. All the contingents were, as among sailors, on the friendliest of terms unofficially, and Admiral Bristol, the American admiral, sent a wireless message *en clair* to the British admiral to ask if he could lend a supply of fresh meat from his spare stores. It happened at that moment that a British supply tender had just dropped anchor in the harbour off Galata. This tender bore the name of S.S. *Dago*. The British admiral replied, also *en clair*, 'Apply to the *Dago* for your fresh meat.' The American admiral cheerfully sent off a pinnace at once to the Italian flagship. I have no idea how the little affair was straightened out, but for some time to come Italians and Americans were not on speaking terms.

The winter had come on in full blast. Whoever imagines that a winter on the Golden Horn is like a winter in Algeria should spend one among the cypresses of Stamboul! Biting blasts blew day after day from across the Black Sea, iced by frosts from Siberia. Snow and sleet made the muddy streets almost impassable and we slithered down the slopes of Pera in unspeakable slime. Constantinople is probably one of the coldest places in the Mediterranean at all times of year. Even in August its temperature rarely rises above 80°.

But the winter did not bother us, for we were all happy as we had not been for years. The lifting of that dead weight of war had put new life into us all. The certainty that we could rise each day and know that the life before us would be more or less normal, that somewhere in the near future we should all be back in England and that the world was at peace, at last made the things of peace into realities. I used to wander round the lovely Ottoman Museum and recover some of that almost forgotten knowledge that I had acquired at Oxford. Parties of soldiers used to be taken round the sights of the city and shown the works of art. Everyone was stimulated by the things they saw. The deep inner love of beauty and of knowledge was faintly stirring like the germ of seeds long kept underground in a frozen soil.

We had also some semblance of a social life. Those British citizens who had stayed in Constantinople during the war—and there was a large British population which had been unable to depart on the outbreak of hostilities—did their best to entertain us. Dances and dinners enlivened things, though it was pathetic to see the drab and dreary costumes which the European civilians had to wear. There was a textile famine and suits for men or dresses for women cost fabulous sums.

Among the interesting people we met were one or two families of cultured and delightful Armenians, a few Greeks and occasional Turks. But, in the main, the Turks naturally kept to themselves.

A round-up of suspected persons, particularly of Turks who were known to be dangerous intriguers against us, and of some few rascals who were known to have organised massacres in Armenia during the war, took place during the winter. A large batch of prisoners was sent to Malta. Anxious to protect the city, we arrested all possible suspects. At the time we naturally did not know that many of our suspects were innocent and that among them were men of high probity. But we had to act on what information we had and a good deal of it came, naturally enough, from informers, who, like spies, invariably gave incorrect information.

General Milne had his headquarters in the villa once owned by Krupp, at Therapia, on the shores of the Bosporus. The interior of the villa was an amazing spectacle; it enlightened us on the taste of German profiteers. Bronze statues of Venuses holding electric lamps, red plush sofas and execrable pictures, made this palatial home into a perfect imitation of a Brighton boarding-house. I think it was in this villa that I saw an example of that finest of all industrial works of art—a plaster Venus de Milo, with a clock inserted in her stomach!

Among my manifold tasks was to deal with any and every oddment who merely expressed a desire to see the Commander-in-Chief. Seldom have I met so many human curiosities. One day a White Russian *émigré* was shown in. He had a great invention, he said, and he had been all his life a scientist at Moscow. He explained that his invention would revolutionise both the whole textile industry and the whole machine-making industry. He proposed to sell us his secret. He invited me to tea with him to meet his numerous family who were all living, as only Russians can, on hope. We drank vodka and tea and ate endless cakes, and after a time he explained to me that he had discovered a substance which would withstand a heat of almost 4000° Centigrade. With it he could make crucibles, in which quartz could be so efficiently melted that it could be drawn off into threads as fine as the finest known silk. I knew well enough that such quartz threads had long been made by scientists but that they were always brittle. His invention apparently would wind off these gossamer threads from the viscous quartz and so use them for the making of imperishable textiles. 'Imagine,' he said, 'I can make you a complete suit of clothes of quartz fabric. It will never wear out at all and when it gets dirty you merely throw it on the fire.' Similarly from welded quartz he proposed to make all those parts of machines which soonest perish. I referred him to our Ordnance Department. They told me later that no doubt his experiment was theoretically possible, but that a suit of clothes made to his specification would cost at least five hundred pounds.

Another inventor came my way, also a White Russian. He had with him a model electric gun which he placed upon my table. He fastened a plug to the electric light, placed a number of pellets in the gun and fired them. The barrel of the gun had no breach, it was just a tube through which you could see. The electricity somewhere about the centre of the tube projected the pellet as it was put in at one end of the tube. 'So,' he said, 'you see that I have a model gun which can be used for all future fortress guns. All you have to do is to get the electric charge and merely insert the shells as fast as you can.' How it worked I have no idea, but the Ordnance Department told me that in the full scale gun the amount of electricity required for each shot would be several million volts, and that to fire one shot would cost about £10,000. So another good invention went west and another recruit was found for the Paris taxi ranks.

One of my strangest visitors was a Frenchman who said that he had just arrived from Astrakhan where he was a caviare merchant. He was prepared, as one ally to another, to give me all the information about that Bolshevik stronghold that he could provide. I thanked him warmly and gave him a cigarette. He expatiated at length upon affairs at Astrakhan, which were as fishy as I had expected. When he sat down, I had noticed that he placed upon a table a small rectangular package, neatly tied with string and covered with brown paper. As he talked I happened to notice that a large lense protruded from the package and was carefully aimed at one of my maps of the Caucasus on the wall. The map in question was covered with little flags which I had placed to indicate various troop-movements. I need hardly say that the map was out of date and represented a state of affairs long past. I never kept important and recent information on wall maps in any case, as a natural precaution. With acute pleasure I watched him manœuvre his packet and, during the course of conversation, make his exposure with the utmost tact. Our conversation at length came to a close. I rang a bell. He was just about to take up his neat little camera when my corporal entered. 'Forgive me,' I said to the Frenchman, 'but before you leave I must ask you to submit to the formality of having the plates removed from your camera.' 'Camera, monsieur!' he replied, with well-simulated surprise. 'C'est mon déjeuner.' 'Nevertheless,' I countered, 'it is best to remove the plates from it.' The corporal bore it off, and later returned it empty. I often wonder for whom exactly that poor caviare merchant was spying. It certainly gave me more pleasure than it gave him.

In the evenings, for entertainment, we used to repair to the Petits Champs music-hall. Here on a tawdry stage wretched artistes performed their sad songs and music blared incessantly. There were always episodes. Once at the playing of the 'Marseillaise' a Turkish officer remained seated.

A bunch of French officers rushed over to him and dragged him by his ears to his feet. On another evening an attractive little Austrian girl was singing inoffensive Viennese melodies. A half-drunk French subaltern rose unsteadily to his feet and with a shout of 'Sales Bosches' threw a chair at her. We all rose and suppressed the Frenchman, and the curtain came down hurriedly. The poor little Austrian collapsed in tears. Fortunately, the chair had not hit her.

I could not complain. My life was now more full of variety than for many years past. But I ached to get home. Yet I was to find it hard, for those who were first demobilised had to declare their professions, and those whose professions were held to be essential for the well-being of England were the first to go. As I could claim to be nothing more than a student of archæology with no post and no salary, I saw myself mouldering for years in the Near East. However, as a student, I had definite claims more than most, on the assumption that my studies had been interrupted by the war and that in consequence the sooner I was home to continue them the better.

So I pulled all the wires at home that I could pull and waited. Meantime my intelligence work became daily more interesting and less *opéra-bouffe.* Fortunately the White Russian *émigrés* who were now flocking to Constantinople in thousands from Odessa did not come within my sphere. For this I was profoundly thankful, for a more useless, fatuous set of people it would be hard to imagine. Naturally they were nice enough—or at least as nice as the typical denizens of Mayfair—but how ultimately they were ever going to get a living baffled the imagination. They arrived in fur coats and all the elements of luxury, with their jewel cases and their mounds of luggage, and those that could made one swift dash to Paris. Those whose jewels or fur coats were insufficient capital to provide them with a fare to Paris stayed in Constantinople. Russia was certainly getting rid of its non-productive population.

But Asia and Asia Minor were now beginning to show developments. Almost immediately after the occupation we had sent a large contingent of troops to occupy the Caucasus and police it. They had no mandate to govern it, still less to treat it as an enemy region. And so the Caucasus sprouted happily into republics, as I have shown above, while we policed it and saw that law and order was maintained. On our arrival we found chaos. For up to the last moment of the German armistice there had been warfare. A Turkish division and a German division—the latter under General Kress von Kressenstein—had by November 1918 carried on a bitter rivalry for the control of Batum and Baku. Germans wanted German influence to prevail, and Turks wanted a Caucasian province of Turkey. Late in the autumn of 1918 the British force known as Dunsterforce, operating from North Persia, had been pushed out of Baku by a strong Turkish division, and their departure had been celebrated by Turks and Tatars by a dreadful massacre in which 80,000 Armenians had been slaughtered at Baku. Germans remained for the most part in Tiflis, the capital of Georgia.

Into this chaos came at last the most powerful British forces. With them came a naval contingent bound for Baku, whose job it was to arm and equip certain merchant ships there and to commission them into the British Navy for purposes of policing the Caspian. The railway line from Batum to Tiflis was our main line of communications to the east and our main headquarters were at Tiflis. German troops were quickly evacuated and the Turks dispersed. General Kress von Kressenstein was sent to Batum, a prisoner. There he was given a berth on a transport to be sent for exchange to Constantinople and so back to Germany. But the gallant general stood on his dignity. He wanted to go only on a warship, he declared, as befitted his rank and dignity. He refused the berth on the transport. So he waited in Batum and later was put on a cattle ship. We had no time for Prussianism of this sort. Everyone was very busy and there was a shortage of ships anyhow. He was told that if Germany had not torpedoed so many ships we might have managed to spare him a transatlantic liner.

One evening G.H.Q. was electrified to hear news of Enver Bey. That slippery rascal, to whom most of Turkey's woes were due, had escaped at the moment of the Turkish armistice and we had never succeeded in getting on to his tracks. All we had found was his house and his luggage and a huge consignment of the finest Turkish cigarettes in it, each cigarette tastefully inscribed with the name of 'Zita,' the Hungarian ex-queen. (We found no explanation of this touching tribute.)

Suddenly Enver materialised out of the blue. A telegram from headquarters at Batum stated tersely that he had been reported as hiding in a house some ten miles north of that city. The British general proposed to send cavalry to surround the house at midnight. We waited for the next report. It came at dawn, to say briefly that the house had been raided, that property definitely identified as that of Enver had been found in it, but that Enver had once again slipped away. Nor did we ever hear of him again, and as far as is known he was finally killed in some obscure fighting in Turkestan, near Bokhara, a year later. He was no fighter of lost causes, and to have ended almost unknown and certainly unsung was appropriate enough. Had he had a fraction of the stern determination of Mustafa Kemal or even a hint of Mustafa's organising genius, he might have raised all Asia against us. He was from start to finish a mere upstart. Never in our dealings with Turkey during 1918 and 1919 did we detect the faintest traces of his character or influence or meet with any hint of his power. Yet all this while Mustafa Kemal was walking among us, unknown and unsuspected, even by his friends, to be the great power that he has become.

There were coloured patches on the Black Sea. It was not as drab as it looked. Its coasts were certainly a brilliant kaleidoscope. From the Symplegades at the northern exit of the Bosporus to the Turko-Bulgarian border was a *terra incognita* where nothing happened and nothing mattered, and there were no towns or ports. The inhabitants were mainly Greeks, accustomed since the time of Homer to agriculture and wrecking, like the inhabitants of Cornwall. On the quiet Bulgarian coastline there was the large port of Varna where British gunboats kept the peace and where the now peace-loving Bulgars urgently cultivated their gardens at the foot of the Balkan ridges. North of here was the sole coastline of the new and inordinately satisfied Rumania, with Constanza, a lively and industrious port. Northwards again was Akkerman at the Bessarabian border and then Odessa, as violently disturbed as were the southward coasts at peace. Here was the centre of White Russian aggression against nascent Bolshevism. In the Crimea, farther east, was again a vast White Russian organisation. But immediately east was the Sea of Azov, into whose narrow and shallow depths no one had penetrated. Here, as far as Novorossiisk, where the coast bends south again, was an unknown patch, for which I could provide no flags on my variegated map. Novorossiisk, on the other hand, was certainly a White Russian port. Then to the south again came that coast where the mighty Caucasus dips steeply to the sea and makes coastal traffic hug the rocky shores. From there south was full British control with its centre at Batum. There the coast turns westwards, and from near Batum right all the way along to the Bosporus again was the vast stretch of the coast of Asia Minor, wooded, unknown, unpenetrated and controlled by us solely from the sea. Its ports, Trebizond and Samsun, held our ships, but of the hinterland we knew almost nothing. Here indeed was a pretty problem for the Army of the Black Sea.

Across its dark and heaving waters British destroyers

scurried here and there, and transports sailed regularly between Constantinople and Odessa, Varna, and Ekaterinodar with supplies. To and from Batum was a regular service of ferries taking reinforcements to Batum for the Caucasus and bringing back a regular number of men for demobilisation. Many even of the troops from Mesopotamia were sent home *via* Baku and Batum to England, and at last we had this mighty line of communications working easily.

It was all profoundly interesting. Even the uncertainties were now a matter more of amusement than alarm. One day the naval authorities at Constantinople decided that they would clear up some of the uncertainties, so they despatched a destroyer with orders to 'proceed to the Sea of Azov to investigate whether Bolshevik forces had control of this region.' The gallant captain of the destroyer set forth upon his quest. Cautiously winding his way through the uncharted Azovian shoals he descried a small town. Entering its harbour he dropped anchor, hoisted the Union Jack, landed in a pinnace, in his best uniform and accompanied by his lieutenant. Lighting their cigarettes they pushed through a curious crowd until they found one who looked like an official. 'We should be obliged,' said the captain, 'if you would inform us whether this port is in the hands of the Bolsheviks.' 'It is,' replied the official, who then conducted them to the Town Hall from which floated the red flag. At the Town Hall there was a scene of great activity. Commissars and soldiers hurriedly donned their uniforms and hastened to welcome the naval officers from the destroyer. The Russian love of piquant situations had not failed them. A banquet was arranged, the officers and crew of the destroyer were dined and wined regally, much vodka was drunk, the assembly sang the 'Internationale' and 'God Save the King.' The guests were conducted back in the small hours by bibulous and happy hosts. The Mayor and Corporation spoke: 'Inform your admiral, with our compliments, that the Sea of Azov is definitely in Bolshevik hands.' The destroyer departed the next morning to the accompaniment of brass bands and salutes.

This story I was told by one of the naval officers concerned. I have no reason to doubt his veracity. For things were like that on the Black Sea.

Captains and officers of transports on the Black Sea indulged in one hobby which made them the envy of all Constantinople. The Russian ruble could be bought in Constantinople in unlimited quantities for threepence a ruble. At Odessa, Novorossiisk, and Batum it could be sold for the equivalent of sixpence in French or Turkish currency. So those with a little capital had no trouble in doubling that capital in a trip!

It was astonishing how little we knew all this time of Asia Minor. A system of Control Officers had been set up in all the main towns. At Eski Shehir, Angora, Konia and at a few other cities was one solitary British officer, usually a subaltern, whose duty it was to send in periodical reports of the state of affairs. Vague rumours reached us in the spring of some kind of organisation of Turkish officers in the inner parts round and near Angora. Many of these officers were known to have slipped quietly out of Constantinople and among them, though we did not know it, was Mustafa Kemal, of whose part in the defence at Suvla Bay we were then wholly unaware. Indeed he had the supreme gift of keeping himself as an unknown quantity until the moment came. Few men can withstand the lure of publicity when organising a movement, but Kemal, with that quiet confidence and immense secrecy, which is one of the great virtues of Turks, managed his affairs unseen. He was in no sense a conspirator, merely an organiser of national spirit and national resistance, thinking out every move carefully in advance and at no point showing his colours prematurely. Our officers in Asia Minor hardly knew of him. He was merely a 'movement,' and as such was not accounted seriously at Headquarters in Constantinople. We thought we had power enough to deal with movements, but, as ever, we relied more on coastal power than on inland control. And against us were the great long-suffering mass of the peasants of Anatolia and behind them the untraversed highlands of their plateau, their forests and woods of the Cappadocian hill country and the unknown tracts of Taurus. With a handful of inexperienced officers as our guides we imagined that we knew all about Asia Minor.

But what a complex situation we had to handle, made the more complex by the complete inactivity of our late Allies. Or perhaps it would be more just to say the obstructionist activity, for wherever a spoke could be put into our wheels there was always a Frenchman or an Italian to do it.

Alone we attempted to bring some semblance of order into the two and seventy tribes of the Caucasus, into the patchwork coasts of the Black Sea, and into heterogeneous and unknown Asia Minor.

Nor did we stop there. In March General Milne went on a hurried tour of inspection eastwards. On his return we were at last informed of the half-known British Army far off in Turkestan which he had inspected and about whose fate we were now to decide.

My curiosity was now more aroused than ever, and I longed to get away from this frowsy city and its fake civilisation. I think the germ of war was not yet fully eradicated from my blood, and I wanted to see what fighting there still was. Imagine therefore my joy when I was notified a week or so later that I was to go with the Chief of Staff and two other officers to this actual field of events to make preparations for the evacuation of those very British troops in Turkestan whose existence had so long intrigued me.

I gathered maps, I packed, and suddenly received orders to go to Therapia to General Milne's house prepared to embark for the frosty Caucasus and distant Transcaspia.

* * * * * * *

With snow drifting in the air I set out from Headquarters for Therapia early on a March morning. At the diminutive quayside at Therapia was a slim destroyer. We embarked, with a small escort of a dozen infantrymen and a sergeant, who were to accompany us all the way there and back. Up the grey shores of the Bosporus we sped and past the Symplegades. Once out in the open inhospitality of the Black Sea we pitched and rolled with the utmost violence for the rest of the day and the night. At dawn we at last saw that most splendid of all views—the snowy ridge of the Caucasus appearing like a great white slash across the sky. Slowly the coastline emerged from the mists of the lowlands and we saw endless foothills with neat white villas dotted along them. At the quayside we saw long avenues of palms, for, strange to say, this land was almost tropical, protected as it was from Siberian blasts by the barrier of the Caucasus. Batum itself was a lovely town of golden Russian churches and bulging domes, neat streets and avenues of trees.

On the quay were vast heaps of manganese, mined from the hills behind. Among them was a special train waiting for us.

I wandered through the town during the few hours of leisure we had. In a shop I found an elderly Greek with whom I talked about Greece and Greeks. Delighted to hear his own tongue from a foreigner he chatted amiably and told me of the many Greeks who live in the Caucasus—at Batum there was quite a small community. He gave me a book, which I still have, written by a learned Caucasian Greek entitled *Greeks in the Caucasus*.

Our train was the most luxurious train I have ever seen. The Railway Transport Officer told me that it was originally that of the Russian Viceroy of the Caucasus. It had four sleeping rooms, a kitchen and a superb observation drawing-room, carpeted with the finest of Persian rugs. The line was, like all the Caucasian lines, broad gauge, so that the width of our apartments was great. At the end of the short train were the quarters for our infantry escort and a small office with a typewriter which would serve me for our records.

In the afternoon we started off through the green pastures of Phasis, the ancient home of pheasants.

We passed through park-like country, rich in oak and chestnut, with endless streams that sparkled among the trees. Away behind rose the precipitous foot-hills of the mighty Caucasus. It was early spring and the snows were just beginning to melt. Slowly the railway wound its way up a steep gradient and the cliffs closed in until we found ourselves passing over a ridge that was the watershed between Phasis-land and the open valley of the Kura, which flowed eastwards into the Caspian. Near the summit of this great Caucasian watershed, that divides all Asia from all Europe, we saw the narrow cleft that cuts northwards and leads over the Caucasus itself into Russia, the cleft along which runs the famous Russian military road over Mount Kazbek. Soon we passed, on a rocky spur above the upper waters of the Kura, the ancient city of Mtzkheta, a name as unpronounceable as most Georgian words. Georgia more than any other part of the Caucasus deserved independence on a self-determinative basis, for it has an honourable history as a kingdom from early Byzantine times, with a people accustomed to a rule of their own choosing. The passing sight of Mtzkheta, a cluster of venerable churches and crumbling walls, brought me once more into an ancient land, but a land of which I knew almost nothing. I could not even quite make out where I was, for the recently established republic had caused to be replaced all the old Russian railway station name-titles with large signs inscribed in the peculiar Georgian script. Consequently the maps I studied as we went along were useless for purposes of identification, since I could not read the Georgian names. I had to guess by the reading on my map the ordinary conventions of hill and dale, river and peak. But I was also now in a region known to the Greeks—the far-famed

Colchis, the home of Medea, the destination of Jason in his search for the Golden Fleece. Here was the Far East of the Greeks, whose old proverb said:

'To Phasis, where is the last voyage in the world for sea-ships.'

Batum was near the capital of ancient Phasis, or Colchis, and we had now left behind us on the western side of the watershed the famous River Rion, which empties itself into the Black Sea, and we were slipping gently down the eastern slopes, with the Kura, still keeping its ancient name of Kyros, foaming in ravines at our side, on its way to Tiflis and the great eastern plains. For the first time since the beginning of the war I had carried with me a copy of Herodotus. At last I felt I could really enjoy great literature without pretence or pedantry. In my text I found a creditable account of the Caucasus, composed from the stories of ancient merchants whom Herodotus had met. Later on I found that his description of Turkestan was even more satisfying, indeed astonishingly full and accurate. Greek merchants from Black Sea ports seem to have penetrated to unheard of distances. To-day their descendants have stayed on these ancient routes.

Tiflis swung into our sight, perched on the lower slopes of mountains on the southern side of the Kura, mountains whose roots ultimately ran up to the great main trunk of Ararat, for whose snowy peak we looked, but in vain.

Our excellent train was parked in a siding, and we walked out into the town through a very modern and well-equipped station.

The town was broad and dignified, indeed it was a city. We proposed to spend but the one night there, in our train, and then to hurry forward on our main task. At Batum we had been joined, unexpectedly, by General Gough, sometime Commander of the 5th Army in France. He had joined us, not as part of our mission, but simply to reach Baku as conveniently as possible on affairs of his own. We all visited our headquarters at Tiflis and dined with our friends. In the evening we were taken to the Opera, where we saw as fine a performance—in Russian—of *La Bohème* as one could hope to see. Since March 1916 to March 1919 I had been only once on leave home, and apart from the entertainments during that one leave, I had not seen anything that could properly be called a theatre during those three years. At Tiflis I found real pleasure. The audience was most diverting. All round us were Cossack officers in their superb uniforms, or else they were Circassian princes. Their ladies were of two distinct types, the dark almost Latin Georgians and the extremely blonde, amazonian, bobbed-haired, blue-eyed Circassians. But I was bitterly disappointed in their standards of beauty. The Georgians were merely swarthy, mainly aquiline, and in no sense lovely. The Circassians were like young Prussian girls, bony-faced, a trifle untidy, and only remarkable for their pronounced blondness. There is an old book published in the fifties of last century called *The Beauties of the Bosporus*: it usually appears in second-hand book catalogues under the classification of 'Curious, Erotic and Facetiæ.' [1] Many people buy it eagerly to see the lurid contents. Inside is a fine collection of steel plate engravings of cypress trees, mosques and sea-scenes. A similar feeling of having been deceived overcame us when we saw the Beauties of Circassia and Georgia. On the whole we decided that the natural beauties of their land were superior.

Our friends told us that the fiercest quarrels often took place at the opera among the Georgians. Only a few nights before there had been shooting at the exit-door as people came out from the opera. Georgians, apparently like Irishmen, favour the genial habit of having the entertainment first and the fun afterwards.

A cursory glance over Tiflis the next morning and we

[1] D. G. Hogarth's book on travel in Cyprus, called *Devia Cypria*, is also frequently so classified!

were off on our still long journey. Our train descended the downward gradient alongside the Kura, and soon we were passing through the loveliest open pastures imaginable. The type of scenery had totally changed. Now we could see a clear thirty miles over open grassland to the main range of the Caucasus itself, cloaked with snow. Here and there a lonely horseman, armed with a long javelin, served to emphasise the immense loneliness. Bands of nomad Tatars also appeared and we were already in a different world. Soon our small train approached the frontier between Georgia and Azerbaijan, its quarrelsome sister republic. A few miles short of the frontier the train stopped at a wayside station, contrary to schedule. I jumped out—for the running of the train was one of my tasks—and found the stationmaster in heated conversation with our engine-driver. The driver, it appeared, according to our interpreter, refused definitely to cross the frontier with his engine. He explained that once across the frontier the engine would be kept by the Azerbaijanlis, and perhaps himself as well. There was, he added, no sort of communication between the two republics, for the simple reason that each side impounded whatever crossed the border. Nor, as we had already found out, was the paper money current in Georgia recognised in Azerbaijan. Wilson's great invention had already begun to creak and groan! In the light of recent events it is amusing to look back on the defects of these first essays in self-determination, for they foreshadow almost everything that has since happened in Europe.

However, we had no intention of letting our affairs be hindered by the fears and feelings of incompetent republicans. I detached two of our escort, told them to fix bayonets, and mounted them in the cab of the engine. Off we steamed with the engine-driver making protesting noises. For all I know he never got back to Georgia and is in Azerbaijan still. But as the distance is not great I imagine he has not felt completely exiled.

Soon the lovely pastureland began to look withered and rusty. The cliffs and rocks of the Kura changed to yellow and livid red hues. There were no sheep and no villages. Here and there black greasy pools among the dusty yellow rocks appeared, covered with a film that reflected strange colours. Round a bend in the line I suddenly saw an immense plain on which appeared to be a dead forest of shattered tree-trunks, like some lunar landscape, but dun-coloured and grimy. It was the great oil-field of Baku that lies to the west of the city. Through it wound our train and there was scarcely a sign of life. Then Baku appeared, shoddy, modern and dusty, with clamouring Tatars at every side station, each and all covered with grease and grime. Here was our terminus, and our train puffed slowly to a dead end. Away in the background behind houses I could just detect the hint of a sea-horizon, misty and pale, a mere haze of blue. Friends met us and we spent a night at the headquarters of our garrison. Tatars seemed to me to be by far the least attractive of all the inhabitants of the Caucasus. They crowded and jostled us and each other; they fought and shouted; there was none of the calm of the immemorial East here. It was the noisiest place I had seen for a long time.

We were given much useful information, in particular of the appalling massacre at Baku by the Tatars in late 1918. I read reports by all the neutral consuls. There was no doubt about the horrors. One consul said that the Tatar population was, after a time, so sated with killing that men were to be seen leading batches of prospective victims, roped together like fowls, offering them for sale to other killers less exhausted than themselves for a few rubles each.

In the harbour we were astonished to see the white ensign floating at the stern of several merchantmen. It was the first time since the days of Antony Jenkinson that British ships had ever dropped anchor in the Caspian.

These were, of course, Russian vessels hired from merchants at Baku and commissioned into the British Navy, armed and equipped for naval action.

After a glance at the main sights, if such they can be called, of Baku, we embarked in a comfortable old Russian passenger ship at the quayside, late at night. It smelt violently of anti-bug powder, and had evidently been recently de-loused and de-bugged for our benefit. It was a ship that had been built in the eighties and had all the stately accommodation and rich ornament of a Margate steamer. The captain was an amiable Russian with a white goatee beard and a sympathetic manner.

On a windy night, with a heavy sea, we set out. To my astonishment all lights were dimmed or covered, for fear of submarines, as we were told. We laughed aloud at so comical a situation, for this sea was a lake with no exit but the River Volga. Yet rumour had it that the Bolsheviki—with whom we were at last in touch—held Astrakhan in force and were there assembling a submarine brought in sections by river from the Baltic!

On a brilliant morning we saw the low roofs of Krasnovodsk and skirted the ancient mouth of the River Oxus, which a few centuries ago changed its course and now discharges itself into the Sea of Aral instead of into the Caspian.

At the quay our serious task began. The Caucasus was peaceful and settled. But Transcaspia was in a ferment, for Bolshevism was spreading slowly but surely round the arid Caspian shores from Astrakhan and from the far north-east at Tashkend.

To me, personally, Bolshevism did not seem a deadly enemy, nor our combating of it in these remote regions a burning necessity. But what a chance of seeing some of the forbidden parts of the East, and what humours there would be by the wayside!

Nor was I kept long waiting for my entertainment. First of all we went to the president's house at Krasnovodsk, for Krasnovodsk was a republic all on its own, with its own worthless paper money and its own slightly more valuable president (for he had charge of the bullion which was at the back of the paper money). At last we saw the president. His name was Kuhn. He came down the main road of this ramshackle town (rather like what I imagine Klondike to have been) in a cloud of dust with a bodyguard of four mounted Turkomans on ponies. All five were riding at full gallop—'to avoid bullets,' as the president later explained, for he was not at the moment at the height of his popularity with his republican friends.

A brief conversation explained our needs, which were, in brief, a special train of two carriages to go to Merv, six hundred miles east. We had our own guard of a dozen English infantrymen to go with us, in case of minor troubles on the way. The president was delighted. 'Consider it arranged,' he told us. 'Just tell the stationmaster I authorise it,' he added. 'And by the way, on your return journey, which you tell me is next week, would you be so very kind as to take me with you to Baku? You see, things are a little difficult here. The Bolsheviki keep sending people over from Astrakhan to assassinate me, and, to tell you the truth, I was not appointed president by what you would call popular election. I merely took over the post from my predecessor.'

He was a very large man and he gave a very large smile. I felt rather sorry for the predecessor. But I felt rather sorry for the president, too. So we agreed to take him back with us, but could not guarantee that that agreement would hold valid with any successor whom we might find in his place on our return. For lives were brief in Transcaspia in those days. But he was supremely satisfied and undertook to do his best to survive until our return. In fact he did, and we took him.

Imperial Bolshevism has long since swallowed this and all the Caucasian and Asiatic republics and made larger units that now form well-organised states in the Soviet Union. But in those days of 1919 it was profoundly interesting to see how the pronouncements of President Wilson in 1918 had led to the mushroom growth of countless hopeful republics, some genuine enough, like Georgia, some wholly bogus, like Krasnovodsk and, as we found later, the republic of Askhabad.

I must confess I liked that president more than any of the many presidents of republics that we met *en route*. He was physically so splendid a type of the northern Russian. More still, he had all the personal attraction of the habitual homicide. For, as they darkly told us in the town, he had slain with his own hand at least sixteen of the notables in the process of forging his way to presidential eminence. There was nothing of the Chicago gangster about him; he was rather the 'wide open spaces' type of the cheap novelette, simple, generous, even sympathetic, and quite definitely firm.

But our time was short, and I felt rather uncertain about the facilities of the Central Asiatic Railway. So off to the station we went and I interviewed the stationmaster, a sombre and untrusting man. Quite clearly this stationmaster was a Bolshevik in sympathy. He looked upon us as the intruders that we were. He made us feel that we were uninvited guests—which we were also—and he was quite adamant about the special train. Without any Oriental politeness or circumlocution he told us flatly that he would not procure and could not find, even if he wished, any sort or kind of special train. We told him that we were looking for a mislaid war and hoped to end it, but he was unimpressed. I threatened him with reprisals, but could not for the life of me imagine what they would be. He remained disdainful and unmoved. So I produced my trump card and sent a hurried note to the president. In a few minutes I heard the galloping bodyguard and saw the dust of his approach. The president appeared, bowed and smiled to the stationmaster as if to his oldest friend, and offered him a cigarette. I explained my difficulty with tact and caution. The president turned to the stationmaster and said gently, 'Just get that train ready.' 'It is already under steam in the siding,' replied the stationmaster suavely. We rose, bade farewell to both dignitaries, and prepared to entrain.

That charming president had, I felt, considerable force of character. What he said went.

So off we started upon a journey that remains in my mind as the most unusual and most interesting that I have ever made. There are many books written by travellers who penetrated these parts before the war, particularly in the eighties of last century, when the imperial Russian armies had just subdued with blood and slaughter the marauding and head-hunting Turkomans of those days. The famous General Skobelev had with an iron hand transformed nomad tribes of considerable savagery into sedentary cotton-growers, and built small colonial cities along the trade route that soon was transformed into a railway. This region was certainly one of Russia's most successful imperial enterprises.

But we saw it under conditions which were unique. None of the many books would now be even tolerably accurate. They were, too, written by travellers who were there only with special privileges, who were allowed only to see what was thought good for them, and who were personally conducted by officials or governors. But we saw it stripped of its Russian bureaucracy, freed from its Russian rule, and thrown back for a brief and exciting period on to its own resources. And these resources were peculiar. The Turkomans, magnificently tall, picturesque, and dignified, still retained the elements of Russian civilization and the discipline of Russian rule. Many of them had served in the Great War with the Russian armies in Galicia and Austria and bore the medals of the Russian army. All, in a sense, were pro-Russian, and yet there stirred within them the same germ of self-determination that stirred all around

Orad Sirdar, leader of our Turkoman allies

Austro-Hungarian officer prisoners on the quay at Krasnovodsk

them, although in their case it had not developed to the stage of any specific organisation; they still remained a tribal people ready to move and act on a tribal basis. But we found them our friends because all they wanted was peace and quiet and to be left alone, and they were mortally afraid of being exploited and taxed and pillaged by the Bolsheviki in the north-east from Tashkend and near Bokhara.

The other element was the Russian population, colonists in type, who lived mainly on and for the railway. Like all railwaymen, they disliked drastic change which was likely to alter their settled life, and the discipline of a railway system was in their blood. They, too, wanted to be left alone and would have welcomed an independent Trans-caspian republic. But, instead, they had to endure a series of presidents and local republics, each independent of the other, each with a currency which was not current a few miles farther on and a president who changed from week to week.

Our train left Krasnovodsk and set forth optimistically. We skirted the old Oxus estuary and at last came into sight of the bastion ridge of mountains that was the frontier between Persia and Turkestan. To the north and north-west stretched an endless plain of fertile mud washed down from the hills and dotted every few miles with cotton-growing villages. The snow had only just left the plain, for Turkestan has as hard a winter as it has blazing a summer. Everywhere were careful irrigation and apparent prosperity. At every station we found the same scene: Turkomans in their long robes and shaggy sheepskin caps, occasional black-hatted Persians, and Russian railwaymen. No one seemed curious to see us; no one, in fact, seemed surprised at anything. The Turkomans showed a polite interest, while the Russians were phlegmatically helpful.

The desert over which our train passed was not the desert of the novels or of the films. It was perfectly smooth and had no sand. Beyond the fact that caravans of camels and bushes of camel's-thorn were to be seen on it, it bore no resemblance to the deserts of Egypt. And all the time there loomed in the background the unending ridge of mountains that screened Persia.

One town only of any size did we pass before reaching Askhabad, the capital of the province. This was Kizil Arvat, and here we found the first traces of our forgotten war in the shape of English soldiers on the platform. They were men of the Hampshire Regiment, a mere handful stationed at this town (six men in all, I think) to govern it, keep it in order, protect it from external attack and internal sedition. They assured us that in fact these onerous duties were purely nominal, for nothing of any sort at all had happened there for a month and they were all living in complete comfort on the best of terms with their neighbours.

So we passed on and at length came in sight of a lovely oasis of trees with fine houses rising above them. This was the considerable settlement of Askhabad and here the mountain ridge at the back rose up to a greater height and was snow-covered. Behind it was no longer the peaceful land of Persia, but the uncertainties and ambiguities that went under the name of Afghanistan. Here we were met by British staff officers, by Russian officers whose allegiance was to the far-off armies of Denikin, and by Indian troops. Here at last was our forgotten war apparently in full swing.

Askhabad, with its long avenues of planes and poplars, its old-fashioned Russian stucco-fronted houses, its drainage and water system, and its electric light, was a model townlet. Forgetting the war which we had just found, we visited the main square and the market-place. In the centre of the square were two muzzle-loading guns which we found were British, dated 1838 and 1849 respectively. As British had never fought Russians in Turkestan, we were driven to assume that they were British guns captured from us by Afghans and captured from Afghans by Russians.

The market was the cleanest and the most interesting which I have ever seen in the East. There were for sale all the nicest things one can imagine: dried peaches from the oases, fish from the Caspian, apples from the 'Garden of the Hesperides' in the Caucasus, of enormous size and fabulous redness; joints and heads of wild ibex in the meat shops, skins of Persian lamb, of marmot, fox, and snow leopard, rugs of Bokhara and of the Tekke-Turkomans, and, most popular of all commodities, brand-new bicycles, for bicycling on the mud flats seemed to be the favourite pursuit of the Turkomans. A hospital, government offices, and even a museum added to the amenities.

Over a pleasant dinner we were told the nature and condition of the war which we had been sent to inspect. It was evidently a good war, if any war can be so called. But it was good in the sense that there were hardly any casualties, no front, no trenches, practically no artillery, and certainly no gas, mines, or other horrors. And then there were the entertaining extras, such as a local currency struck by the British general (General Malleson) in charge; the local Republican Committee, who had other sources of income independent of ours, and were nominally our advisers; and, last but not least, our Intelligence Service, which brought information that would have made Edgar Wallace or Phillips Oppenheim envious.

It was, in short, just the sort of war that our regular officers had always longed for, the sort of war that many of them thought the Great War should have been.

But to those of us who had been in France it was hardly a war to be taken seriously. True, it had a certain importance outside itself. It gave us a means of knowing, at least in part, what was fermenting in that vast mysterious region south of the Urals, west of the Pamir, and east of the Volga, that most romantic of all regions, whence so much of barbarism or potential culture has always throughout endless centuries pushed westward and forced its way either into

Asia Minor or round the north of the Black Sea into Europe. Here germinated the Huns, the Tatars, the Bulgars, the Sarmatians, and the Scythians, and hence they moved out at intervals westward, either driven by the pressure of Chinese and remoter Eastern tribes or forced to seek new pastures by the periodical desiccation of the land and the decay of vegetation. Here was the very pulse of Asia itself, and we had our hands on it. That and that only justified this strange war and this unwanted expedition. Vaguely, by means of agents, intercepted messages, or deliberate spying, we had learned what was afoot in Astrakhan, in Tashkend, and on the confines of Mongolia and China, at Kashgar in the east and at Balkh, the back door to Afghanistan, on the west. For here we were in the ruins of an empire that had just tottered but not yet completely collapsed, and in such a condition there was much to be found out. Where unity of command has vanished and unity of administration gone, every joint gapes and every rent opens wider in the general fabric. And we could see much of what was inside.

So off we went the next day to see the foremost line of battle. A few hours in the train to the eastward and a scamper on desert ponies for another half-hour brought us to the last eastward point of the British spearhead, near great Merv itself. At a point east still of Merv was the end of all things, the little railway station of Annenkovo, facing Charjui, the Bolshevik bridgehead on the Oxus. It was a curious thing to think that from here I could go westward continuously to London in safety and comfort, but that half a mile farther on I could reach London only by walking to Peking! One felt that if the Allied victory had done nothing else it had at least succeeded in producing a certain unity of control over areas hitherto plunged in inextricable confusion.

At length we reached the 'front.' For there was, after all, something that could just be called that. But it was only four feet in width—for it consisted of the railway line! On that line we had an armoured train, and about a mile farther on, almost on the banks of the Oxus, the Bolsheviki had their armoured train. As ours advanced, theirs receded, and *vice versa*. But of flanks to this 'front' there were no traces, for the railway was well out in the desert and the mountains of Afghanistan were far away to the south-east. To outflank the armoured train, one had to make a circuitous route in the desert, and this was virtually impossible owing to lack of water. Consequently both sides lived in, around, and near their armoured train and moved with it backward or forward. All the ordinary rules of strategy were forgotten or put aside; the whole thing was a game pure and simple.

Then there was the enemy. A few skirmishes showed that he consisted, strange to say, not of Russians, but of Hungarians and Austrians. Imagine this strange little war, months after the Armistice, where Englishmen from Hampshire, Punjabis, and lancers from Bengal fought side by side against citizens of Vienna and Budapest, on the banks of the remote Oxus in the plains where Alexander of Macedon had passed and founded mighty cities! Nowhere, I think, in the whole area of warfare had there been so odd a paradox, so strange a collocation of forces. I had a long talk with an Austrian officer recently captured. He was delighted with his fate, for his chances of seeing his home had hitherto been but slight. He told me that the Hungarians and Austrians had been made prisoners years before and sent to Siberia. He said that they were asked to serve as mercenaries and were well paid; that none of them had heard of the Armistice, and they had been told that their only hope of returning home was to push the British back to the Caspian and so reach Astrakhan. Probably most of them were resigned to the not unpleasant life of mercenaries in this not very unpleasant war.

With our binoculars we could see the enemy sentinels at

the distant station of Ravnino and the steam of the Bolshevist armoured train. But there was no sound of war, no shells—not even an occasional bullet. The war was a thing of spasms and surprises. The trains would push each other backward and forward, unable to do any very satisfactory shooting, since most of their guns pointed out at right angles to the railway line. Once a party of Hungarians had succeeded in carrying their water and creeping round the desert by night. A small battle developed and our forces round the railway drove them back again. A small cemetery by the station marked our casualties, surely the loneliest and strangest of all the many war cemeteries, now, I imagine, utterly forgotten and not within the jurisdiction of the War Graves Commission.

This, in brief, was the war we had been sent to find, a comical enough affair in itself, but with serious issues depending on it. It was obvious that the officers of the Indian army who were 'at the front' thought it was real war, thrilling, genuine, and epic. Nice youngsters, in command of smart Indian lancers, but none of them had even the vaguest idea what war really was. And the senior officers, too, thought it a very serious war; but the north-west frontier is an inadequate training for the horrors of intensive bombardment, mustard gas, and the *Minenwerfer*. The officer of the Indian army still retains the boyish enthusiasm for war which has long ago been knocked out of the veterans of Continental European warfare.

Our 'allies' were in force at this spear-point front. There were the Russians, a very uncertain quantity. Their officers looked upon us as intruders, even as the stationmaster at Krasnovodsk had done. Everywhere I had received the same impression: nobody really loved us. Not that we were not definitely useful to Russians and Turkomans alike, but both felt that we were interfering in affairs that did not concern us. And no doubt we were, but it was a most profitable intrusion from our point of view and it was of no little interest that it was the first time that British troops had ever fought battles in Central Asia.

Our Turkoman allies were undoubtedly the most picturesque of all the allies that helped us on any front during the war. Their leader was a fine old man called Orad Sirdar who had served with high rank in the imperial Russian army. He wore a Russian uniform, but a Turkoman sheepskin hat, about the size of the ordinary English busby. He carried a sword of formidable type, more like a Persian scimitar than anything else. His personal staff were superb Turkomans who wore the usual Turkoman dress of a long gown (cut like a dressing-gown) of silk, and black or pure white sheepskin hats. The general impression of the Turkoman forces was one of efficiency, but we gathered that in action their cavalry, which was their main contingent, was of little value, since, in the charge, it scattered and was not well disciplined enough to reform quickly. Such had been their behaviour at the Battle of Dushakh in September 1918, when the Turkoman cavalry had scattered and commenced looting the abandoned Bolshevist supply train, with the result that the Bolsheviki had reformed and counter-attacked them with some effect.

For the forces on the spot our task was not a cheerful one. We had orders to arrange for the evacuation of the British and Indian troops back by way of the Caucasus and for the general winding up of the enterprise. Our place was to be taken by a new contingent of Russians from the armies of Denikin at Ekaterinodar in South Russia. The reaction of the Russians on the spot was curious. They didn't want to lose us, but they felt that we ought to go. By the Turkomans our departure was viewed as a disaster. So much so that at Askhabad we were asked to meet a delegation of Turkoman headmen of tribes who wished to know our intentions. The meeting remains in my mind as one of the most interesting and impressive affairs which I encountered during the war. Some eight or nine splendid chieftains appeared, each dressed in the purple or brown silk robes of Turkestan, each with his head uncovered, displaying the clean-shaved poll that Turkomans hide beneath their shaggy hats. All were over six feet in height, with clear-cut features and long aquiline faces, exactly like the rare type of Anatolian Turk that one sees from time to time in Turkey, who still preserves the facial characteristics of his desert ancestors from Turkestan.

They announced that if we withdrew our troops they would be at the mercy of either White or Red Russians and that they relished the control of neither. They further said that as soon as we went they would start a tribal move of some two hundred thousand men south-westward into Persia. In fact they did so, and for some time in the last months of 1919 Turkestan became largely nomadic again. But our commitments would have been too large for our forces if we had remained, and in any case our task of holding the equilibrium and surveying the ground in general had already been more than adequately carried out.

So with plans prepared we started on our return journey. Arrangements were made for all our troops to be sent back *via* the Caspian and the Caucasus or by way of Baghdad.

One deep regret remained. Away to the north-east was Bokhara, ruled by an Emir of astonishing ingenuity and courage. His state was a kind of non-Bolshevik enclave in Bolshevik territory. He had resisted all attempts of the Bolsheviki to penetrate his domain or to control him in any way. He had even gone so far as to blow up Bolshevik railway lines in various places and to declare openly his alliance with us! But we on our part were helpless to do anything to help him. As token of his esteem and affection for British arms he had sent, on a famous occasion early in 1919, an emissary, who had made an enormous circuit in the desert and reached Merv, whence he had been taken to Askhabad to General Malleson. The emissary reiterated the professions of friendship of his sovereign and produced

Emissary of the Emir of Bokhara and General Malleson

as proof a package of decorations for the British troops—the 'Star of the Emir of Bokhara,' a lovely and resplendent Oriental adornment. Unhappily sanction was never granted for the wearing of these decorations, which was a pity for those who held them, as they outclassed in brilliance any foreign decoration granted in the whole war.

The Emir was our one deep regret. We could not help him and we had to leave him. Later, when the whole anti-Bolshevik force collapsed and the Turkomans dispersed and Bolshevism established itself firmly in Transcaspia, we heard that the Emir held out to the very end, until overwhelming forces captured Bokhara by storm. The Emir escaped before the final fall and went, I believe, to Afghanistan. But his lovely city of Bokhara was looted and its autonomy ceased. Turkestan became virtually an imperial province once again.

Our journey back was as diverting as our arrival. Just as we were about to leave the station of Askhabad and had said our farewells to the British Staff, a strange and swarthy man appeared. He introduced himself as the president of Askhabad! Behind him were two men carrying a heavy box. With the greatest politeness he begged permission to be given a place on our train in order that he might 'pay a visit to Tiflis.' There was room enough on our train, but we did not wish to involve ourselves in complications, as our task was a purely military one, with no political issues to consider. Nor did we feel that we were in any way indebted to the president, and above all we distrusted the look of that large wooden box. Later our suspicions of it were found to be justified, for it had held the contents of the republican treasury. So we proffered our sympathy and regret and left the unhappy president behind us. I can see him now lighting a cigarette and gazing despondently after us as the train steamed out, for he knew that his presidential career would be a chequered one if he stayed much longer.

Our journey back to Askhabad was uneventful and we were able to enjoy the loveliness of this remote province. For it was lovely in colour and in form. The railway skirted the mountain ridge the whole way along, and to the north the plain lands had a beauty all of their own. Soft fawn-coloured earth with vivid green crops and trees at the infrequent settlements, pale turquoise-blue distances, and pale rose-coloured skies at evening. It is a land of no sharp outlines or tremendous contrasts. And it has everywhere the imprint of a most ancient world. Here and there along the line—for the railway follows the only route possible along the desert, the only route where water, which comes from the mountains, can be found—were great mounds of prehistoric settlements, links of a great chain that runs east and west across the valleys south of the Caucasus ridge and so across Turkestan to Balkh and the Pamir. One group near Askhabad has been excavated by American archæologists and the results show affinity with Europe on the one hand and Mesopotamia on the other. The railway here, as in the Caucasus, follows the ancient road, perhaps the most ancient road in the world.

At Krasnovodsk we took ship once more, accompanied by our friend the president, who had managed to survive. But this was our only interference in local politics.

A few months after the evacuation of our troops was completed the whole of Transcaspia fell into Bolshevik hands. White Russians and Turkomans alike were scattered like chaff, and the first steps were taken which ended in the establishment of Turkestan as a semi-autonomous Soviet Socialist state. For Russia its potentialities are great. The mud plains are the finest of cotton-growing areas and the organisation of the whole province in material ways is quite excellent. As a colonial province it leaves nothing to be desired, for after the conquest of Skobelev fifty years ago it was made as perfect as an imperial province could be. In export of rugs and carpets alone it contains immense wealth. And for Russia it is of the greatest strategic importance. It forms the background of Afghanistan, the Russian counterpart of our North-West Provinces. From Merv runs the only strategic railway that Russia possesses against the Afghan frontier. And it was precisely in these parts that Germany, during the war, spent much time and effort with anti-Allied propaganda, conducted by two able and enterprising agents, Captain Wagner and Dr Niedermeyer, who in ability, though not in results, were almost the equal of men like Colonel T. E. Lawrence.

The history I have related is now ancient history. All the chief characters have vanished and the situation is so completely changed that it seems to belong to another age. For Central Asia is the least static of all the regions of the East. But every change there has its counterpart on the southern marches of Afghanistan, and the mighty mountains of that unruly state link up rather than sunder the affairs of the plain lands south and north of them.

But those who curiously read the words 'Central Asia' among the list of places recorded upon the war memorial at Hyde Park Corner in London will now know to what a strange forgotten war it bears witness.

* * * * * * *

On our way back from this remote visit we came once more to the gilded domes of Batum. Here a small passenger ship awaited us to take us up on a hurried trip to Novorossiisk, main port on the east for the White Russian forces. We sailed close inland along the Abkhazian shore, round the very roots of the mighty Caucasus and up to the flat shores of the Kuban. In a large and roomy harbour we saw the nondescript little port that served the Russian armies. Here we were shown vast warehouses, crammed to the roof with machine-guns and grenades and small arms ammunition, all British made, destined for Wrangel and his men and Denikin, to aid them in what we then believed was their righteous war of freedom. Tanks had just been landed and there were many guns: indeed, so armed, the White troops might well have fought their way to the Arctic. But, as it so happened, a few weeks later these very troops came running helter-skelter over the hills to the port pursued by ill-armed but very fierce Bolshevik troops, and the whole vast accumulation of arms fell, ready packed, into the hands of the Reds. For those vast armaments I am now paying in part through the British income tax. But what was a million or two to us then?

From Novorossiisk we took train for some hours across the rich black plains of South Russia, incredibly fertile, well populated and prosperous. But there was no charm about this country. It was bleak and dull and held nothing of the interest and beauty of Turkestan. A day and a night at the Denikin headquarters at Ekaterinodar and we learned all we wanted. For White Russia came only incidentally into our plans. All we wanted was to ensure that Denikin would provide troops to hold those Turkoman lands that we were just on the point of evacuating. In due course those troops were sent, and held our Turkoman domains for exactly a week, before they ran as fast as they could to the Caspian, pursued by Bolsheviks who burst in the moment we had left. I never heard again of any of the strange characters who were in Transcaspia while we were there. The whole scene changed, and now once more Merv and Askhabad and Kizil Arvat are peaceful cities in a well-organised province of the new Russia.

At the headquarters of Denikin we saw confusion and incompetence. No one seemed to have any reliable information about the enemy, and, as an experienced Intelligence Officer, I was shocked to find that no one seemed to know or to care where the enemy was. It was not long before their ignorance was transformed to more definite knowledge.

CHAPTER XIV

DEMOBILISATION

BACK across the Black Sea once more, this time obliquely from north-east to south-west. The dark and heaving waves were as unfriendly as before and I was overjoyed to see the quay of Therapia again. At Headquarters I resumed my normal routine, but a week later my demobilisation papers suddenly materialised. Just as in 1914 I had received that simple order to go to my unit, so now I was told that I should proceed at once to Southampton. These brief telegrams covered a period of my life of no little length. It was over four and a half years since I had put on my uniform, and now I had the strange feeling that I was nobody's property any longer. My friends smiled enviously; I handed over my job to a successor, went round to say good-bye to all I had known; packed my very small possessions in my canvas valise and obtained a ticket for Salonika. A few days later I was sitting in a luxurious sleeping compartment of the International Wagon Lits Company at Sirkedji Station in Stamboul waiting to take the winding journey westwards over hills of eastern Thrace to the coast of Macedonia and so past all the old battlefields, up the Strymon valley and past Doiran to Salonika. Off we creaked with an ancient and battered engine to pull us. Fifty miles out the engine broke down and we waited some hours. After two days along the coast we saw the grimy houses of Salonika again. On the way we had stopped at every station and looked for the first time with eyes of tourists on the lovely mountains of Macedonia. Bulgar soldiers crowded the platforms along the coast between Dedeagatch and Kavalla, for this region was still held and still claimed by Bulgaria. Only at the Peace Treaty did she finally lose it and withdraw her troops into the mountain fastnesses, raging and cursing that this coveted outlet should have been awarded to Greece. But Bulgaria had been beaten to the ground, her armies dispersed or captured and her capital occupied. Alone of all the belligerents she took her defeat bravely and acknowledged that she was utterly beaten. I am tempted to wonder if an Allied occupation of Vienna and Berlin would not have had a similar effect on our other opponents. For force can only be destroyed by force: war admits of no compromise and must be fought to the ultimate end. I am a pacifist by nature and by conviction, but I do not believe that reason or justice can intervene when once force has been named as arbiter. Our enemies called on force to serve them, and on the ultimate implications of force we too should have called when dealing with Germany, for then the Germans knew no other reasoning. The issue was plain enough: one group of nations had started out to show Europe, by making an example of Serbia, that force is the surest diplomacy. The other group took on the challenge and decided to show to the world that force as an argument leads to its own destruction. But the weapon used to prove this purely idealistic conception was itself the weapon of force. We won our illogical and unreasonable point and proved to Germany and Austria that force is no argument. We proved it by force alone. In a word, we were trying to give our opponents the *reductio ad absurdum* of their own argument. And I think we succeeded, though we made the fatal mistake in the case of Austria and Germany of abandoning our argument in favour of reason at the very end of the debate. In November 1918 we decided that Force had gone far enough. In doing that I think we were wrong. For in 1935 again we are driven to organise against Germany precisely the same arguments that we left suspended in 1918. Again we have mobilised force against Germany, and all Europe once more is holding up the warning finger to the Germans and saying

'Be careful: if you threaten force, look first at the weapons we hold in our hands!' Yet with Bulgaria alone we pushed our argument to the logical conclusion. We utterly routed one of their three mighty armies; its soldiers were mown down as they retreated in droves, the survivors fled into their mountain villages, threw away their arms and donned civilian clothes to escape being made prisoners: our pursuit stopped only at the gates of Sofia, and stopped there because the prospect of a Serbian army in the Bulgarian capital was one likely to embitter Balkan relations for a generation to come. That was our one concession on this front to the demands of Reason. Of the other two Bulgar armies one surrendered intact and the other was ordered to march home and demobilise. Three hundred thousand troops of the enemy were thus disarmed and dispersed in a matter of a week or so. The plenipotentiaries of the enemy accepted our terms without argument. They handed over enormous material of war and withdrew their control from all areas which had not originally been Bulgarian. From that day to this Bulgaria has kept her word, observed the terms of the Peace Treaty, abandoned all her demands for territories outside her borders and returned to her natural boundaries. Her peasants now cultivate their gardens, her politicians keep to Bulgarian politics. Bulgaria deserves after all these years the rewards due to a trusted opponent. More honest than Germany, more truthful than Hungary and more faithful than Austria, she deserves the full honours of war due to an honourable and stubborn enemy. Her soldiers fought fairly and with valour; her generals were able and skilful, beaten only by generals more skilful than they. I am glad to have served on the Bulgarian front and I am glad to have made many friends since the war in Bulgaria.

From Salonika, now a mere depot for discarded army goods, I and another officer took passage on an Italian transport bound for Taranto. Once more I sighted the Acropolis from Phalerum Bay as our ship stopped to coal.

Once again I sighted Cape Matapan as we coasted to the Ionian Sea and across the Adriatic.

At Taranto we went to a rest camp on the shore, among vineyards and fig-trees. The next day we were put aboard a troop train with six hundred happy soldiers bound for England. Our train was to find its way up the eastern Italian coast, across the Alps, and so to Le Havre and Southampton. We were told that our trip would take about a fortnight! It did.

Past Brindisi and Bari and Molfetta we went, trundling along. I and my friend shared a grimy second-class carriage and slept precariously on the seats. It was a marvellous feeling at last to know that I no longer owed allegiance to anybody. True I was still an officer, that I was still bound to His Majesty by unbreakable bonds. But actually nobody wanted me to do any sort or kind of duty. We all helped marshal the men each evening as our train stopped at some halt where they were given a meal: we marched them in still as soldiers, but they knew and we knew that there was no more need of the formalities of military life. We were all good friends with one object in common—to get home. No one got drunk, because he knew that if he did he would probably get left behind. No one complained, because we knew that whatever we suffered by way of discomfort would end in a fortnight. We were all continuously happy for that entertaining fortnight. At some of our innumerable stoppings, if we happened to be at a village, some of the men would jump out and play with the children beside the line, or give presents of jam and chocolates to the startled peasants. One idiot had obtained somewhere a red wig and a mask and he delighted crowds of Italians by capering along the train and chasing the children. With such diversions we whiled away our lengthy journey. We were well looked after. Once or twice we stopped the night and slept in rest camps. One such at Faienza was as pleasant an evening as I had had during the war. We wandered round the ancient city and felt that we were getting a free trip to Italy.

Modane and the colder air of Switzerland gave us a change. Then came the almost interminable fields of France, and as Paris neared many of us wondered how the train would go. For the proximity of Paris was too great a temptation for us to imagine that six hundred men would still be found in the train when we left Paris. But a far-sighted demobilisation staff had taken all due measures. As the outskirts of Paris appeared we suddenly found that our train was making a vast circle round the city and not stopping except at St Germain. Two experienced soldiers, however, did vanish at St Germain. They knew their Paris. But when our train, five hours later, skirted round the northern suburbs, there were our two absentees, waiting for us at a small station. They were greeted with roars of applause.

At Le Havre we spent another night in a rest camp and the next day were on a boat for Southampton. There are few places in England so lovely at dawn as Southampton Water. As we slipped gently alongside the quay I felt that this was England unchanged and unmoved by all the chaos and killing I had seen: an immemorial place that nothing had ever shaken. It was early April and there was a gleam in the air and a cold clear sunlight. All those low red houses of an English town that I had almost forgotten seemed so very English and so very unruffled. They seemed to look at me and say, 'Who are you and what has all the trouble been about? Why are you so pleased to get back? This is only Southampton, nothing very lovely!'

I disembarked on the quay. It was early and there was no one about except a solitary policeman who ignored me. At last I saw a small shack bearing the notice 'Demobilisation Office.' I entered. A sleepy corporal handed me a small form. I filled it up almost mechanically. I signed it. I was demobilised. 'Am I really out of the army at last?' I asked him. 'Yes,' he said, and smiled. I walked to the station, found there was no train for some time and went for a stroll in the streets of that ancient city. I now had no one in the world under my orders and no one who could ever command me again. It was unthinkable. My life was my own to do as I liked with. I could plan every moment now exactly as I wished. But it still didn't seem true or possible.

I stopped in shops and talked with people about anything I could think of. They seemed exactly as people had always been in England years and years ago. Everything seemed perfectly ordinary. What on earth had been happening all these years, and what had I been doing? I was back again in that world of real existence that I seemed to have left for so vast a space of time. I felt as if I was waking up at last and my dreams passing.

In London I found my father and my mother and sister. All was unchanged. Now, I thought, what on earth am I going to do with myself? How shall I start to do whatever I am going to do? Here I am, back in the home that I had always known after being away in a strange nightmare land of unreason where there was nothing but killing and destruction. I am a barbarian still for I remember it all.

I met friends who had also returned. They, too, had that taint of that barbarism on them. But I felt happy to be with them, for we had been savages together and I still felt that I had more in common with them than with any one else. We met together and talked furtively of the war. We felt rather like escaped convicts.

But now we all had to begin to do something, and, harder still, to think what that something was to be. It was inconceivable that it could be anything which did not involve the giving or the receiving of orders. Yet we knew that we should have to be independent.

One of my friends who had just come back told me that he had that very day encountered one of his sterner and more forbidding maiden aunts at lunch. 'Well, James,' she said crisply, 'now you have come back you had better settle down and begin to do something serious at last.' James had had four years of service behind him and had been wounded five times!

But the aunt was right, as aunts always are. We all had to start to do something serious again. We had all been like naughty children, mad to kill and break and destroy. We were at last growing up.

CHAPTER XV

FINAL PHASES

AFTER a week or so in London seeing friends I hastened up to Oxford for one simple purpose, to take my overdue M.A. degree, which I thought would at least give me the feeling of being civilised again. I arranged to stay there for a short while, as there were formalities to be gone through and old friends to be sought out. Also I had no civilian clothes of any kind. My last surviving civilian suit I had had sent out from London to Constantinople in order that I might exchange it for a Persian carpet of a value of some ten times the suit; for, as I have explained above, there was a famine of textiles and clothing in Turkey! My deal was a good one, and that rose-coloured carpet now lies in my study.

So up I went in my uniform to Oxford and the first man I visited was my tailor. In a week or ten days I should be properly garbed again.

Then I began to look round and search for my friends and hear the news. For I had no means of knowing what had happened to them. Some I knew were dead, but my information was meagre. But I learned soon enough. Roger Heath, who won the Newdigate in 1910 with one of the loveliest poems of the decade, was among the killed. I had roamed Greece with Heath in 1913 and the very winter before the war he and I had discovered and copied out a fine unrecorded Greek inscription in the sunny bay of Megara, almost touching the island of Salamis. Balleine, who had been my tutor in Roman history, was dead, but my philospohy tutor, Walter Moberly, had survived and been given the D.S.O. for untold gallantry. Guy Dickins, who had been mainly instrumental in my ever going to Greece at all, whose scholarship and archæological learning had helped and guided me and inspired me, was dead, shot through the head. Of those who had been at school with me, or who had been of my year at college, I could find none. Arthur Roe, brilliant classic and scholar, who had taken his first in Greats almost as the war broke out and who had at once passed almost at the top of the Indian Civil Examination, had disobeyed the orders of the Government that he was not to join the army and been killed a year after he joined. Cox, scholar of New College, with whom I had made so many expeditions from school and from Oxford during vacations was among the missing. Woodhouse, mercurial President of the Union for 1911, who was of my own year at Lincoln, was dead. It seemed only yesterday that we had all talked and met. I was making appalling discoveries, and I felt more lonely than ever.

There was a strange atmosphere in Oxford. Gone were the early patriotic raptures of 1914. There was not the faintest echo of that first demand that none but the lame and the blind should be educated. Indeed I felt that, just because I was in uniform, I was looked at askance. 'What are the licentious soldiery doing here?' these glances seemed to say. 'This is a home for learning, not for playing at soldiers.' I felt the caustic breath of the maiden aunt who had put my friend James in his place. Oxford had put on very firmly all her lace collars and bugles and whalebone corsets and was holding up her lorgnettes most superciliously.

On reflection I think that this attitude towards the licentious soldiery was mainly due to an unconscious reassertion of the real purpose of Oxford. For Oxford was now no longer a place for strutting soldiers—and in khaki and red tabs I was a trifle obvious. Oxford was beginning to be a university once more after lying dormant for five years. I felt this curious anti-military atmosphere most of all among the older folk. But that was because so few of the younger dons had returned. So many were dead or still away. I dined at various common rooms and everywhere I felt the same curious atmosphere. The war was never mentioned at all. They were trying so hard to take up the old threads that had been broken in 1914, that people still apparently soldiers struck them as an intrusion and an offence. And I felt it all exceedingly unpleasant. It was hardly a welcome home after an Odyssey! Had I done my duty by the military training which my University had given me only to be treated as a kind of unclean outcast?

Fortunately my civilian suit arrived and I was subjected to no more of this unspoken criticism. The first day I wore my new suit I felt as if I should fall to pieces. For so many years my waistline had been held firm by a belt and a close-fitting uniform and my legs in leggings, that no belt and soft trousers made me feel almost decadent.

Like my elders and betters I decided to forget the war. I set to work on the text of Herodotus and reread all that he had written about the frosty Caucasus and the deep-lying Caspian—for the spell of those distant parts was still upon me. Carefully I compiled a paper which I sent off to a learned journal which promptly published it. I was overjoyed, for at last I felt I was back again in the world of learning and research.

It was strange but delightful to go to dinner in lovely June evenings in different colleges and see the same customs and the same conversation continuing as if there had been no war. Oxford was trying so very hard to recover, but beneath the calm and the sanity of those dinners lurked the knowledge of all those dead men who should have been there too. Yet not one word did we ever have of them. We talked of almost everything else. Those who talked were either the elders or else those very few dons younger than myself who, from physical infirmity, had not been able to serve, and so had taken their courses regularly during the war and then been made fellows of this that or the other college. But there were not many such. Those I met seemed unreal and improbable people. Those of them who are still in Oxford remain now as unreal and improbable as they were then.

About this time T. E. Lawrence returned to Oxford in the guise of a Fellow of All Souls. But as he slept all day and worked all night he was not as sociable as had been expected. Sometimes he emerged during the day and I used to see him drifting like a wraith along the lanes and byways of the Bodleian Square. I believe that he hardly ever mentioned the war at all.

Early that summer I was offered a post at the British School at Athens. I took it with alacrity, for England was to me a strange and wild place in 1919, and I was glad to get out of it.

In January of the next year, while still at Athens, I was elected a Fellow of New College, but I could not yet tear myself away from the Balkans and I arranged to spend part of the year in Oxford and part in Athens for a time.

* * * * * * *

In 1920 I was working quietly at Athens. Poor Greece was still in turmoil. While the Great Powers who had dragged her into the war were settling down to the reconstruction of peace, there was no rest for the Greeks. The growing menace of Nationalist Turkey, and the ambiguous position in Asia Minor in which the Greeks were placed by the decisions of the Great Powers, had left Greece a heritage of hate and confusion in the Balkans. And not only did no one attempt to help her except with words, but her ancient allies, the Protecting Powers, did much to impede her in what she could do for herself. The French actively armed the Kemalist forces in Asia Minor, Italy collaborating. Russia was out of the picture and England did nothing.

Nor could I any longer take much interest in wars or politics. I was deep in my work again and had, as I thought, and as all of us thought, put the war into the category of forgotten things. What ostriches we all were to be sure, for the war's baneful influence controlled still all our thoughts and acts, directly or indirectly.

One day in the spring of 1920 a friend at the Legation told me that the mother of Rupert Brooke was anxious to have a tomb placed over his grave in the remote little island of Skyros. He had died in 1915 and been buried in a glade near the harbour. No one had been to see the grave since the burial and no one knew much about it. I had never met Rupert Brooke before or during the war. But my friend asked me if I would undertake this task. I was of Brooke's generation and there seemed to be no one in Athens more suitable than myself. So on a windy day in early April I set out in a ridiculous little steamship that plied once a week between the northern islands of Greece. The marble tomb, which had been cut at Athens from a design made in London, was sent on ahead in a small sailing ship, whose captain had made rendezvous with me at the remote port where the grave lay. I started out at sunset in the little steamship, but off Sunium we ran into one of those ferocious storms for which Sunium is famous, and our ship fled to Laurium harbour for safety for the night. During the night we dragged our anchor and drifted aimlessly round the rocky harbour in some danger. In the morning we set forth again, as the storm had subsided. We tried the Doro channel just south of Eubœa, but the channel was a sheet of surf and the captain wisely turned tail and sailed up the inner passage between Eubœa and the mainland. The next day we arrived at Skyros and I disembarked at the little white-roofed port-village. A wild sky showed behind the steep cliffs of the island, but the sun was soon bright and the storm gone for good. I set out for my rendezvous, which was at the other end of the island, some four hours journey from the only village. I took mules and provisions and at length came to the beautiful bay of Treis Boukes, which had served during the war as a meeting place for warships and transports and a refuge from German submarines. In the Middle Ages it had served as a refuge for pirates. Its rôle had been curiously inverted. No house or sign of human occupation was visible. It was an utterly deserted bay. As a harbour it was perfect. Its waters were deep and it had two entrances, covered from storms by a small rocky islet. But its use by pirates had made it useless to the inhabitants. As often in the Greek islands the town was built on a hill as far away from the best harbour as possible; for pirates congregated in all harbours and if the town was near at hand they could sack it at their leisure. And so wherever there are fine harbours in Greek islands you must search for the towns and villages anywhere but on the harbour itself. At Lemnos and at Melos I had noted the same thing.

I went to the shore and to my surprise and satisfaction found my trusty lugger captain already there. He was anchored a few fathoms off shore. There was no quay of any kind and a shallow beach. So that we were immediately faced with the problem of how to unload two and a half tons of marble tombstone. To heave them recklessly over the gunwales would have ended either in their dropping into the sea or in the breaking of the ship. So we decided to build a small quay! By this time some curious peasants had collected. They were shepherds from the hills above. On learning of our dilemma they at once offered us the hospitality of their shack. We accepted and I remained their guest for three weeks, living the life of Greek shepherds of all ages. It took us three days to build our quay and then my captain and his sailor assistant departed, paid and content. By this time I had summoned the help of three expert quarrymen from the marble quarries at the other end of the island. With them I now had to solve the next problem. We found the grave placed in an exquisite and secluded dell some three hundred feet above the sea, reached by a rough goat-track from the shore. It was then surrounded by olive-trees and turf which was covered with variously coloured anemones and fritillaries, as lovely a spot as there is in the Aegean.

We had to face the task of transporting our two and a half tons of marble up that goat-track of three hundred feet ascent. The tombstone was packed in six or seven wooden crates; the main part of the stone weighed one and a half tons. In addition there was a set of heavy iron railings to go round the completed tomb. So we set to work. We cut wooden rollers from pine trees and started to level with crowbars the more preposterous protrusions of rock on that winding path. We spent a week in this task. Then came the more formidable work of pushing yard by yard the marble fragments along the rollers up that three hundred feet. Never before have I so deeply admired and respected the architects of Stonehenge as when I indulged in this primitive megalithic undertaking.

In the evenings we would cease work and go with the shepherds to watch them as they drove the sheep into the pen. I marvelled to see the shepherds use the device of Cyclops as they counted their sheep. One man stood astride the entrance to the pen and the sheep were driven between his legs. As they passed he counted them. At supper we would sit round an open fire with the patriarch of the community, an old man of eighty, and drink the bread and milk which he ladled from a wooden bowl of immense proportions. The rest of the party consisted of five young men, all nephews of the old man. I found that one had served near me in the Struma valley and another had been as a soldier to Odessa with a Greek division which was sent with other Allied troops there. All were the most charming and delightful companions. At nights we curled up on shelves in the shack and wrapped thick blankets round our shoulders.

At length we had the marble tombstone at the site of the grave. I ordered a pause in the task, and went back

Grave of Rupert Brooke on Skyros immediately after its erection

Skyros Castle. (Norman Douglas, Greek priest and gendarme)

hurriedly to Athens to get various implements and materials which were needed. I found that I could catch a boat that went from Skyros to Kyme on the eastern shore of Eubœa and from there would get by car to Chalkis, where a train to Athens was an easy matter. At Athens I found, newly arrived on his first visit, Norman Douglas, anxious to see all that he could of Greece. So I asked him to join me on the return trip and help in the completion of the work. So back he came with me. I have seldom met a more engaging travel-companion. As we walked the four-mile path from Skyros village to Treis Boukes harbour he regaled me with such wealth of lore and learning that I found a walk on a Greek island a hundredfold more interesting than I had imagined. He showed me flowers I had not noticed and told me of the strange minerals that protruded here and there from the ground. He repeated all the legends and stories that have ever been written or invented about plants and stones and insects and animals that we saw around us. The island seemed to be a perfect storehouse of gems and rare fauna and unusual flowers. I remember at one moment he bent down and picked up a large block of green stone. 'This is nephrite,' he said. I knew nephrite well enough in the guise of prehistoric axes, but I had never noticed it as raw material. With the shepherds he was immensely popular, for he had the gift of getting on with all men, even when he could not speak their language. When he found that one of my marble-masons spoke Italian he was overjoyed and a flood of conversation ensued.

The masons now completed their task and the tomb was laid. Round its edge runs an inscription in English and in modern Greek. We next had to arrange to have the tomb officially consecrated. So we returned to the village and sought out the head of the monastery of St George that stands behind a mighty Frankish tower above the village. With him we returned and one quiet afternoon he put on his stately Byzantine robes and mitre and intoned the burial service of the Greek Orthodox Church. At that service were only Norman Douglas and myself, the three stonemasons, and a few shepherds who stood curiously in the background. I wondered what Brooke would have thought to see this strange assembly. I came away sadly to think that here was still another of my generation accounted for. It was a lonely world now for men of my age.

* * * * * * *

During 1921 and 1922 I revisited the old front north of Salonika, for during the war I had noted several places where an archæologist would find much to delight him. One such, that struck me as the most promising, was on the edge of a marsh just behind the line. It was near a ruined railway station on an abandoned railway that joined the Salonika-Vienna route to the Salonika-Constantinople route. The site was known by the name of Causica. It had been under shell-fire and among the bivouacs of the troops in reserve. It was not half a mile from the front line, which was on the forward slopes of the Doiran hills, at whose foot on the marsh was this ancient settlement, or whatever it may have been. All I knew was that an industrious and enterprising member of the Y.M.C.A., who was here in charge of a canteen, had in his spare time unearthed various antiquities, the nature of which was so unusual as to inspire me with a longing to know more.

So one early summer day I set forth with a dozen Greek workmen and some tents from the railway station of Karasuli, some twelve miles from my site, and we arrived at sunset at this desolate and abandoned place. Here were the endless scars on the hillside that were the remains of dugouts and shellholes; the prodigious litter left by a vast army, showed how populous the place had been a year or so ago; now it had the silence of a complete desert. There were no villages, no shacks or houses, nothing but the littered waste of low hills in a setting of scenery so lovely that I wondered why I had never during the war fully recognised its loveliness. As night fell the silence was strangely punctuated at irregular intervals by rifle shots. Shepherds, whose sheep grazed here and there on these precariously pastured hills, had found old army rifles among the wire and skeletons of the front line and had made them serviceable for use against the occasional prowling wolves that still haunted these wilder parts. Also there was the rare chance of marauding Serbian bandits from the frontier, a mile away.

We set to work and in a day or so discovered that our one-time Y.M.C.A. canteen was an ancient cemetery of warriors, whose spears and shields and gallant ornaments we found in grave after grave. As, with the ruthless curiosity of the archæologist, I dug them up, one by one, I thought of those countless other skeletons of my friends and fellow-soldiers which still lay white and scattered in the ravines of Doiran and along the moorland of the 'P Ridges' (as we had called that terrible bastion of defences which the Bulgars held to the end). It was not until two years later that the War Graves Commission succeeded in finding the last of the forgotten bodies of British soldiers.

My ancient Greek cemetery proved to be of the Homeric period, from about 1000 B.C. As I found the graves of these well-armed warriors I could not but reflect on the progress of civilisation, for above those graves I had first, before excavation, to clear away countless shell-fragments, cartridges and all the oddments of modern war, before I could arrive, a few feet lower down, at the armaments of our ancestors. There is nothing so sobering to the optimism of those who believe in progress, than to find cheek by jowl the concrete evidences of man's failure to achieve steady spiritual advancement. Who were we, with our shells and our vaster instruments of death and destruction, to talk of the barbarians of ancient times, of the ruthless slaughter of the Homeric armies, of the massacres of the uncultured invaders of ages past? What we miscall Progress is merely the unsubdued optimism of man that urges him now and again to make new adventures in the world of ideas. And as each adventure is made it fails. The optimist can claim only that the aggregate of adventures leads to greater self-realisation in the human soul—for what that is worth. All archæologists must be of necessity somewhat callous in their outlook on the great process of the Preferment of Man. For they have the concrete evidence in their hands of man's wickedness and man's goodness. And for the most part they will find more traces of wickedness. Away in the Valley of the Somme you will find the earliest and the latest weapons made by man, buried side by side in the same soil—his first Palæolithic axes, and his most cunningly fashioned shells and bullets. Boucher de Perthes discovered prehistoric man of the dawn of history by the Somme. Twentieth-century man has discovered there also that he has not changed much in that million years that have passed.

In the evenings I would wander on the quiet hills, where there was no sound but the call of an occasional jackal or the rifle-shot of a shepherd or the cry of a curlew. There was the old Front Line where my friends had been; there, still untouched, was the great belt of barbed wire that had protected the Line, and facing it the dark ripple of the Bulgar wire. Both ran over the smooth hills like a rusty dragon, undulating and billowing with the contours. Below were the flat plainlands where so short a time ago had been the bustle of life and the sparkle of camp-fires. I could not tear myself away from this place, for there was something of home about it. It was like looking at an old house where one has lived in one's childhood; one creates over again the old scenes and recaptures the old experiences. And, above all, one feels an odd affection for what is but an empty shell.

A second year I returned to my hunting ground and completed my excavations. My workmen were curious refugee Greeks from the Caucasus, who had fled to Greece as Turkish power increased. Some of them could speak no Greek at all, only Turkish; one spoke Georgian. All knew the places I had seen on my eastern trip. All my experiences were continuous, and it seemed that I could not yet escape the war.

One evening at full moon, to celebrate the arrival of a new supply of food at our camp, the men staged a dance. One of them played a queer one-stringed instrument and chanted an ancient Caucasian tune. The rest wound slowly and silently round in a circle, making the intricate steps of some ancient ceremony. The moon was vivid and their moving shadows on the turf made strange patterns. I watched them for an hour, as I smoked a pipe in the cool night air, and felt that for once the war was forgotten.

* * * * * * *

Later I chanced to visit Constantinople again to investigate the possibilities of archæological research. There I found the Army of Occupation still in control, but the government now that of Kemalists. The Sultan had fled for his life and the old order was finished. At Headquarters I found many of my old friends and made many new ones. The Brigade of Guards was now the garrison of the city, and a superb garrison it was. They stood no nonsense from Turks or Christians.

To my delight I was offered the chance to go to Gallipoli, which was then held in strength by our army, who anticipated a possible conflict with the new army of Kemal, which had arrived at the Straits, flushed from victory over the Greeks, and bombastically threatening to cross into Europe and seize what Turkey demanded by force of arms. The world was once more in a ferment and there was talk of war. I arrived at Gallipoli just as the 'Chanak crisis' reached its height. I was bound on a purely archæological examination of the peninsula, but I could not fail to be excited by the events that were impending. I went by a troop transport to Kilia Bay and there found many of my old headquarters friends of Salonika times. General Milne had returned to England the previous year and General Harington was now the Commander-in-Chief at Constantinople. He was an able commander, but he had not that swift and compelling way with Turks that commended General Milne to the army. He preferred negotiations, but you cannot negotiate with an army flushed with victory and convinced that no one can stop it. I made the rounds of the Gallipoli defences. No Turk could have crossed the Straits. Of that I was certain. Every quarter of a mile along the southern shore of the peninsula was a heavy howitzer, registered on the opposing shore. At every landing point were troops in reserve and endless barbed wire. In a bay were all the aircraft in the Mediterranean ready to disperse the Turkish attacks. Against us were Turkish divisions of infantry, cavalry divisions and little or no heavy artillery, and only two or three aircraft. How those forces hoped to cross the Straits I could not imagine. Yet they put up a superb bluff. We had a defended bridgehead across the Straits at Chanak, where a brigade sat solidly behind barbed wire waiting for attack. The true policy was to let the attack come and exploit the consequences, but the prospects of a new war, even on so small a scale, alarmed the British public. We should in fact have considered this small affair as the concluding contribution of Great Britain to her policy in the Near East. Turkey would undoubtedly have received a severe check and subsequent negotiation would have been on a reasonable basis. As it was, no conflict ensued and there followed the Conference of Mudania and that of Lausanne, where Lord Curzon rescued for Great Britain a few fragments of her self-respect.

The cause of the débâcle was clear enough. By avoiding hostilities we evinced weakness. And we were forced to avoid them by a campaign carried out in London which was as unscrupulous as it was ill-informed. 'Get out of Chanak' was the cry which humiliated our whole Near Eastern policy. When Lloyd George and Churchill made their famous appeal to the Dominions to help to wind up the Turkish trouble the Dominions immediately responded. New Zealand promised a contingent at once; Australia stated that she would send one 'if circumstances required.' Canada, less interested, asked for fuller information. South Africa did not reply owing to the absence of General Smuts. It was left for the *Daily Mail* to decide that the British Army was to get out! and the Conservative Party seized on this as an admirable opportunity to eject Lloyd George and Winston Churchill also! I was amused to see how our principal fire-eaters eat their fire.

The old smell of wartime was in my nostrils again. That queer combined scent of bacon fat, axle grease, beer, and canvas, that permeates every camp, once more brought the recent past before my eyes and nose. In civilian garb I breakfasted on the tawny shore of Gallipoli with old friends, and watched soldiers at their endless tasks. I felt like the 'superannuated man' back in his office.

I was lent a motor boat and rounded Cape Helles, to Anzac Bay. I saw all the famous beaches and the terrible slope up to Achi Baba. The cemeteries then were hardly made, and the ravines were still full of bones. I tried to forget the war and to do what I came for, which was to reconstruct the ancient Gallipoli of Miltiades, to find those ancient Athenian colonies, and to make an archæological survey. I roamed over the whole peninsula.

Later I crossed to Chanak. I was determined to see Troy. With two adventurous friends I set out from Chanak; we passed the sentries at the barbed wire defences and drove in an ancient and rickety Ford over the incredible bumps and potholes of the coastal road. Strictly speaking we were now in enemy territory, except that the war had not begun! Soon we encountered Kemalist troops, who took no notice of us. As we rounded Erenkeui and approached the plain of the Maeander we entered a small and battered village. Some Turkish privates came running out to us, brandishing rifles. My friends loosened their revolvers, desperately resolved to fight if called on to do so. The soldiers stopped at the car and smiled. 'Please tell us which is the best way to Hissarlik,' we asked. Hissarlik is Troy. They smiled again and explained the best road, and retired. Here was no enemy anxious to invade Europe. What nonsense it all was. For here were we, fifteen miles in the territory of the Turks, and no one made the smallest attempt to stop us.

So we went to Troy, roamed its mouldering battlements and gazed across at the distant peak of Samothrace and the low shore of 'smoky Lemnos' with the Scamander in its marshes below. Here at Troy we found that Turkish soldiers had made it into a redoubt, and trenches followed the ancient walls of Priam. The same old battle-field was in use again.

We returned that evening to Chanak, after as delightful a day as I had had for many a month. Somehow there was more friendship in visiting these ancient places with fellow-soldiers than with other men. For there is no friendship so solid and so lasting as that which develops in the mutual experience of war.

The Chanak crisis passed a week or so later, and with it our prestige in the Near East for several years to come. Politicians and journalists between them had taken charge at home and armies were in disgrace. Perhaps after all they were quite right. Yet if armies are disgraceful things I am not convinced that politicians and journalists are more graceful.

With Chanak and all I saw on Gallipoli the war finally fluttered to a close as far as I was concerned.

I have set down these experiences for what they are worth. I watched the war in its first glimmerings, and I watched it as it spluttered out into darkness, leaving only its smoke and dirt behind it. It is good to have seen it as an organic whole. Those younger than myself, who went into it without knowing exactly how it began, cannot always

Royal Air Force official—Crown copyright reserved

The site of Troy from the air. The trenches of the Turks can be seen running by the ancient circuit walls

estimate the importance of its various stages. The facts I have tabulated concern one individual person alone—myself. They have no other value than to illustrate the development of one single and utterly unimportant life during five years or so of desperate confusion and constant battle.

The world will have to develop a civilisation that is infinitely more intelligent and sane before the belief in war can be abandoned or before the leaders and dictators erase from their guns that ancient slogan *ultima ratio regum*. War has only one purpose that can justify it, and that is to prove to those who seek hegemony that hegemony in material things is a worthless vapour, an unsubstantial flame that flashes in a marsh of corruption. Germany sought, and seeks still, for hegemony. To-day the ancient strife has broken out again. Europe is corrupted with the belief that he who has at his disposal the greatest force can impose his will and his ideas on others by a backing of brute power. In the last war the whole world was brutalised beyond belief; in the next it will be ground to powder. Slowly but certainly we move down the inexorable slope. The ancient fallacy has raised its head, Hydra-like, and we must cut and hack at it again. For it seems that what emerged in 1914 has not yet been extirpated: it grows again, fed on its own corruption. To fight two world-wars in a lifetime may seem too heavy a toll of years to give. But I would rather serve in war to see vindicated once again the ideas for which we fought, than would I see the structure of civilisation preserved in its present precarious form. Better to crash over the abyss and start again than live in perpetual fear. In my own lifetime I may well see the complete reversion of the existing mode of life to plain barbarism, our cities heaps of rubble, our habits of existence a half-forgotten memory—"*quae oppida quodam tempore florentissima fuerunt, nunc prostrata et diruta ante oculos jacent.*" But even that were preferable to the alternative set before us.

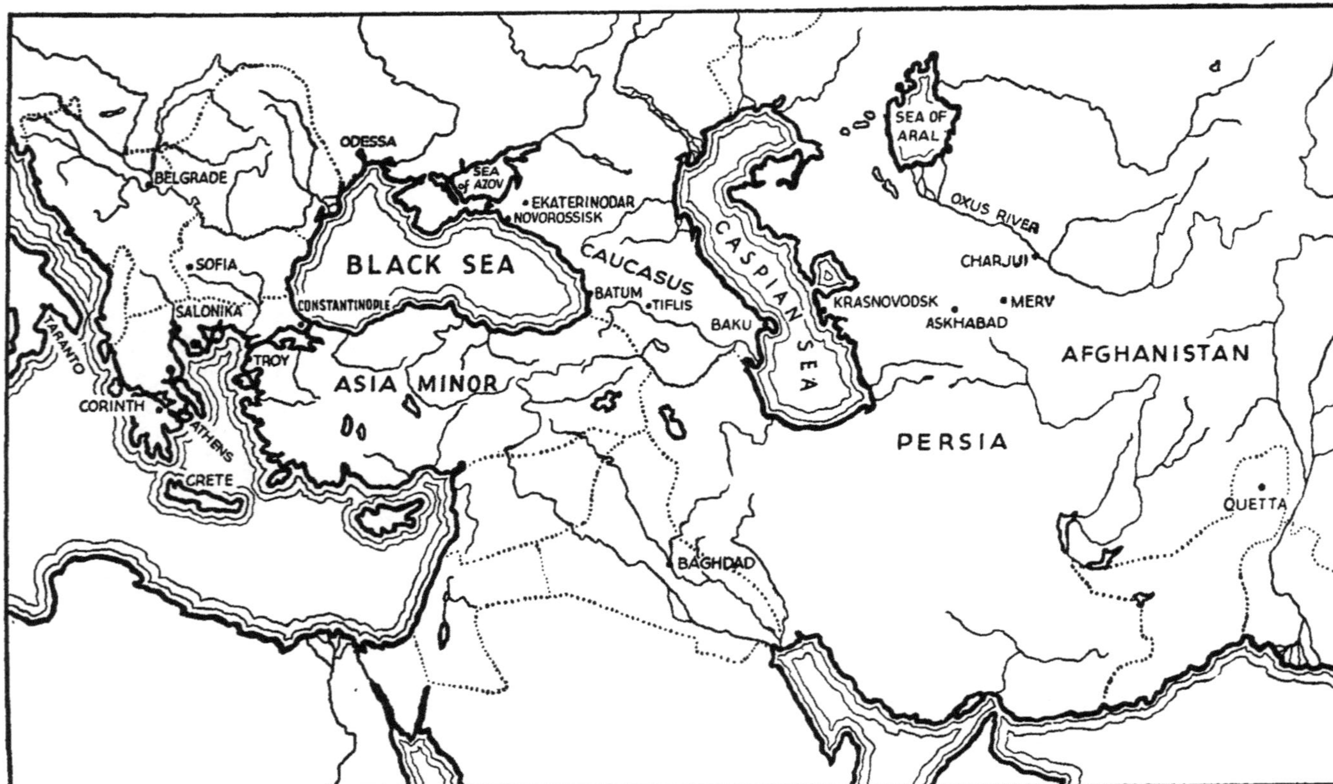
ODESSA
BELGRADE
SEA of AZOV
EKATERINODAR
NOVOROSSISK
SOFIA
BLACK SEA
CAUCASUS
CONSTANTINOPLE
BATUM
TIFLIS
SALONIKA
TARANTO
TROY
ASIA MINOR
CORINTH
ATHENS
CRETE
CASPIAN SEA
BAKU
SEA OF ARAL
OXUS RIVER
CHARJUI
KRASNOVODSK
ASKHABAD
MERV
AFGHANISTAN
PERSIA
QUETTA
BAGHDAD

Lightning Source UK Ltd.
Milton Keynes UK
UKHW011051120422
401447UK00006B/970

9 781845 749231